A HISTORY OF THE THEATRE IN AMERICA

FROM ITS BEGINNINGS TO THE PRESENT TIME

BY

ARTHUR HORNBLOW

FOR NINETEEN YEARS EDITOR OF "THE THEATRE MAGAZINE"
AUTHOR OF "TRAINING FOR THE STAGE," ETC.

WITH PHOTOGRAVURE FRONTISPIECES AND
188 ILLUSTRATIONS IN DOUBLETONE

VOLUME II

PHILADELPHIA AND LONDON
J. B. LIPPINCOTT COMPANY
1919

WINDHAM PRESS
CLASSIC REPRINTS

CONTENTS

3

CONTENTS

4

CONTENTS

ILLUSTRATIONS

VOLUME II

7

ILLUSTRATIONS

ILLUSTRATIONS

A HISTORY OF THE THEATRE IN AMERICA

CHAPTER XV

HACKETT AND MACREADY

NEW THEATRES IN NEW YORK. LAFAYETTE AS A PLAYGOER. FIRST
INTRODUCTION OF ITALIAN GRAND OPERA IN AMERICA. TRIUMPH
OF MME. MALIBRAN. JAMES H. HACKETT AT THE PARK. A
FAMOUS FALSTAFF. COMING OF WILLIAM CHARLES MACREADY.
ANECDOTES OF THE DISTINGUISHED ENGLISH TRAGEDIAN. BUILD-
ING OF THE HISTORIC BOWERY THEATRE. ITS FOUNDERS AND ITS
AUDIENCES. QUARREL BETWEEN WOOD AND WARREN OF THE
PHILADELPHIA THEATRE. BUILDING OF THE ARCH STREET THE-
ATRE. FIRST APPEARANCE OF JAMES E. MURDOCH.

A NEW place of amusement was opened in New
York in 1822, which at one time seriously threatened
the supremacy of the famous Park Theatre. This was
the Chatham Garden and Theatre, situated between
Duane and Pearl Streets, with an entrance through
private dwellings on the west side of Chatham Street.
The house was well patronized from the first night
and at once became the resort of beauty and fashion
of the metropolis, being as popular in its day as
Niblo's Garden was forty years later. So successful was the place that two years later a permanent
theatre was erected called the Chatham Garden
Theatre. This house was opened May 17, 1824, with

"The Soldier's Daughter," the cast including: Messrs. Kilner, George Barrett, Allen, Moreland, Joseph Jefferson, Jr., Stone and Mesdames Entwistle, Durang and Walstein.

General Lafayette honored this theatre with a visit the following September. The distinguished French soldier was very fond of playgoing and full of amusing anecdotes of actors, especially of his famous compatriot, Talma, who, he declared, preferred Shakespeare to any other dramatic author. On September 20 Francis Courtney Wemyss made his New York début at this theatre as Marplot in "The Busybody," and on October 6, 1825, a pastoral opera in two acts by Samuel Woodworth, an American dramatist, entitled "Forest Rose, or American Farmers" was produced here for the first time on any stage. This piece, which introduces the Yankee character of Jonathan Ploughboy, was later made very popular by J. H. Hackett.

The following year Mr. Barrière, the proprietor, died and Henry Wallack took a lease of the Chatham which he reopened March 20, 1826. Among other well known players who appeared here under the Wallack management were H. J. Conway, Mr. and Mrs. John Duff, Mr. Dwyer, John Bernard, Thomas Placide. Later that same year, Junius Brutus Booth became stage manager and was himself seen in Shakespearian repertoire. The season, however, was not a success, and at its close Wallack found himself a bankrupt. After this the house lost ground rapidly. The fashionable clientèle it had enjoyed so long fell away and the Park resumed its former position as the city's leading theatre. Later lessees were Kilner [1] and Maywood, J. H. Hackett and Charles R. Thorne.[2]

Another theatre, called the Lafayette, situated on the west side of Laurens Street, near Canal Street, was opened in 1825, but failed to gain any great popularity. Rebuilt in 1827, with a façade of white granite and the interior beautifully decorated, it was pronounced at the time the largest and most splendid theatre in America. The company included H. Wallack, H. Eberle, Mr. Fisher, T. Placide, W. Conway, Mr. Burroughs (stage manager), Mr. Scott, Mr. Thayer, Mr. Faulkner, Mr. Hyatt, Mr. Anderson, Mr. Walstein and Mesdames Hill, Stone, H. Wallack, Fisher, Alexina Fisher. Standard comedies, operas, and melodramas constituted the attractions at this house, the existence of which was destined to be short. On April 11, 1829, it was destroyed by fire and never rebuilt.

At the Park Theatre, late in the fall of 1825, was tried the interesting experiment of giving Italian opera. Musical works such as the popular " Beggar's Opera " and various adaptations of the Italian operas were already familiar to the American stage, but this was the first time that any attempt had been made to present Italian opera in the original language and with Italian singers. The Park Theatre was, therefore, the first home of grand opera in this country. The first production, Rossini's " Barbieri de Sivig-

---

[1] Thomas Kilner was born in England in 1777, and made his American début at the Park Theatre, New York, in 1815. In 1821 he was joint lessee with Clarke of the Federal Street Theatre, Boston. He was an excellent actor in "old men's parts."

[2] Charles R. Thorne, Sr., was born in New York in 1814, and made his début at the Park Theatre in 1830 as Octavian in "The Mountaineers." At one time he was also manager of the Federal Street Theatre, Boston.

lia " was made on November 29, the singers being: Garcia, De Rosich, Angrisani, Crivelli, Garcia, Jr., and Maria Felicita Garcia (later the celebrated Mme. Malibran).

Signor Manuel del Popolo Vincent Garcia, founder of the famous family of Spanish musicians, was born at Seville in 1775 and began his career as chorister at the Seville Cathedral at the age of six. In 1808, the year his daughter Maria Felicita was born, he made his début in Paris where he soon became first singer. His fame grew all over Europe both as singer and composer until 1817 when he went to London where later he founded his famous school of singing. His daughter Maria Felicita, one of the most distinguished singers the world has ever known, made her début under his guidance. In 1825 he conceived the project of taking grand opera to America and sailed to New York from Liverpool with a company. The operas given by the Garcia troupe during this first season in America were " Il Barbieri de Siviglia," " Tancredi," " Il Turco in Italia," " La Cenerentola," " Semiramide," " Don Giovanni," " L'Amante astuto," " La Figlia del Aria."

The experiment was a decided success. The receipts on the opening night amounted to $2,980 and the house, crowded to the doors with an exceptionally well dressed audience, presented a spectacle of unusual brilliance. The display of jewelry and luxurious toilettes, which has always been an inseparable feature of grand opera, was not absent on that occasion. " An assemblage of ladies so fashionable, so numerous, and so elegantly dressed," says a chronicler, "had probably never before been witnessed in an American theatre."

Signorina Maria Felicita Garcia, the most famous songstress in Europe, was of course the star of the evening. "Her lovely form," says Ireland, "her passionate attitudes, her commanding gestures, the expressive play of her features, her noble brow, her tread on the stage as of a goddess on Olympus, her soul lighted eyes, and, above all, her inconceivable singing impressed an ineffaceable picture on every mind." [*]

At the height of her success in America, on March 23, 1826, Signorina Garcia contracted a marriage with Eugene Malibran, an aged and wealthy French merchant of New York, expecting to retire from the stage. The match is said to have been compulsory and prompted by filial duty alone. But the sacrifice was of little avail. Business misfortunes soon overtook her husband. In a short time he went into bankruptcy and Signorina Garcia had to return to her profession for support. On January 15, 1827, tempted by the offer of $500 per night made by manager Gilfert, Mme. Malibran made her appearance at the Bowery Theatre as Count Belino in Bishop's opera "The Devil's Bridge," from which all the music had been cut, except songs incidental to her part. Although she spoke with a slight foreign accent, she was as successful in this field as in the more familiar scenes of Italian opera.

The season of 1826 at the Park Theatre was notable for the début of an American actor who later rose to a position of great prominence on our stage.

[*] Records of the New York Stage. By J. N. Ireland.

This was James H. Hackett, who made his first appearance before a New York audience March 1, 1826, as Justice Woodcock in " Love in a Village." All the players of distinction who had appeared on the American stage up to Hackett's time were English. There were, of course, many native players of ability appearing in the different theatres throughout the country, but none were gifted with conspicuous talent. The Merrys, the Oldmixons, Duffs, Coopers, Keans, Booths, Mathews, Wallacks, all came from England. No player of consequence previously before the public could be pointed to as an American product.

James Henry Hackett was born in New York in 1800. His father, Thomas G. Hackett, a Hollander of distinguished lineage, traced his ancestry back to one Baron Hackett who crossed from Normandy into England in the train of William the Conqueror. After serving in the life guards of the Prince of Orange, he sailed for America where he settled down and married a daughter of the Rev. Abraham Keteltas of Long Island. Through this marriage the Hacketts became indirectly connected with the Duanes, Beekmans, Roosevelts, De Peysters and other old American families.

Thomas Hackett died three years after his son, James Henry, was born and to the widow fell the duty of rearing and educating the future actor. The boy received a classical education and very early showed an extraordinary fondness for Shakespeare. His mother wanted him to be a lawyer, but he preferred the stage and he actually acted in public when only sixteen in a small rôle at a theatre in Newark,

N. J. In 1819 he married Catherine Leesugg, a favorite soubrette of that day, and this association naturally sharpened his thirst for the theatre. But no opportunity presenting itself, he went to Utica, where for some time he engaged in the grocery and crockery business. Having made a little money, he returned to New York determined at last to try his fortunes on the stage. The appearance at the Park followed. The début was not a success, and gave no promise of his future development. Some well intentioned friends even advised him to abandon the stage and go back to mercantile pursuits.

A week later, when he acted Sylvester Daggerwood in the younger Colman's " New Hay at the Old Market " and introduced clever imitations of the elder Mathews, Kean and other actors, he was more successful, and on October 25 his Dromio of Ephesus also added to his rapidly growing reputation.

Two years later he crossed the Atlantic and acted in London—the first American player to appear on the English stage as a star. On his return to this country, he appeared in several new rôles. In 1827 he was seen at the Park as Richard, and three years later originated the character of Rip Van Winkle. Of this impersonation Sol Smith, the manager, said: " I should despair of finding a man or woman in an audience of 500 who could hear Hackett's utterance of five words in the second act, ' but she vas mine vrow,' without experiencing some moisture in the eyes." It was not, however, until May 31, 1832, when he played Falstaff to Charles Kean's Hotspur in " Henry IV " in Philadelphia, that he achieved the triumph on which his whole reputation rests. He

Կ

ranks as the best Sir John Falstaff that has ever
enacted the character of the fat knight, although the
critics differed in their opinion as to the merit of his
impersonation. George William Curtis found the
conception devoid of unctuousness. To him it was an
" acted " rôle too carefully studied to be natural.
William Winter accords it unreserved praise.

His Falstaff was a symmetrical and extraordinary blending
of intellect and sensuality. The external attributes were perfect.
The burly form, the round, ruddy face, the rimy fringe of gray
whiskers, the bright, penetrating, merry eyes, the rows of even,
white teeth, the strong, hard voice, the pompous, gross, selfish,
animal demeanor, tempered at times by wily sagacity and by the
perfect manner of an old man-of-the-world, combined to make it
an admirably distinct and natural embodiment in all that relates
to form.[4]

A man of scholarly attainments and fine ideals,
Mr. Hackett was held in the highest esteem both in
his private and professional life. In 1829 and 1830
he became manager of the Chatham and Bowery
Theatres, and he was manager of the Astor Place
Opera House at the time of the fatal riot. He died
in 1871.

Another distinguished actor, the Englishman,
William Charles Macready, who was even more
closely connected with the Astor Place riot, came to
America a few months after Hackett's first appearance at the Park Theatre, and made his début October
2, 1826, at the same theatre in the rôle of Virginius.

The tragedian's great reputation in England had
preceded him here, and there was much curiosity to

[4] From " The Wallet of Time." Copyright, 1913, by William Winter.
Moffat, Yard and Company, Publishers. Reprinted by permission of Jefferson Winter, Esq.

see this actor of whom William A. Conway had stood so much in awe that he suddenly left New York and went into retirement when he heard that he was coming to America. The New York critics the day following his début pronounced him second only to Cooper. Further acquaintance with his merits as displayed later in " Macbeth," " Damon," " Hamlet," " William Tell " and " Coriolanus " soon compelled the acknowledgment that he was the most chaste, finished and classic actor seen up to that time on the American stage.

Macready was born in London in 1793. His father, an Irishman, had been a popular actor on the Dublin stage, where he had formed a friendship with Macklin. Through the latter's influence, he obtained engagements in England, and in 1793, when his wife, also an actress, presented him with a son, he was already a member of the Covent Garden company. When not engaged in acting, Macready, Sr., wrote plays and managed theatres in the provinces. His business fortunes fluctuated, but one important thing he succeeded in doing—he gave his son a first-class education. In fact, young Macready's boyhood was spent largely in schools. He hardly knew the meaning of the word home. After preliminary studies at Birmingham and Cheltenham, he was sent to Rugby where he received that academic training which all through life stamped him as a gentleman and a man of marked intellectual force.

At Rugby dramatic performances were occasionally given and Macready particularly distinguished himself in recitation. A natural inference was that he would eventually take to his father's profession, but that was not his ambition. His own desire and that of his parents was that he should go in for law. It had been planned to send him to Oxford, but the elder Macready got into such serious financial difficulties that he was imprisoned for debt, and his son in this emergency had to leave Rugby and take charge of his father's affairs. Thus he became a manager when only sixteen years of age.

His own début as an actor occurred at Birmingham, June 7, 1810, when he appeared as Romeo. Next he was seen as young Norval, Zanga and George Barnwell. In 1811 at Newcastle he first essayed the rôle of Hamlet. At Newcastle he acted with Mrs. Siddons in " The Gamester " and " Douglas." Her acting, he always said, was a revelation to him and its lessons remained. Other parts assumed with success at that time were Orestes, Marc Antony, Beverley, Hotspur and Richard III. The news of his success in the provinces soon reached London and before long he received offers both from Drury Lane and Covent Garden. He made his début at the latter house September 16, 1816, as Orestes in " The Distressed Mother." Hazlitt declared him " by far the best tragic actor that has come out in our remembrance with the exception of Mr. Kean." Three years later, when he was seen as Richard III, he showed his capacity for the highest tragic parts, and in 1820 his performance of Virginius in the new play by Sheridan Knowles added even more to his reputation. An English critic says of him:

Macready's performances always displayed fine artistic perceptions developed to a high degree of perfection by very comprehensive culture, and even his least successful personations had the interest resulting from thorough intellectual study. He belonged to the school of Kean rather than of Kemble; but, if his tastes were better disciplined and in some respects more refined than those of Kean, his natural temperament did not permit him to give proper effect to the most characteristic features of the great tragic parts of Shakespeare, King Lear perhaps excepted, which in some degree afforded scope for his pathos and tenderness, the qualities in which he especially excelled. With the exception of a voice of good compass and capable of very varied expression, Macready was not in a special degree gifted physically for acting, but the defects of his face and figure cannot be said to have materially influenced his success.

Macready's method of arriving at his effects was entirely mechanical. Each move on the stage he planned out carefully beforehand. In this way he differed entirely from the elder Booth who did nothing with premeditation and acted solely on the impulse of the moment. Joseph Jefferson comments on this marked difference in the methods of the two actors. He says:

As soon as Macready entered the theatre he began to assume the character he was going to enact. He would remain in his dressing room absorbed with the play; no one was permitted to enter; his dresser was not allowed to speak to him, but stood outside ready to open the door just before it was time for the actor to go upon the stage. If the mechanism of the play remained intact, he became lost in his character and produced grand effects, but if by some carelessness he was recalled to himself, the chain was broken and he could not reunite it. He now realized that his acting would be tame, and then his rage knew no bounds; he would seize the unlucky actor who had " ruined him," shake him, throw him aside, and, rushing to his dressing-room, fall exhausted upon the sofa. This was not affectation, it was real; he could not conquer his unfortunate temper. In my youthful days it was the fashion of thoughtless actors to ridicule these " Macready tantrums," and I regret to say I often joined in the sport; but as I look back on his suffering and read the pages wherein he chastises himself for his ungovernable temper, and when I know how useful and benevolent he was in the closing scenes of his life, I feel a great sympathy for him. "He poured a flagon of Rhenish on my head once," but—I forgive him.[5]

Although priding himself on his scholarship, which in his day was the distinguishing mark of the gentleman, Macready was, as we have seen, a man of irascible temper and strange moods. Coleman, Murdoch and others who acted with him, represent his rehearsals as very serious affairs. "Beast!" was a favorite expletive and flattery would not always mollify him, "Don't humbug me, sir," being his reply to propitiatory phrases. Discontent, morbidness, temper and envy were his besetting faults. William T. Price, in his estimate of the characteristics of the English actor, says:

Macready's impatience at bad acting does not explain his execrable temper and his treatment of subordinate actors. There was no excuse for his brutality. It would be false biography to deny that his general conduct towards his inferiors was simply brutal. His views of life were false, and this was a mere incident of an unhealthy state of mind. It was not a matter of indigestion. He admits again and again his failing, and repeatedly characterizes his own conduct as vile. He prays over it, moralizes over it, and the next day is as insulting, overbearing, and unreasonable as before.[6]

Joseph Jefferson has given us some idea of the sudden outbursts of rage to which the English actor was subject. He relates this experience:

Macready was acting Werner. I was cast for a minor part. In one scene a number of characters had to rush off, bearing lighted torches, in search of some delinquent. At rehearsal the tragedian particularly requested that we should all be sure and make our exit

[5] From the Autobiography of Joseph Jefferson. Copyright, 1889. Reprinted by kind permission of the Century Co.
[6] From A Life of William Charles Macready, by William T. Price.

22

at night at just the same time and place, so that we might not disturb the arrangement of the scene. All went well up to the time for making our hurried exit, when, to my horror, I found Werner standing exactly in line with the place of my exit at rehearsal. I presume that when he gave his directions in the morning he did not observe me. What was I to do? The cue was given, and there was no time for argument. I rushed past him, torch in hand. I heard his well-known groan; but as I flew by an unmistakable odor of burnt hair filled the atmosphere, and I knew that I had singed his wig. When the curtain fell I turned in horror to see the effect. The enraged Werner had torn his wig from his head, and stood gazing at it for a moment in helpless wonder. Suddenly he made a rush in my direction; I saw he was on the warpath, and that I was his game. And now the chase began. I dodged him up and down the stage; then around the wings and over " set " rocks and gauze waters. He never would have caught me but that in my excitement I ran head first into the stomach of a fat stage carpenter. Here I was seized. The enraged Macready was so full of anger and so out of breath that he could only gasp and shake his burnt wig at me. Of course, I was disgraced and not allowed to act again during his engagement.[7]

Macready made three visits to America. The last time he came was in 1849. On his second visit in 1843 he opened at the Park Theatre, New York, to extraordinary receipts, and later in Boston some of the most celebrated men of the country assembled to do him honor. He would certainly have taken up his permanent residence in America but for the disastrous Astor Place riot which, of course, made any such desire impossible of realization. The part he played in that unfortunate affair, the bitter controversy with Forrest and the causes that led up to the quarrel will be related in their proper place.

It was during Macready's first American tour, on

[7] From the Autobiography of Joseph Jefferson. Copyright, 1889. Reprinted by kind permission of the Century Co.

October 13, 1826, at the Park Theatre, that William Wheatley, then only a child, but who afterwards became one of the best light comedians on the American stage as well as a prominent manager, made his first appearance on the boards as Albert to Macready's William Tell. He was born in New York, December 5, 1816, his father, Frederick Wheatley, being a member of the Warren and Wood company at Baltimore while his mother was a favorite actress. William continued acting with Macready, accompanying that actor on his tour through the United States. Later, he returned to the Park and was seen in " Tom Thumb," a production made especially for him. In 1842 he went to Philadelphia and made his début at the Walnut Street Theatre on September 22 as Doricourt in " Belle's Stratagem." He was tremendously popular in Philadelphia, and in 1853 he became lessee of the Arch Street Theatre in conjunction with John Drew. On Mr. Drew's retirement, he became sole manager of that house. Later he took a lease of Niblo's Garden, New York, which opened under his management April, 1862, and in 1863 he assumed the management of the Chestnut Street Theatre, Philadelphia.

On December 16 Thomas Barry, an English actor-manager who later played a prominent part in American dramatic history, made his first appearance here in the title rôle of " The Stranger." A cultured man, of fine personal appearance, he was a great favorite in such rôles as Lord Townly, Joseph Surface, Duke Aranza, etc. After serving for some years as stage manager at the Park, he went in 1833 to Boston where he was offered the management of the

24

Tremont Theatre. In 1839 he returned to New York and for a time was manager of the Bowery, later resuming his old position at the Park. From 1850 to 1854 he was acting manager at the Broadway Theatre and later went to Boston to take charge of the new Boston Theatre.

Early in 1825 a number of New Yorkers interested in the drama conceived the idea of erecting in New York a playhouse which in size and beauty of design should rival the famous Park Theatre. Messrs. Gouverneur, Graham, James A. Hamilton, George W. Brown, P. M. Wetmore, T. L. Smith and Charles Gilfert were the projectors of the enterprise, and a company was formed for the purpose of erecting such a theatre in the Bowery just below Canal Street, on the site of the old tavern and cattle market known as the Bull's Head. The reason that this location was chosen was that the wealthy people of the city were building their residences in that neighborhood, and with the constant tendency of the better classes to move uptown, along the Boston Road, the Park Theatre had come to be considered a little out of the way.

The new playhouse, the tenth to be erected in the city of New York, was opened October 23, 1826, with " The Road to Ruin " followed by the farce " Raising the Wind." The company included: Mr. and Mrs. Duff, Mr. and Mrs. Young, Mr. and Mrs. George Barrett, Mr. and Mrs. Roberts, Messrs. Edwin Forrest, Faulkner, Hyatt, Stone, Bernard, Lamb (the singer), C. Durang, Logan, J. Scott, Hamilton, Kenyon, Essenden, Laws, Read and Beckwell, Mrs. Gilbert, Mrs. Hughes, old Mrs. Barrett.

25

Mrs. Brazier, Miss Devlin, little Miss Kent and others. The management was entrusted to Charles Gilfert, a manager and musician of experience, who had been musical director at the Park Theatre and later manager of the Albany Theatre.

A novelty, which excited much interest at the opening, was the experiment of lighting the house by gas.[*] This was the first time that the new method of illumination had been tried in a theatre in New York.

The house was first known as the Bull's Head Theatre. Its real name was the New York Theatre, Bowery. When Thomas Hamblin[*] and J. H. Hackett assumed managerial control in 1830, they called it simply the Bowery. Under this name the house became one of the most famous of all American theatres and had a long and glorious career of almost a hundred years, most of the illustrious players of our stage having at one time or other trodden its historic boards. In 1879 the old theatre became the home of German drama and its name was changed to the Thalia.

When the Bowery Theatre was first built it created a sensation. The size of stage and auditorium was larger than in any other theatre in the country, the seating capacity being about 3,000. Externally, it was one of the most imposing structures in the city. Classic in design, it had the appearance of white marble, with a spacious portico and lofty Corinthian

[*]Attempts at introducing gas as a new method of illumination had begun in America about 1820, but it did not come into general use until many years later. When the theatres first began to use gas, it was usually manufactured upon the premises, and its methods of control were necessarily crude.

[*]Thomas S. Hamblin, an English actor, came to America in 1825 and made his début at the Park as Hamlet. He then toured the United States until 1830 when he returned to New York and became manager of the Bowery Theatre. He died in 1853.

columns. In the late fifties, its early magnificence
eclipsed by more modern theatres, the Bowery lost its
standing as a first class house and rapidly deteriorated
to the third and even fourth rank until at last it became the home of lurid melodrama. But even in
these later days it still retained a hold on the affections of playgoers who enjoyed strenuous acting. To
watch its audiences was alone worth the inconveni-
ence to which the out of the way location of the
house put the visitor. Describing the theatre at this
period a writer says:

> We have often expressed the opinion that those who never go
> to the Bowery theatre miss many great treats. To say nothing of
> a multitude of good plays—in their way—they miss really crowded
> houses and really appreciative audiences. Broadway audiences
> never applaud like the Bowery audiences, and never hiss like the
> Bowery audiences. On the west side of the town hissing is a lost
> art. Thank Providence, it still flourishes in the Bowery!

Though melodrama and pantomime now held
first place on the Bowery stage, its patrons were not
averse to Shakespeare now and then. Preferably,
however, they crowded the house whenever a play
was given which called for the services of dogs and
horses. Charles Burnham, the well-known manager,
gives this interesting description of the kind of entertainment offered in the sixties:

> Whenever a holiday came around, the managers were more
> than generous with the quantity of the entertainment offered and
> the quality compared more than favorably with that given at some
> of the more higher-toned houses on Broadway. Imagine a bill like
> the following being given in these times: "The performance will
> begin with the petite Comedy of 'The Youth That Never Saw a
> Woman.' (Dance by Miss Minnie Jackson.) After which the
> roaring Irish Farce of 'Paddy Carey,' with songs and Irish Jig.

THE THEATRE IN AMERICA

To be succeeded by the local drama of ' Fast Women of the Modern Time,' introducing the celebrated Female Minstrels and Female Target Scenes and a new and beautiful programme of Songs, Jigs, Walkarounds, and Essence of Old Virginny. Interspersed with Wit, Fun and Frolic; Odd, Strange, Droll Sayings, Quips, Quirks, and Quidditities. Concluding with G. L. Fox's Comic Pantomime of the ' Four Lovers.' " All these various pieces were interpreted by a company that ranked high in the list of artists of the theatre at that time.[10]

The Bowery Theatre was destroyed four times by fire. The first time in 1828, again in 1836, again in 1838 and again in 1845.

While New York was celebrating the building of its fine new playhouse, the theatrical situation in Philadelphia was not so promising. In 1826 the long partnership between William B. Wood and William Warren was brought to a sudden end. The two men had never been on very friendly terms, and the friction continued until separation papers were signed, Wood retiring from the management, but being retained in the organization as an actor. On August 31, 1826, Warren opened the new theatre in Washington for a six weeks season with stars as added attractions, but the experiment was not a success, and Warren returned to Philadelphia to give all his attention to the Chestnut Street Theatre which opened December 4, 1826, under his sole management. The company now included the following: Jefferson, Wood, Warren, Cowell, Wemyss, John Jefferson, Porter, W. Forrest, Heyl, Singleton, Meer, Jones, Wheatley, Webb, Darley, Hallam, Green, Bignall, Hosack, Parker, Murray, Garner, Howard, Kleet,

[10] From an article by Charles Burnham, in the *Theatre Magazine* for March, 1918.

Mrs. Wood, Mrs. Jefferson, Mrs. J. Jefferson (late Burke), Mrs. Anderson, Mrs. Francis, Mrs. Greene, Mrs. Darley, Mrs. Cowell, Mrs. Meer, Mrs. Murray, the Misses Hathwell.

The season began with "The Stranger." This was followed by Macready's first Philadelphia engagement, and later J. B. Booth, Mr. and Mrs. H. Wallack and Edwin Forrest in "King Lear" appeared there. The general business, however, was far from satisfactory and bankruptcy seemed not far distant when Mr. Wood was approached by a number of gentlemen who had built a new theatre in Arch Street, and asked to undertake its management. In due course the new house opened its doors, but Wood found himself confronted by all the difficulties incidental to a new and ill prepared enterprise. The company he finally succeeded in getting together was undisciplined and ill assorted, the manager was at all times subject to interference by the owners, and finally Wood gave up a hopeless and thankless task and handed in his resignation. Meantime, things had gone no better with Warren. The Chestnut Street Theatre closed soon after the Arch Street house, and the actors proceeded to Baltimore.

On January 1, 1829, Messrs. Pratt and Wemyss took over the Chestnut Street Theatre, Philadelphia. The Walnut Street Theatre was reopened three months later under the management of S. Chapman and J. Green, Mr. and Mrs. W. B. Wood being engaged as members of the company. To the Walnut Street house William Warren—now feeble and discouraged after his many failures—also went seeking an engagement as actor.

The Arch Street Theatre, meantime, had resumed under the direction of Mr. Phillips, and at this house on October 13, 1829, James E. Murdoch, an American actor with a style entirely his own, and whose ability ranked him with the best artists of his day, made his first appearance on the stage as Frederick in " Lovers' Vows."

Born in the Quaker City in 1813, of good family, young Murdoch began, continued and ended his career as a close student, paying particular attention to the art of elocution, to which circumstance and a steadfast belief in himself his success was largely due. Of medium height, with a fine, manly face, graceful and pliant gestures, " he was," says a critic, " admirably adapted physically for tragedy or comedy. Only moderately endowed with the dramatic temperament, in genteel comedy—in such parts as Charles Surface, Young Mirable, Rover, Benedick and Mercutio, he was unsurpassed." In 1842, he retired from the stage to give a series of Shakespearian lectures and lessons in elocution to law and divinity students. He was also the author of an interesting volume of theatrical impressions entitled " The Stage."

In 1831 the Arch Street Theatre passed under the control of Messrs. Jones, Duffy and W. Forrest. An unusually large company was engaged and here Edwin Forrest laid the foundations of his future fame.

CHAPTER XVI

EDWIN FORREST

THE TRAGEDIAN'S EARLY BEGINNINGS. BARNSTORMING OUT WEST.
SUCCESS IN NEW ORLEANS. DÉBUT IN NEW YORK. GROWING
FAME. VISIT TO LONDON. QUARREL WITH MACREADY. THE
ASTOR PLACE RIOT. THE TRAGEDIAN'S PERSONALITY. HIS CASTLE
AT FONTHILL. ENDOWMENT OF THE EDWIN FORREST HOME.

ON November 6, 1826, Edwin Forrest, a native
American actor and the most dominant personality
our stage has known, made his début at the Bowery
Theatre in the rôle of Othello. It was not his first
appearance in New York for he had been seen a few
months earlier at one performance at the Park
Theatre. He had been acting in Albany, playing
second rôles to Edmund Kean, when opportunity presented itself to appear in New York, at the benefit of
his friend, Jacob Woodhull. He selected the rôle of
the Moor, and his success on that occasion at once
brought him offers from Manager Simpson of the
Park and Manager Gilfert of the Bowery. He signed
with the latter manager at a salary of $800 a year.

Forrest at this time was only twenty years of age.
It will be remembered that six years previously—
when only fourteen years old—he had made his first
appearance on any stage at the Walnut Street Theatre,
Philadelphia, as Young Norval in Home's tragedy
" Douglas," when he was billed as a " young gentleman of Philadelphia."

Edwin Forrest was born in Monroe Street, Philadelphia, March 9, 1806. His father, a Scotchman,

having failed in business, became a runner for the old United States Bank. His mother was an American woman of German descent. Forrest senior died when Edwin was still in his childhood, and, the widow's slender means not permitting her to give him a liberal education, he was taken from school at the age of ten and put to work, first in a printing office and later in a ship chandler's store. But the boy had no taste for office routine. He early displayed talent for the stage and began taking part in amateur theatricals. With his brother William he joined a juvenile dramatic club and acted in a wood-shed before enthusiastic boy audiences. Before he was eleven he made his first public appearance in a female rôle at the old Southwark Theatre. The venture was a ludicrous failure, but, not discouraged, he persevered, and three years later asked Manager Wood to give him a trial at the Walnut Street Theatre. The début followed on November 27, 1820. His success was decisive. A leading Philadelphia paper said of the performance:

Of the part of Norval we must say that it was as uncommon in the performance as it was extraordinary in just conception and exemption from the idea of artifice. We were much surprised at the excellence of his elocution, his self-possession in speech and gesture, and a voice that without straining, was of such volume and fine tenor as to carry every tone and articulation to the remotest corner of the theatre.

The play was repeated on December 2. Three weeks later young Forrest assumed the rôle of Frederick in Kotzebue's drama " Lovers' Vows " and on January 6, 1821, he played Octavian in "The Mountaineers." The veteran Cooper was living in Philadelphia at that time and the boy went to him and asked advice in regard to his future. Cooper told him he must not trust to his raw triumphs as an amateur, but that if he really wished to make a name for himself, he must be willing to serve a regular apprenticeship in the actor's art and climb the ladder rung by rung and not try to climb by great skips. Realizing that the advice was sound and seeing no opportunity in the East where well trained actors abounded, the boy wrote to Manager J. H. Caldwell, who was then operating in New Orleans, offering his services. To this letter he received no answer. In 1822 Manager Jones of the Western firm of Collins and Jones visited Philadelphia for the purpose of recruiting players for the Western circuit, and Forrest applied to him for an engagement.

Impressed by the young man's bearing and earnest manner, Jones at once struck a bargain with him. Forrest was to receive $8 a week and play whatever he was cast for, no matter how good or how poor the parts might be. Forrest agreed, said good-bye to his family and started West. His first stopping place was Pittsburgh. The theatre in which he acted was so dilapidated that on rainy nights the audience sat holding up umbrellas. He played Young Norval to great applause, and all that season appeared in tragedy, comedy, farce and ballet. On the conclusion of that engagement, the company gathered up its properties and took passage on an Ohio flatboat for Maysville, Ky. From there the players went to Lexington and finally to Cincinnati. When travelling by land, Forrest and the other actors rode on horseback while the women of the company followed in covered wagons with the theatrical paraphernalia. They opened at the old Columbia Street Theatre in Cincinnati March 6, 1823, in " The Soldier's Daughter," Forrest taking the part of Young Malfort. A little later J. H. Caldwell, who had previously ignored the young actor's application, wrote Forrest, offering him a position in the New Orleans company at $18 a week. Sol Smith at that time was prompter of the Cincinnati Theatre and he wrote a piece called " The Tailor in Distress " in which Forrest appeared as a negro. Later, Sol Smith organized a company of his own and Forrest wanted to join him, saying he preferred going with him for $15 a week rather than undertake the long trip to New Orleans. Sol Smith, however, refused to take him and advised the young man to accept Caldwell's offer. Angry at this refusal, Forrest joined a circus and when Sol Smith went to remonstrate with him, he found the young man turning flip flops. Finally, he was persuaded to proceed to New Orleans, where he arrived in February, 1824, opening as Jaffier in the tragedy " Venice Preserved."

Other rôles in which Forrest was seen during this New Orleans engagement were Iago, which he played to Conway's Othello, and the title rôle in Howard Payne's " Brutus," a part in which he later became famous. The manly bearing of the handsome young actor, together with his robust physique and fine voice, made him at once a warm favorite, but he did not stay long in New Orleans, owing to a quarrel with his manager. Caldwell had at first made much of his new protégé, but later became jealous of his popularity. The leading actress of the New Orleans company at that time was Jane Placide, a young girl of remarkable beauty. Forrest fell deeply in love with

34

her, and when she rejected his advances he discovered that he had a rival in the person of his manager. He challenged Caldwell to a duel, but the manager paid no attention, and the baffled and angry Forrest, having " posted " his former manager, went to cool his wrath and disappointment in the wigwam of an Indian chief with whom he had formed a close friendship.

In 1825 he was back in New Orleans, from whence he sailed for New York. Reports of his success in the West had already reached the Eastern cities, and Charles Gilfert at once engaged him for the Albany Theatre, where he acted with Edmund Kean, playing Iago to that tragedian's Othello, Titus to his Brutus, and Richmond to his Richard III. Then followed the successful appearance at the Park Theatre, New York, and the engagement at the Bowery Theatre, his salary making a leap from $28 to $40 a week. " From this success," says Lawrence Barrett, " may be traced the first absolute hold made by Edwin Forrest upon the attention of cultivated auditors and intelligent critics." [1] He was later re-engaged for eighty nights at $200 a night. This was the beginning of Forrest's career as a star, though he had only just completed his twenty-first year.

After this he played in every city in the United States, acquiring rapidly both fame and fortune. The rôles he played at the Bowery with extraordinary success were Damon, Jaffier, William Tell and Marc Antony. On the death of Manager Gilfert in 1829, he went to the Park Theatre, appearing in the rôle of Damon. At this theatre on December 15, 1829, he

---

[1] Edwin Forrest. By Lawrence Barrett.

was first seen as Metamora in John A. Stone's tragedy of that name, and two years later he was seen as Spartacus in " The Gladiator," a tragedy by Robert M. Bird, " both of which plays," says William Winter, " were written to fit his talents and peculiarities and in both of which his acting was the perfection of physical realism. . . . Forrest was then in the prime of manhood and the first flush of popularity, a person remarkable for muscular force, a voice of prodigious volume and melody, and a cogent style of depicting the emotional experience of turbulent characters. He had, within a brief time, acquired an extraordinary vogue and distinction. The local stage, not then able to exult in much tragic talent distinctively American, proudly claimed for the American actor a rank equal with that of the best foreign representatives of tragedy." [1]

In 1836 he was seen for the first time as Lear, which many critics considered his finest part. Forrest was of the same opinion himself. His magnificent physique, rugged exterior, tempestuous style of acting, all lent verisimilitude to the kingly rôle. A friend once remarked to him: " Mr. Forrest, I never saw you play Lear as well as you did last night." Whereupon the actor drew himself up to his full height, and replied indignantly: " *Play* Lear! What do you mean, sir? I do not *play* Lear! I *play* Hamlet, Richard, Shylock, Virginius, but by God, sir, I *am* Lear!"

In October of that same year he made his first professional visit to London, appearing at Drury

[1] From "The Wallet of Time." Copyright, 1913, by William Winter. Moffat, Yard and Company, Publishers. Reprinted by permission of Jefferson Winter, Esq.

Lane as Spartacus. The play failed to make any impression, but the American actor was greeted with great applause. There were loud cries for Shakespeare, and Forrest satisfied the demand by giving "Othello," "Lear" and "Macbeth" twenty-four times out of the thirty-two nights of the engagement. The *Times* wrote of him: "He is a tall, rather robust man, not remarkably handsome, but with expressive features and that cast of countenance which is well suited for theatrical effect. His voice is remarkably powerful, his figure rather vigorous than elegant, and his general appearance prepossessing." While in London he met and wooed Catherine Norton Sinclair, the beautiful daughter of the well known English vocalist. They were married at St. Paul's Cathedral the following year, and when Forrest returned that fall to fill his engagement at the Chestnut Street Theatre, his English bride accompanied him. The marriage, however, did not prove a happy one. Charges and counter charges were made on both sides until, in 1850, Mrs. Forrest secured a divorce and went herself on the stage.

From Philadelphia, Forrest proceeded to the Park Theatre, New York, where on May 24, 1841, he was seen as Aylmere in "Jack Cade," a tragic drama written for him by Robert T. Conrad, of Philadelphia. In 1845 the tragedian paid a second visit to London and appeared at the Princess' as Macbeth. The audience did not like his impersonation and hissed him. Without any justification, Forrest at once attributed this hostility to the machinations of Macready. The English tragedian had acted in America two years previously and some of the critics had pitted him against Forrest, thus creating considerable rivalry and partisanship among theatregoers. Shortly afterward, Forrest was in Edinburgh where Macready happened to be acting Hamlet. Still smarting from the hostile reception he himself had received in London, and still believing Macready the instigator, Forrest went to the theatre, stood conspicuously in a box and hissed the English actor. "This act, opposed to good taste," says Lawrence Barrett, "was at once reported in the newspapers, and led to letters of crimination and recrimination, which made the quarrel an open scandal, not only in England but in America." In 1848 when Macready paid his third visit to America and was hissed in Philadelphia he alluded publicly to Forrest's conduct in Edinburgh. Forrest replied in the newspapers and Macready made a rejoinder. "The honors in this wordy squabble," adds Barrett, "were all with Macready, who preserved his dignity while defending his cause." [1]

From this trivial misunderstanding grew the fatal riot outside the Astor Place Opera House, New York, May 10, 1849, which resulted in the killing of twenty-two persons and the wounding of thirty-six others.

The Astor Place Opera House had been opened in 1847 by Sanquirico and Patti with the opera "Ernani." The following year the mother of Adelina Patti, Signora Catrina Barilli-Patti, made her début as Romeo. The theatre was centrally situated, but never had much success as an opera house. William Niblo and J. H. Hackett next took a lease of the house and announced a four weeks' engagement of Mr. Macready, beginning May 8, 1848. The adher-

---

[1] Edwin Forrest. By Lawrence Barrett.

ents of Forrest at once determined on a hostile demonstration. The house did not open May 8 as announced, but on May 9, J. H. Hackett appeared in " The Merry Wives of Windsor." On May 10, Macready was announced to play Macbeth to the Lady Macbeth of Mrs. Coleman Pope. Forrest's adherents declared boldly that he would not be permitted to play. There were rumors of impending trouble all over town. The feud had been fanned until it was no longer a squabble between two rival actors, but a reopening of the old time enmity with England. On the city walls appeared posters worded as follows:

Workingmen, shall Americans or English rule in this city? The crew of the British steamer have threatened all Americans who shall dare to express their opinion this night at the ENGLISH AUTOCRATIC Opera House! We advocate no violence, but a free expression of opinion to all public men. WASHINGTON forever! Stand by your Lawful Rights! AMERICAN COMMITTEE.

Apprehending a serious disturbance, the authorities at once took measures to preserve order. " As early as half past six," says T. Allston Brown, " persons began to assemble about the theatre and at seven o'clock the rush to get admittance was tremendous." The writer continues:

The theatre was crowded to the dome. A large body of police were distributed all over the house in detached parties. When the curtain rose there was an outburst of hisses, groans, cheers and miscellaneous sounds. During the opening scenes, several persons who hissed and hooted were seized by the police and immediately conveyed to an apartment underneath the boxes. A vociferous welcome was given to Mr. Clarke, when he appeared as Malcolm. The entrance of Mr. Macready, in the third scene, was the signal for a perfect storm of cheers, groans, and hisses. The whole audience rose, and the nine-tenths of it who were friendly to Macready cheered, and waved their hats and handkerchiefs. The tumult lasted for ten or fifteen minutes, when an attempt was made to restore order, by a board being brought upon the stage, upon which was written, " *The friends of order will remain quiet.*" This silenced all but the rioters, who continued to drown what was said upon the stage. Not a word of the first act could be heard by any one in the house.

At this time the scene outside the house was most exciting. In front and rear the fierce assaults of the mob, as they thundered at the doors, resounded over the theatre, while the shouts and yells of the assailants were terrific. As the mob increased in magnitude so did the ferocity with which they assailed the building. Several despatches were sent to the City Hall, where the military were stationed. At length about ten o'clock, the sound of cavalry, coming up Broadway, was heard, and in a few minutes afterwards two troops of mounted men, of the First Division of the State Militia, and a battalion of the National Guards were seen approaching. A troop of horse then turned from Broadway into Astor Place and rode through the crowd to Bowery, receiving showers of stones and other missiles on their way. In a few minutes afterwards the National Guards made their appearance, and attempted to force a passage through the crowd to the theatre. The mob hissed and hooted at them, and finally attacked them with stones, which were at hand in consequence of the building of a sewer in the neighborhood. The soldiers were thrown into disorder by the attack upon them, and retired on Broadway, where they rallied and made another attempt to reach the theatre. The officer in command then said to the sheriff, who was on the ground, that if he did not get orders to fire, he and his men would abandon the streets. Accordingly, the sheriff directed the military to fire a round over the heads of the people, which was done, but without effect. The people continued to pelt them with paving stones, as before. An order was then given to the troops to fire at the crowd, and it was done, two men falling, one shot in the arm and the other through the right cheek. The first was sent to the hospital, but the other was found to be dead.

After the volley, the crowd retreated a short distance, but rallied and renewed the attack with greater vigor than before. Paving stones and other missiles were then thrown by them in great quantities, and another volley was fired by the military, killing and wounding several more. After this volley, the crowd retreated again, and the military and police took advantage of it to form a line across the street at both ends of Astor Place, so as to prevent any connection between Broadway and the Bowery. Major General Sandford then issued an order for more troops, and two brass pieces loaded with grape, to be brought to the scene immediately, as it was rumored that the crowd intended to arm themselves and renew the attack. The cannons were placed in front of the theatre, ready for a renewal of the attack. At one o'clock, A. M., quiet prevailed, and the play came to an end The performance of the afterpiece commenced, and had proceeded but a short way when the discharge of musketry startled the whole house—some one calling out that " the house was to be blown up." All started to their feet, when ex-Justice Merritt addressed the house, and requested the audience to keep their seats, as there was no danger. This somewhat restored order till a few minuets afterwards, when it was announced that a man had been shot outside. The performance was instantly stopped, and the audience rushed out of the building.

There were a great many persons wounded in addition to those referred to, seriously or slightly, who either went away or were taken away by their friends. Sometimes heavy stones would crash through the boards which had been nailed up as a protection, and a number of policemen were constantly occupied in nailing up and securing the defences. A shower of stones assailed the windows of the theatre. News then came from the street, through Captain Tilley, that a man known to be Edward Z. C. Judson was heading the mob outside, and calling upon them to stone the building. He was promptly arrested by the Chief of Police. As one window cracked after another, and pieces of bricks and paving stones rattled in on the terrace and lobbies, the confusion increased till the Opera House resembled a fortress besieged by an army. Finally, in the last scene of the act, Mr. Matsell, Chief of Police, made his appearance in the parquet, and, followed by his aides, marched directly down the aisle to the leader of the disturbance, whom he secured after a short but violent struggle.[4]

---

[4] History of the New York Stage. By T. Allston Brown. Copyright, 1902, by Dodd, Mead & Co., Publishers.

Macready barely escaped with his life. If the mob could have got at him there is little doubt what his fate would have been. As it fortunately happened, he managed to get safely away. Disguised and accompanied by a few friends, he went to the stage door where the party was not permitted to pass. Returning to the stage, they climbed over into the orchestra, and mingling with the audience moving out, succeeded in reaching Broadway. Macready at once went to a friend's house where he sat up all night and at daybreak next morning was driven to New Rochelle. From there he went by train to Boston, whence he sailed for England.

The disgraceful disturbance in New York, coupled with his scandalous domestic dissensions, at once lost for Forrest the support of the better classes of theatregoers, while, says a biographer, "he became more than ever an idol of the 'common people' who saw in him a champion of American resistance to English assumption."

Critics are not unanimous in according to Forrest rank as the greatest player this country has yet produced. Some of his adherents have made of him a god-like man in the possession of gifts vouchsafed to few mortals, but in the opinion of William Winter, Forrest "was not a man whom it is desirable to canonize." He continues:

. . . In youth and early manhood he was boisterous, sensual, revengeful, and profligate. In age he was misanthropical. He was capable of good impulses and kind actions, but the impulses were often checked by distrust, and the actions were often prompted and moulded by selfish aims. His vanity was prodigious. He thought himself the greatest of actors and of men. The least expression of dissent from his opinion, or of disapproval of what

42

EDWIN FORREST

he had said or done, would sting him into an outburst of fury, or madden him to a long fit of sullen resentment. . . . Although there were always persons who neither admired, nor liked, nor praised him, no man in America ever attracted larger crowds of followers, or elicited more copious and emphatic adulation. . . . There was no reason outside of himself why he should not have lived a triumphant and happy life. Yet his existence was a tempest and his career a magnificent failure. . . . In youth he revolted against wholesome discipline. In manhood he revolted against culture, the restraints of good breeding and right social custom, the duty of consideration for other persons, the supremacy of spiritual law, and even those iron dictates of destiny which, for each individual, flow out of personality. He was constitutionally savage and always in rebellion.˙ . . . The actor temperament, in the nature of things selfish, was in him selfishness incarnate. He recognized neither fault in his character nor error in his conduct.[5]

His biographers, James Rees, Lawrence Barrett, William R. Alger and other critics, on the other hand, are lavishly eulogistic of the tragedian. The late Edmond S. Connor, a distinguished actor who frequently played with Forrest, though off the stage they were not on speaking terms, after dwelling at some length on Forrest's remarkable powers, exclaimed: "And oh, the majesty of the man!" Alfred Ayres, another keen student of the drama, says of him:

No one that saw Forrest in the first scene of "Lear," when Lear parcels out his kingdom, ever could forget the Jovelike majesty of his aspect. Mr. Forrest made many people dislike him—he could not be, and he would not be, diplomatic with the indolent, the untruthful, or the dishonest. On the other hand, no man ever made warmer friends. He was bountifully endowed by nature. His features were regular and in early life pleasing. His height was five feet ten, and his figure was symmetric, but would have been better if it had been somewhat less herculean. Even in such parts

[5] From "The Wallet of Time." Copyright, 1913, by William Winter. Moffat, Yard & Company, Publishers. Reprinted by permission of Jefferson Winter, Esq.

43

as Othello, Coriolanus, Virginius, Jack Cade, and the Broker of Bogota, had his figure been less Samson-like, he would have pleased the eye better, while in Hamlet, Richelieu, and Claude Melnotte, for example—characters that from a strictly art point of view were among his best personations—he appeared to be miscast. Heavy, however, as Forrest was in build, he was never ungraceful in his movements. No man could bow more gracefully than he. His voice was phenomenal. I never have met any one that did not unhesitatingly concede to Forrest's voice the first place among all the voices he had ever beard. But it was not Mr. Forrest's face, grace, and voice that made him by critical—if not by common—consent the greatest English-speaking actor born in the last century—and I doubt not the greatest actor born in any century—it was his wonderful elocution. Forrest, probably, made the greatest part that ever has been written—the part of King Lear—more effective; got more out of it, than any other actor ever has gotten out of it, which rightfully gives him the first place among the players of all time. To a greater extent Forrest united those gifts, physical and mental, and those habits and tendencies that count in an actor than has any other man known to history. Indeed, among the players of whom we have any knowledge, Forrest was a colossus, as well intellectually as physically.[6]

Herman Vezin, the American actor, thought Forrest lacked " the polish of art," although physically endowed beyond any actor he had ever seen. Another critic says " he excelled rather in delineating tumultuous passion than in the portrayal of intellectual subtleties and poetical grace."

In the opinion of Lawrence Barrett, " his obtrusive personality often destroyed the harmony of the portrait he was painting, but in his inspired moments, which were many, his touches were sublime. He passed over quiet scenes with little elaboration and dwelt strongly upon the grand features of the character he represented. His Lear in the great scenes

---

[6] America's Greater Players. By Alfred Ayres. *Theatre Magazine*, December, 1901.

rose to a majestic height but fell in places almost to mediocrity. His art was unequal to his natural gifts."[7]

All agree as to the vital importance of his work and the impetus he gave to the American drama. " He was," says a critic, " the first American actor to whom the attribute of greatness fairly belongs. He had not only a splendid physique and magnificent voice, but also great force of character, which gave a stamp of authority to his every act and judgment, so that he may be credited with having so moulded the public taste, as touching his art, that his successors had to reckon with the Forrest tradition. That he became one of the most powerful tragedians of this or any other country is undoubted; he ranks high among Shakespearean interpreters. He had for professional competitor Junius Brutus Booth and yet retained his friendship. Both in England and America he competed successfully with Edmund Kean and Macready."

William Winter tells us that Forrest " revolted against culture," that he was " always the slave of his ignorance," that " he had knowledge enough to know that there is such a thing as learning, and he resented, with fierce irritation, the nevertheless irrefutable fact that this was possessed by others and was not possessed by him."

But James Rees, Forrest's biographer, presents an entirely different picture of Forrest's mentality and culture. He says:

We never entered his library but we found him either with a book in hand or engaged at the writing table. The former, how-ever, was his chief employment in his hours of ease. No one could

[7] Edwin Forrest. By Lawrence Barrett.

THE THEATRE IN AMERICA

have imagined for a moment that the quiet, calm student before
him was the terrible Lear and Othello of the stage. A writer has
said of him: " Having received but little instruction in his boyhood, from the time fortune dawned upon him, he sought by every
means that wealth and determination could give him to make himself an accomplished man. His library in Philadelphia, of which
everybody has heard, was his home, his resting-place; and here he
gathered such a store of literary knowledge as but few men acquire,
even in a longer life than sixty-seven years. Mr. John W. Forney
has been heard to say on returning from a visit to Mr. Forrest, that
Forrest was a fresh surprise to him each hour he spent in his company. His knowledge was not confined to dramatic literature alone.
He was a good classical scholar, a remarkably acute and learned
lawyer; and his knowledge of science and arts alone would have
made him a foremost man in any country." [8]

For many years Forrest continued to act all over
the United States and rapidly accumulated great
wealth. His castle of Fonthill on the banks of the
Hudson, his mansion in Philadelphia, and his extensive library were the talk and envy of the theatrical
world. During his last appearance at the Fourteenth
Street Theatre, New York, in 1871, his engagement
was brought to a sudden termination by illness. His
last appearance as an actor was on the stage of the
Globe Theatre, Boston, April 2, 1872. He died December 12, the same year. He left at Holmesburg,
Pa., a permanent home for aged and indigent players,
and in this peaceful, secluded haven to-day a dozen or
more actors and actresses, stage favorites of another
era, spend the last days of their lives waiting the final
call as " Mr. Forrest's guests."

In his will, in which he provided for the endowment of the Edwin Forrest home, he said: " My professional brothers and sisters are often unfortunate,

---

[8] A Life of Edwin Forrest. By James Rees.

and little has been done for them, either to elevate them in their profession, or to provide for their necessities under sickness or other misfortunes. God has favored my efforts and given me great success, and I would make my fortune the means to elevate the education of others, and promote their success, and to alleviate their suffering, and smooth the pillows of the unfortunate in sickness, or other disability, or the decay of declining years."

CHAPTER XVII

THE AMERICAN DRAMATIST—1690–1890

FAMOUS MEN OF LETTERS WHO ATTEMPTED THE DRAMATIC FORM.
THE EARLIEST NATIVE PLAY ON RECORD. FIRST PLAY PRINTED IN
AMERICA. FORREST OFFERS PRIZES FOR NATIVE PLAYS. THE
CREATOR OF JONATHAN PLOUGHBOY. JOHN HOWARD PAYNE'S
PLAYS. THE PHILADELPHIA SCHOOL OF DRAMATISTS. INDIAN
PLAYS. OTHER AMERICAN DRAMATISTS.

WHATEVER niche in the hall of theatrical fame
posterity eventually awards to Edwin Forrest, the
actor, no theatre lover eager to see this country one
day produce a great playwright, a modern Shakespeare who shall reflect and glorify the enormous
vitality and peculiar genius of our people, will fail to
give him credit for what he did, as a patriot, to promote the cause of the American national drama.

Up to Forrest's time, America had no dramatic
literature. It was the golden age of American letters
in every form except the dramatic form. Webster,
the lexicographer; Prescott, Motley, Bancroft, Park-
man, the historians; Longfellow, Edgar Allan Poe,
James Russell Lowell, William Greenleaf Whittier,
Walt Whitman, the poets; Washington Irving, Feni-
more Cooper, Nathaniel Hawthorne, Charles Brock-
den Brown, J. K. Paulding, Bret Harte, the novelists;
Oliver Wendell Holmes, Ralph Waldo Emerson, the
essayists and philosophers; Mark Twain and Artemus
Ward, the humorists—these made up a glorious company that shed lustre on American literature wher-
ever the English tongue was spoken.

Of these literary titans only Longfellow, Irving,

Holmes, Paulding, Poe and Brown ever attempted to write for the stage, and only Paulding and Brown had any success in that field. Longfellow wrote several plays, none of which were acted. His blank verse drama " The Spanish Student " was published in 1843 and the Tragedies in 1868. Irving collaborated on more than one play with John Howard Payne, but insisted on his share being concealed. Poe wrote a play called " Politian," from which he claimed Longfellow had plagiarized his " Spanish Student." Oliver Wendell Holmes, in 1831, contributed a " Scene from an Unpublished Comedy " to a Boston monthly. James Russell Lowell's translation of Professor Child's operetta " Il Pesceballo " was acted by amateurs in 1862.

One reason, undoubtedly, for the aloofness of polite literature was the Puritanical prejudice which still persisted against all things theatrical. Another was the indefinable hostility against, and the open contempt for, the stage which literary workers have always affected. This attitude of literature toward the theatre is succinctly expressed by Gertrude Atherton, the well known author:

A novelist is not entirely trained to the humiliation of a playwright, and is entirely opposed to the autocracy of the producer. Since a novel is an intimate revelation of real character, I am afraid that the theatre can never do entire justice to the author. I am very fond of the theatre, but I always wish there were better taste, a nicer selection of language, and a closer attention to untheatrical atmosphere than we usually find in plays on the American stage.[1]

A still more potent reason for the absence of our early literary workers from the theatrical field was

[1] See article in the *Theatre Magazine*, February, 1918.

perhaps the fact that they fully realized the difficulties of dramatic construction, that the drama had a
technic of its own entirely different to the one gov-
erning their own art, and which was only to be
acquired by a long and arduous apprenticeship. The
late F. Marion Crawford told the present writer that
the stage appealed to him most strongly as a medium
of expression, but that he had always recoiled from
any attempt in that direction, awed as he was by the
enormous difficulties of the craft.

Many of our literary men have taken a keen interest in the theatre. Both the parents of Edgar Allan
Poe were players. Washington Irving was a constant frequenter of the playhouse, and wrote about it
most entertainingly. He and Bret Harte and Oliver
Wendell Holmes have on occasion written addresses
in verse for the opening of theatres.

Up to the year 1830, America had no national
drama. As previously noted, there had been some
desultory writing done for the stage by native authors,
but nothing had been produced characteristic and
vital enough to deserve being classed as national
drama. Yet the American drama is older than the
American theatre itself. That is to say, American
authors wrote plays long before there was in this
country a single theatre in which to perform them.

Very early in the Seventeenth Century, refer-
ences to America in English plays were frequent.
Shakespeare in " The Tempest " makes allusion to
the " still vexed Bermoothes " (Bermudas). In
" Eastward Hoe," written in 1605 by George Chapman, Ben Jonson and John Marston, there is a
scene in praise of Virginia, which colony was then the

fashionable topic of the day, and Sir William Berkeley, governor of Virginia in 1641, while in America,
wrote a play called " Cornelia " which was acted in
London in 1662. In Mrs. Aphra Behn's play, " The
Widow Ranter, or Bacon in Virginia," the scene is
laid in America, the subject dealing with the insur-
rection known as Bacon's. We also have Anthony
Aston's own word that when in America in 1702 he
" wrote a play on the subject of the country."

The earliest play written by a native of this country, of which we have any knowledge, was " Gus-
tavus Vasa," acted by the students of Harvard
College in 1690. Its author, Benjamin Colman, was
born in Boston in 1673 and died there in 1747. He
was graduated from Harvard in 1692 and entered the
pulpit the following year at Medford, Mass. " On a
voyage to England in 1695," says John Malone in his
introduction to Oscar Wegelin's [2] valuable compila-
tion of titles of early plays by American authors, " his
vessel was attacked by a French privateer. He fought
with the crew and was taken with them and confined
in France as a prisoner of war. He was finally ex-
changed and was enabled to go on to London. He
preached there several times and was urged to remain,
but was called to be first minister of Brattle Street
Church in Boston where he officiated until his death."

Another early play of native origin acted in
America was written by a French officer, Le Blanc
de Villeneuve. This piece, entitled " Le Père
Indien " and dealing with the voluntary sacrifice of
a Choctaw father to save his son's life, was produced
by amateurs in New Orleans in 1753.

[2] Early American Plays. By Oscar Wegelin.

THE THEATRE IN AMERICA

The first play to be printed in America was a farce in three acts called " Androborus " (The Man Eater). It was written by Robert Hunter, governor of New York, in collaboration with Lewis Morris, a native New Yorker and chief justice of the New York colony. This piece, printed in New York in 1714 by William· Bradford and bearing the fictitious imprint of " Monoropolis " (Fool's Town, meaning New York), was a satire on the political conditions of the day, and was doubtless put out to check the meddling of Trinity Parish officials in the affairs of the colony. From the viewpoint of dramatic construction it was not without merit. " The play," says Paul Leicester Ford, " was seemingly never intended for stage production, for a part of the plot turns on so filthy an incident as to preclude its performance even in the coarse and vulgar time of its writing. The piece is dramatic, however, despite its politics and lack of women's parts, the characters are admirably drawn and it abounds in genuine humor. The trick played on Androborus, of making him believe himself dead, is both quaint and effective, and the part of Tom of Bedlam is notable in its Mrs. Malapropisms." [a]

Only one copy of this play is to-day known to exist and in the eyes of collectors of rare Americana it is literally worth considerably more than its weight in gold. The single copy which has survived is fortunately in this country. After having been in turn the property of Garrick, Kemble and the Duke of Devonshire, it is now in the library of Mr. H. E. Huntington of New York City.

[a] The Beginnings of American Dramatic Literature. By Paul Leicester Ford.

The first American printed play to be acted had only two characters and was entitled " An Exercise Containing a Dialogue and Ode Sacred to the Memory of George II." This was acted May 23, 1761, by the Students of the College of Philadelphia. A year later, at the College of New Jersey (now Princeton), the graduating class presented " The Military Glory of Great Britain." As significant of the times, it was only fourteen years later that the tragi-comedy " The Fall of British Tyranny," by John Leacock, made its bid for popular patronage. The tragedies of Hugh Henry Brackenridge, the American lawyer-author (1748-1816), have been mentioned elsewhere.

A tragedy in blank verse " Ponteach, or the Savages of America," written by Major Robert Rogers, the Indian ranger and a native of New Hampshire, was printed in London in 1766, but never acted.

The first play written by an American to be acted by professional players and also printed, was, as already noted in an earlier chapter, " The Prince of Parthia," by Thomas Godfrey, Jr., produced by Douglass in Philadelphia in 1765. Twenty years later (1785) the students at Yale produced another tragedy by an American author—Barnabas Bidwell's " The Mercenary Match."

The first American woman known to have written plays was Charlotte Lennox, daughter of an English government official. She was born in this country, but later took up her residence in London where she became intimate with Dr. Johnson, Goldsmith and other celebrities. In 1748 she went on the stage, and some years later wrote a play called " Philander, a Dramatic Pastoral," which was printed but never acted. In 1769 she wrote a comedy entitled "The Sister," a dramatization of her own novel which was produced at Covent Garden. It proved such a failure that the author would not permit it to be given a second time, yet it was translated into German in 1776, being the first play by an American to be translated into a foreign language.

These and other early efforts at native dramatic composition, including the political satires of Mercy Warren, and the Revolutionary and other plays dealing with the passions of the time, are to-day chiefly interesting as literary curiosities. They had little, if any, bearing on the development of the native American drama. It was not until Royall Tyler and William Dunlap began to write successful American plays and Edwin Forrest held out substantial pecuniary inducements to native authors that the native American drama was born. As Edith J. R. Isaacs says:

From the days of "The Contrast" there has been an American drama in and out of the theatre, struggling for expression, fighting for survival. Its history can be traced as clearly as a vein of gold by any one who cares enough to look for it. It is always vital, always American, always dramatic; it is not always good art. Until Bronson Howard's day, it had little respect in the theatre and practically none in literature. Therefore, much of it has disappeared and the rest will disappear unless we can help to breed that high sounding but exceedingly simple thing, a "national consciousness," toward the drama as an art and the theatre as an institution which is taken for granted in every other civilized country.[4]

The period of American playwriting that lay between William Dunlap and the so-called Philadelphia school, was bridged over by several native dra-

[4] Article in New York *Times*. December 10, 1916.

matists of ability: Charles Jared Ingersoll (1782–1862), James Nelson Barker (1784–1858), Samuel Woodworth (1785–1842), Mordecai N. Noah (1785–1851), George Washington Parke Custis (1786–1857), Richard Penn Smith (1790–1854), John Howard Payne (1791–1852).

Charles Jared Ingersoll, a Philadelphia lawyer of note, wrote a five act tragedy " Edwy and Elgiva " which was performed in Philadelphia in 1801, with Mrs. Merry in the part of the heroine.

James Nelson Barker, whom Ireland characterizes as " one of the best of American authors," was mayor of Philadelphia in 1820. All his plays are on native themes. His comedy " Tears and Smiles " was first acted at the Chestnut Street Theatre, Philadelphia, in 1807. His next play " The Indian Princess," the first of the many plays having the Indian maiden Pocahontas for heroine, was produced at the Chestnut Street Theatre April 6, 1808. " Marmion," a dramatization of Scott's poem, was first acted in New York at the Park Theatre in 1812. " Superstition," one of the earliest plays based upon Colonial history, was first seen in Philadelphia at the Chestnut Street Theatre March 12, 1824. According to F. C. Wemyss, who acted the part of George Egerton, the piece was a success, but was seldom performed because Mary Duff, who played Mary, outshone Mrs. Wood as Isabella.

Samuel Woodworth, the creator of Jonathan Ploughboy, a Yankee character made familiar by J. H. Hackett, Alexander Simpson, G. H. Hill, Henry Placide and Joshua Silsbee, was born in Scituate, Mass., and began his career as a printer. In

1810 he went to New York, where he was one of the founders of the *New York Mirror*. He wrote five plays, all of which were produced: " The Deed of Gift," comic opera produced at the City Theatre, New York, in 1823; " Lafayette," a drama seen at the Park Theatre in 1824; " The Forest Rose," acted at the Chatham Theatre, New York, in 1825; " The Widow's Son," also seen at the Park, and " The King's Bridge Cottage," a Revolutionary drama.

Mordecai N. Noah, journalist and critic, wrote " The Fortress of Sorrento," " The Grecian Captive," " Marion," " She Would be a Soldier," " The Wandering Boys " and other dramas of wide popular appeal.

George Washington Custis, author of " Pocahontas or the Settlers of Virginia," produced at the Walnut Street Theatre, Philadelphia, January 16, 1830, was the son of John Parke Custis, the stepson of Washington. He fought in the War of 1812 and afterwards was well known as a writer of prose and verse. Other plays by him are " The Railroad," a drama produced in Philadelphia in which a steam locomotive was introduced; " North Point, or Baltimore Defended," acted at the Baltimore Theatre in 1833, and " The Eighth of January," performed January 8, 1834, at the Park Theatre, New York.

Richard Penn Smith was born in Philadelphia and educated as a lawyer. He wrote altogether twenty plays, turning out pieces with such facility that the last act of " William Penn," a play dealing with Penn's intervention to save the life of the Indian chief Tammany, he began and completed on the afternoon previous to the first performance. Other plays

by this author are " Quite Correct," produced at the
Chestnut Street Theatre, Philadelphia, in 1828; " Is
She a Brigand? " first seen at the Arch Street Theatre
in 1833; " The Disowned," a melodrama presented
at the Baltimore Theatre in 1829; " A Wife at a
Venture," seen at the Walnut Street Theatre, Philadelphia the same year; " The Deformed," produced
at the Chestnut Street Theatre in 1830; " The Triumph of Plattsburg," dealing with the War of 1812,
produced at the Chestnut Street Theatre in 1830. He
also won a prize offered by Edwin Forrest with his
play, " Caius Marius." Two of his plays, " The
Deformed " and " The Disowned," were acted successfully in London.

John Howard Payne, actor, editor, author and
song writer, wrote and adapted over sixty plays. His
first piece, " Julia, or the Wanderer," was acted at
the Park Theatre, February 7, 1806. An historical
tragedy, " Brutus, or the Fall of Tarquin," was first
seen in London at Drury Lane in 1818. " Charles
the Second," a comedy in collaboration with Washington Irving, was presented at the Park Theatre,
New York, October 25, 1824. Payne was more at
home in the field of melodrama, and such pieces as
" Thérèse, or the Orphan of Geneva," " Clari or the
Maid of Milan " (which contains the song *Home,
Sweet Home,* and first seen in London in 1823) were
very popular.

All these were interesting native productions, but
it was not until Forrest offered substantial money
prizes for plays by American authors and began to
produce the pieces offered, that any real stimulus was
given to the national American drama. The real

beginnings of the native American dramatist may, therefore, be said to date from Forrest's time.

Until then, there was little incentive for the American to write for his own stage. The few native authors who were admitted to the footlights were made to feel keenly the humility of their position. They were seldom, if ever, paid. The author was the most inconsequential person back of the curtain. Sometimes out of compassion the manager would condescend to give him a benefit. His compensation thus came to him in the form of charity. Is it a wonder, under such sircumstances, that the successful literary men of that day saw little to attract their talents to the theatre?

Prejudice against the home-made play was almost unsurmountable and has continued in a minor degree until our own day. Barker relates how, because of this prejudice, his play " Marmion " was put on in New York in 1812 as " an English play by Thomas Morton, Esq.," and further announced as " received with unbounded applause in London." After running several nights with success, the American authorship was given out, when the receipts immediately fell off.

Even so modern a manager as Charles Frohman had little real sympathy with, or faith in, the native dramatist. He produced American plays as a matter of policy, but most of his relations were with Barrie, Pinero, Captain Marshall, Haddon Chambers, Henry Arthur Jones and other British dramatists.

The early theatre managers looked to London exclusively for their plays and had found it convenient to ignore the question of authors' royalties, which in the absence of international copyright [5] they could do with impunity. The English plays were all printed and copies could be purchased for a few pence. Dunlap prints a letter he received from Kotzebue in which the German dramatist speaks of Covent Garden paying him a hundred pounds for each of his plays. Dunlap does not say if he himself took the hint and also paid that sum for the many dramas he adapted from Kotzebue, but if he did it was not because he had to, but merely as a matter of courtesy and good business ethics. Accustomed to getting for nothing the best pieces by the most popular English authors, it is hardly surprising that the earlier managers looked with little favor on the unknown American dramatist. As to the suggestion that managers should pay American authors—the idea was preposterous.

Forrest argued differently. The money incentive was a powerful one. What was worth doing at all, he insisted, was worth paying for, and the sequel proved that he was right. New dramatists of ability were immediately attracted to the stage. In quick succession Forrest produced several plays by hitherto unknown native authors—" Metamora " (1829), by John Augustus Stone; " The Gladiator," " Oraloosa " and " The Broker of Bogota," by Dr. Robert Montgomery Bird. These authors, together with Robert T. Conrad, author of " Jack Cade " (1841), and George H. Boker, author of " Francesca da Rimini " (1856), all of whom were natives of Philadelphia, became known as the Philadelphia School of dramatists.

---

[5] Copyright protection was first granted in the United States to Belgian, French, British and Swiss authors July, 1891.

John Augustus Stone, the author of " Metamora," was born in Concord, Mass., in 1801. After making his début as an actor in Boston at the Washington Garden Theatre, he appeared at the Park Theatre, New York, in 1822, as Old Hardy in " The Belle's Stratagem." Later, he was identified with the Bowery and Chatham Theatres. Afterwards, he took up his residence in Philadelphia, where he acted at the Chestnut and Walnut Street Theatres. When Forrest offered $500 for the best American play suited to his peculiar style, Mr. Stone submitted a drama in verse entitled " Metamora," the leading character being the noble red man depicted in Fenimore Cooper's novels, whom Mark Twain wittily describes as belonging to an " extinct tribe which never existed." The piece was accepted and first produced at the Park Theatre, New York, December 15, 1829. Two months later it was seen at the Arch Street Theatre, Philadelphia. Although the play was inferior as a literary production, it met with immediate success, and, having been written for Forrest's personality, the part of Metamora became one of that actor's most famous and popular rôles. A later play by Stone, entitled " The Ancient Briton," for which Forrest paid the author $1000, had more merit as literature, but never attained the popularity of the first piece. A few years after fame had come to him, Stone committed suicide. One day in 1834 in a fit of mental depression he threw himself into the Schuylkill River, and was drowned. In recognition of his ability, Forrest erected a monument on his grave bearing this inscription: " In memory of the author of ' Metamora,' by his friend, Edwin Forrest."

The success of " Metamora " resulted in the remarkable run of Indian plays, " from which," as
Laurence Hutton puts it, " theatregoers throughout
the country suffered between the years 1830 and
1840." The titles of some of these plays were: " Sas-
sacus, or the Indian Wife "; " Kairrissah "; " Oraloosa "; " Outalassie "; " The Pawnee Chief ";
" Onylda, or the Pequot Maid "; " Ontiata, or the
Indian Heroine "; " Osceola "; " Oroonoka "; " Tus-
catomba "; " Wacousta "; " The Wept of the
Wish-ton Wish "; " Tutoona "; " Yemassee ";
" Wissahickon "; " Carabasset "; " Hiawatha ";
" Narramattah "; " Miautoumah "; " Eagle Eye ";
" Lamorah "; " The Wigwam "; " The Manhat-
toes "; " The Indian Prophecy "; etc.

For ten years and more these Indian plays were
very popular, but at last a reaction set in. In 1846,
James Rees [*] wrote that the Indian drama in his
opinion " had become a perfect nuisance," but it was
not until John Brougham, in 1855, came with his extravagant burlesque, " Pocahontas, or the Gentle
Savage," that the Indian play received its final *coup
de grâce.*

Dr. Robert Montgomery Bird (1803-1854),
author of " The Gladiator," in which Forrest scored
another big success in the character of Spartacus, was
born in Delaware. He began life as a physician, and
later took to literature. He wrote many novels,
among them " Nick of the Woods," which was afterwards turned into a popular play by Miss L. H.
Medina. Forrest was a personal friend of the physi-

[*] Author of "Charlotte Temple," "Washington at Valley Forge," "Life of Edwin Forrest," etc.

cian, and they frequently travelled together. "The Gladiator" was first performed on October 24, 1831, at the Arch Street Theatre, Philadelphia, before an immense audience. The play proved a triumph, the poetic beauty of many of the passages and the bold, impressive language causing it to be considered one of the tragedian's noblest impersonations. The tremendous scene at the close of the second act, when the gladiators break loose from their tyrants and raise the standard of revolt, aroused the audience to the highest pitch of enthusiasm. The play held the stage for seventy years. It was acted in England by Macready, and in America by John McCullough and Robert Downing, but none of these actors reached Forrest's heights in the rôle. Another play by Dr. Bird, "Oraloosa," a story of Spanish cruelty in Peru, produced by Forrest the following year, was also received with favor, and after this came "The Broker of Bogota," also Spanish in atmosphere, which is the most finished, as a work of literature, of all Bird's plays.

Another play, written by R. T. Conrad, a Philadelphian, in which Forrest appeared at the Arch Street Theatre, Philadelphia, in 1841, with great success, was "Aylmere, or the Bondman of Kent." This tragedy, written with lofty purpose and which has a stirring patriotic appeal, at once gave its author high rank among our native dramatists. Robert Taylor Conrad (1810–1858) was a lawyer and mayor of Philadelphia in 1854. The piece, at first entitled "Jack Cade," was originally written for A. A. Addams. Four years later, Judge Conrad rewrote the play for Forrest, and the title was changed to "Aylmere." Subsequently, the original title was restored. The tragedy contains some fine passages. As an example of American romantic classic drama, one of these passages, where Aylmere is in the Coliseum, is worth quoting:

> One night,
> Rack'd by these memories, methought a voice
> Summon'd me from my couch. I rose—went forth.
> The sky seem'd a dark gulf where fiery spirits
> Sported; for o'er the concave the quick lightning
> Quiver'd, but spoke not. In the breathless gloom,
> I sought the Coliseum, for I felt
> The spirits of a manlier age were forth:
> And there, against the mossy wall I lean'd,
> And thought upon my country. Why was I
> Idle and she in chains? The storm now answer'd!
> It broke as Heaven's high masonry were crumbling.
> The heated walls nodded and frown'd i' the glare,
> And the wide vault, in one unpausing peal,
> Throbb'd with the angry pulse of Deity.
>   LACY.—Shrunk you not 'mid these terrors?
>   AYLMERE.—No, not I.
> I felt I could amid this hurly laugh,
> And laughing, do such deeds as fireside fools
> Turn pale to think on.
> The heavens did speak like brothers to my soul;
> And not a peal that leapt along the vault,
> But had an echo in my heart. Nor spoke
> The clouds alone: for, o'er the tempest din,
> I heard the genius of my country shriek
> Amid the ruins, calling on her son,
> On me! I answered her in shouts; and knelt
> Even there, in darkness, 'mid the falling ruins,
> Beneath the echoing thunder-trump—and swore
> (The while my father's pale form, welted with
> The death-prints of the scourge, stood by and smiled),
> I swore to make the bondman free!

After the production of " Jack Cade," Forrest

made several efforts to procure another play suited to him. He offered a prize of $3,000 for a play written by an American, " and promised," says James Rees, " $1000 for that play among the number (provided none realized his first intention) which should possess the highest literary merit. In answer to this invitation, Mr. Forrest received upwards of seventy plays, but none answered his original design. He, however, awarded to G. H. Miles $1,000 for his play, ' Mohammed,' deeming it the best literary production in the collection." This play Forrest did not produce himself. He lent the play to Mr. Neaffie, who produced it September 27, 1852, at Brougham's Theatre, New York, where it was a complete failure.

In the competitions inaugurated by Forrest, two hundred plays were submitted, nine received prizes, and $20,000 in all was paid by him to native dramatists, a mere bagatelle, of course, compared with what actors and managers now pay authors for plays. But to-day it is an established practice to pay liberal royalties to authors. In Forrest's time it was not.

Forrest's offers of $500 prizes and a similar offer made by Manager J. H. Caldwell, of New Orleans, at about the same time, spurred James H. Kennicott, a native schoolmaster of New Orleans, to try his hand at playwriting. The result was a tragedy entitled " Irma," which was eventually produced by Caldwell. This was the first American play, written by an American, to be performed in the city of New Orleans.

A native dramatist who had considerable success at this time was Cornelius A. Logan (1806–1853), who wrote for J. H. Hackett a three-act play called "The Wag of Maine." It was performed at the Park Theatre in 1835. He also wrote the comedy, "Yankee Land," introducing Hackett as Lot Sap Sago, and the farce, "The Vermont Wool Dealer." Later, when manager of a theatre in Cincinnati, he attracted much attention by his bold defense of the stage against the attacks of the pulpit. His younger daughter, Olive Logan, was well known as an actress and author.[7]

Another successful American playwright was Epes Sargent (1813–1880), a once prominent Boston journalist, whose five-act tragedy, "Velasco," produced at the Tremont Theatre, Boston, in 1837, was a phenomenal success, largely owing to the acting of Miss Ellen Tree, who made of the heroine Izadora one of her best parts.

Nathaniel P. Willis (1806–1867), the successful writer, one of the publishers of the *New York Mirror* and later editor of the *Home Journal,* won a prize offered by Josephine Clifton[8] with a verse tragedy, entitled "Bianca Visconti." The piece was produced at the Park Theatre, New York, August 25, 1837, and was seen later in Philadelphia and Boston. J. W. Wallack then encouraged him to write "Tortesa the

---

[7] Olive Logan was born in New York State in 1841. Following the example of her elder sister Eliza, also a well-known and successful actress, she made her début on the stage in 1854 as Mrs. Bobtail in "Bobtail and Wagtail" at the Arch Street Theatre, Philadelphia. Three years later, she retired temporarily from the stage to devote herself to literature. She lived abroad several years, was received at the French court and wrote two novels of French life, one of which was published by the Appletons. Returning to America she reappeared on the stage with considerable success and in 1865 was seen in the play called "Sam" which had a run of 100 nights at the Broadway Theatre. She retired permanently from the stage in 1868 and took to lecturing, being one of the earliest champions in America of Woman's rights.

[8] See page 95.

Usurer," which was produced at the National Theatre April 8, 1839, with great success.

James K. Paulding (1779–1860), who had been associated with Washington Irving in the publication of the *Salmagundi,* wrote several clever comedies which diverted audiences of the middle of the Nineteenth Century. Among his plays, " The Bucktails, or Americans in England," is best known, the dialogue sprightly and the characters well sustained. Another piece by the same author, " The Lion of the West," written for J. H. Hackett, had so popular a character, Colonel Nimrod Wildfire, that Bayle Bernard introduced a similar character in his drama, " The Kentuckian." This favorite stage hero wore buckskin clothes, deerskin shoes and a coonskin hat. " He had," says Laurence Hutton,[*] " many contemporary imitators, who copied his dress, his speech and his gait and stalked through the deep-tangled wildwoods of East Side stages for many years, to the delight of city-bred pits and galleries who were perfectly assured that the *Arkansas Traveller*—and one of the best of his class—was the real thing until they saw Buffalo Bill with actual cowboys and bonafide Indians in his train and lost all further interest in ' The Scouts of the Plains ' or in ' Nick of the Woods,' which hitherto filled their idea of life on the plains."

The foregoing were the principal among the American writers who attempted the stage as a medium until the coming of Anna Cora Mowatt, whose comedy, " Fashion," scored a success at the Park, and of another distinguished American poet, George H. Boker (1823–1890), whose fine poetic tragedy,

---
[*] Curiosities of the Stage. By Laurence Hutton.

" Francesca da Rimini," is the only American work of that period which has stood the test of time and is still played with success on our boards.

The creator of our poetic drama, George Henry Boker was born in Philadelphia. After graduating from Princeton, he studied law, but never practiced. His first play, " Calaynos," a tragedy, was written in 1848. Then came " Anne Boleyn " (1850), " The Betrothal " (1850), " Leonar de Guzman " (1853), " Francesca da Rimini " (1856). Of his plays, the late Richard Henry Stoddard said:

> That his tragedies were capable of effective representation was known to those of us who saw Mr. Davenport and Miss Dean in " Francesca da Rimini" years ago, and is known to those of us who have since seen Mr. Barrett and Miss Wainwright in the same play. The conception of his tragedies and comedies, their development, their movement, and their catastrophes, are dramatic. Poetical, they are not overweighed with poetry; emotional and passionate, their language is naturally figurative, and the blank verse rises and falls as the occasion demands. One feels in reading them that the writer had studied the Elizabethan and Jacobean dramatists, and that they harmed as well as helped him. If he could have forgotten them and remembered only his own genius, his work would have been more original.

En résumé the American drama may be divided into several classes: (1) Revolutionary and other war plays, such as Burk's " Bunker Hill " and Gillette's " Secret Service "; (2) the Indian plays, of which " Metamora " was one of the most popular; (3) Yankee character comedies, J. S. Jones' " The People's Lawyer " (Solon Shingle) and Mark Twain's " Gilded Age "; (4) Dion Boucicault's Irish dramas; and plays of the backwoods, such as " Davy Crockett "; (5) Society plays, Mrs. Mowatt's " Fashion "

and the more modern drawing-room comedies of
Bronson Howard and Clyde Fitch; (6) Sociological
plays, of which James A. Herne's " Margaret Flem-
ing " and William Vaughn Moody's " The Great
Divide " are distinguished examples; (7) Poetic
drama, represented by George H. Boker, William
Young and Percy Mackaye; (8) Farce, Charles H.
Hoyt and Margaret Mayo; (9) Burlesque, in which
Weber and Fields once ruled supreme and which
Brander Matthews has referred to as the Aristo-
phanes period of American drama.

The plays of Yankee character have always been
immensely popular. The first stage Yankee, the
Jonathan in Royall Tyler's " The Contrast," contributed no little to the success of the first American
comedy. From that time on, there set in a steady
demand for the Yankee type on our stage. Hackett
responded with Jonathan Ploughboy and Lot Sap
Sago, two rôles that endeared him to audiences everywhere. Then came Solon Shingle, the simple-minded
old man from New England with the soul which
soared no higher than the financial value of a bar'l
of apple-sass—a delicious character played with great
success for years by " Yankee " Hill,[10] Joshua Silsbee,
J. H. Hackett and John E. Owens. Among local stage
types none was ever more popular than that of Mose,
the tough fire boy, in " A Glance at New York," in
which F. S. Chanfrau won his greatest triumph in
the forties. And what theatregoer of the sixties can

[10] G. H. Hill, nicknamed "Yankee Hill" because of his success in Yankee
characters, was born in Boston, and made his stage début in that city in 1799,
being engaged by Warren to recite Yankee stories between the acts. Later he
went to the Park Theatre, New York, where he made such a hit that he was
started on a starring tour, proving a formidable rival to J. H. Hackett.

forget Jefferson's Asa Trenchard, the rough, kind-hearted Yankee, played in sharp contrast to Sothern's Dundreary in Tom Taylor's "Our American Cousin," or the amusing character Colonel Mulberry Sellers, in "The Gilded Age," which, ten years later, made the fortune of that delightful comedian, John T. Raymond? And who does not remember W. J. Florence as the Hon. Bardwell Slote in Woolf's "Mighty Dollar"—that vulgar politician with all the vices of his class, yet with amiable qualities which made him after all a lovable character? Among more modern stage Yankees, Denman Thompson as Joshua Whitcomb won the affection of millions in "The Old Homestead," and William H. Crane was almost as successful in "David Harum."

Probably the most successful American play ever written, judged from the number of performances given, and the amount of money taken in at the box office, is "Uncle Tom's Cabin," a dramatization of Harriet Beecher Stowe's famous anti-slavery novel. The piece has been acted uninterruptedly ever since it was first produced fifty years ago, and, still performed in the popular houses, there seems no limit to its longevity. Some years ago—in the summer of 1902—there were no fewer than sixteen companies playing the piece under canvas. C. W. Taylor's dramatization was the first seen in New York, at Purdy's National Theatre, in 1852, and a year later the Howard family staged the George L. Aiken version, opening at the same theatre, where the play ran three months. George C. Howard acted St. Clair, "and," says a writer, "he made an ideal Southern planter." The writer continues:

On and off the stage, he invariably wore a black broadcloth frock coat with brass buttons, and he always had on lavender trousers. When he was around the hotels and on the streets of the towns where the show was being given, people who had seen him at the theatre recognized him at once and exclaimed: "There goes Eva's father!" Mrs. Howard was Topsy, and there has never been any one yet to equal her in the character. Little Cordelia, her daughter, was a born actress. Nothing more natural or beautiful than the way she played little Eva could be imagined.[11]

The rest of the cast included Greene C. Germon, who played Uncle Tom; George L. Fox, afterwards the famous pantomimist, who was the Phineas Fletcher; Charles K. Fox, who acted Gumption Cute; Samuel M. Siple, who played George Harris, and Mrs. W. G. Jones, who was the Eliza; W. J. Le Moyne, a popular member of Daniel Frohman's Lyceum Theatre stock company, played the Deacon.

Playwriting, early in the Nineteenth Century, was by no means the profitable occupation it has since become. It is doubtful if any of our earlier dramatists received pecuniary compensation for their plays. There is no record of Royall Tyler being paid anything for his successful comedy, "The Contrast," although it is possible that he was given an author's benefit. It is not known if Dunlap was paid anything for his first play, "The Father." He says nothing about compensation in his History, and, of course, his later assumption of the management resulted in his being rewarded only incidentally for the writing of plays. During the early decades of the last century, it seems to have been the custom to give the author the gross receipts of the third night's performance, and, doubtless, it was on this basis that such

[11] Dr. Judd in the *Theatre Magazine* for February, 1904.

70

early dramatists as James Nelson Barker and John Howard Payne were paid. It is also possible, if not probable, that Payne's plays, having been first produced in England, were used without his consent.

An examination of the manuscript diary of William B. Wood, manager of the Chestnut Street Theatre, Philadelphia, from 1810 to 1827, shows no reference to payments made to dramatists, and in the manager's statements of expenses, no account appears to have been kept of any sums paid for the authors' " third night," if such a night existed in his system. For example, on Tuesday, May 27, 1828, Richard Penn Smith's play, " Quite Correct," was performed, but there is no statement about the dramatist even by name. Throughout all of the performances by John Howard Payne in 1811–12, there is no reference, except to a benefit now and then, which he seems to have received rather as an actor than as a dramatist. James Nelson Barker's play, " Marmion," was performed January 1, 1813. There is no mention made of any payment, although he may have received the receipts of the third night.

As previously mentioned, Forrest started the practice of offering money prizes for suitable plays, and probably found it a good investment, since he secured plays like " Metamora," " The Gladiator," and " The Broker of Bogota " with a comparatively small outlay.

The earliest date at which American dramatists began to be paid certain stipulated sums is not known. They were certainly receiving royalties by 1850, when George Henry Boker's plays were acted. " Boker," says Arthur Hobson Quinn, " seems to have received a royalty of five per cent. on the gross receipts of each night's performance. Statements from the treasurers of the different theatres where four of his plays, 'Calaynos,' 'The Betrothal,' 'The World a Mask,' 'Leonor de Guzman,' were given, show a total of $994.56 paid to him in royalties. These figures omit at least two series of performances of 'Calaynos' and all of 'Francesca da Rimini.' It would seem fair to estimate his total royalties from plays up to the time of their production in 1856 at $1,500." [12]

Down to the eighties, however, the average dramatic author got what he could. Some had a separate agreement with every manager. Sometimes, plays were sold to managers or stars for a lump sum. Fifty years ago John Brougham would write a play to order for $3,000. Lawrence Barrett paid Lester Wallack $50 a night and $25 a matinee for "Rosedale." About 1880 began a practice which still holds —the dramatist receiving either a percentage of the gross receipts, or a weekly stipend until a certain sum was reached. This sum at first ran from $1,000 to $50,000, rarely beyond that. When one recalls that nowadays it is nothing unusual for a popular dramatist to make $500,000 with one play, that the late Clyde Fitch during the eighteen years he was writing for the stage, made $1,500,000 in royalties, it can readily be seen that the American dramatist has made considerable progress since the days of "Androborus."

It is not known what Daly gave Bronson Howard for "Saratoga," probably not very much. Later

<hr>

[12] The Dramas of George Henry Boker. By Arthur Hobson Quinn.

72

Howard charged $5,000 for a play, the manager to assume all the risks. That was what was paid for " One of our Girls." The same author's war play, " Shenandoah," probably marks the first big royalty-payer. For this piece Howard was paid over $100,-000 for its first year alone. It is doubtful if Steele Mackaye got a quarter of that out of the amazing run of " Hazel Kirke."

Augustin Daly went through all the phases of paying authors. He did all the tricks of translation, adaptation, rearrangement at bargain prices, in sums down, salary, and royalty.

Foreign plays were seldom paid for before Albert M. Palmer's time. That manager succeeded in getting a court decision which prevented rival managers from producing unprinted foreign plays which he had contracted for and produced, he paying the foreign authors so much a performance, probably not more than $50. Until the introduction of international copyright in 1891, printed foreign plays were pirated without apology.

CHAPTER XVIII

GEORGE HOLLAND THE ELDER AND MRS. JOHN DREW

A POPULAR ECCENTRIC COMEDIAN. CURIOUS LETTER FROM J. B.
BOOTH. THE LITTLE CHURCH AROUND THE CORNER. A BRIL-
LIANT PERIOD IN PHILADELPHIA'S THEATRICAL HISTORY. MME.
CELESTE. THE VOGUE OF CLARA FISHER. BUILDING OF THE
TREMONT THEATRE, BOSTON. COMING OF CHARLES KEAN AND
ELLEN TREE.

LATE in the year 1827, two English players, destined to become the founders of two of America's
famous theatrical families, made their first appearance in the United States. The first of them was
George Holland, the elder, eccentric comedian; the
second was Louisa Lane, better known as Mrs. John
Drew.

George Holland, the elder, was born in London,
December 6, 1791, one of seven children born to
Henry Holland, an actor and teacher of dancing.
The boy received only a superficial education, being
more remarkable for his athletic activities and mischievous pranks than for devotion to study. Cricket
playing, boating, horseback riding, fencing and boxing hardened a frame naturally robust, while his pro-
pensity for fun making, which made him popular in
every circle, stuck to him all through life and contributed no little to his success in the career he ultimately
adopted. On leaving school, his father secured a situation for him in a London silk warehouse. Before
beginning his duties he was allowed a short vacation,
and most of his holiday he spent at Astley's Amphi-

theatre, of which one of his father's intimate friends was manager, and there he saw " Les Ombres Chinois " (Chinese Shadows), an entertainment consisting of little playlets performed by silhouetted pasteboard figures worked by wire. So fascinated was young Holland by this novelty that he got up a similar show for his immediate home circle, and this experience no doubt first turned his thoughts towards the stage as a means of livelihood.

But some time was to elapse before the ambition could be realized. After six months' trial at the silk house, he resigned his position and became a jack of all trades. After clerking in a bank, he joined the staff of *Newman's Echo,* a sheet which gave in cheap form a synopsis of the " want " advertisements in the expensive daily newspapers. Prosperous for a time, Newman finally failed, and Holland found himself once more seeking employment. It was at this period that he became proficient in rowing, horseback riding, fencing and boxing. Making the acquaintance of the leading prize fighters of the day, he was soon on intimate terms with such classic bruisers as Tom Cribb, Iky Solomons, Dutch Sam, Molineaux and Tom Belcher. Later, aimless wanderings took him to Ireland, where he became a commercial traveller for a Dublin lace house. For two years, he drove his lace cart all over Ireland, where he was long remembered for his fair dealing and irresistible good humor. It was in Dublin, at the famous Peter Kearney's Inn, that Holland first came in close contact with members of the theatrical profession. His wit and amiability won him many friends among the actors who frequented the place, and the encouragement they held out finally led him to give up all thought of a commercial career and make a determined effort to get on the stage.

Elliston at that time was lessee of the London Olympic with Samuel Russell as stage manager. After some parleys, conducted through Russell, Holland was finally offered a six weeks' engagement at the Olympic at five pounds ($25) a week, with a promise of another engagement at the theatre in Birmingham six weeks later. Elliston afterwards repudiated this latter arrangement, but offered to take Holland on again at fifteen shillings ($4) a week. The terms were ridiculous, but, realizing that it was an opportunity, Holland accepted, and was cast for the Monk in " Bertram " and the Baron in " The Broken Sword." A fellow actor helped him make up for the latter rôle and, taking advantage of the newcomer's inexperience, dressed him up in a Pantaloon wig and so grotesque a costume that the audience, on his appearance before the footlights, fairly howled with laughter and hooted him from the stage. The young actor beat a precipitate retreat, and for a long time after was known as " the Baron."

While recovering from his discomfiture, Holland opened a school for fencing and boxing, but after an explanation with Elliston, was soon reinstated in the company. Macready and Vincent de Camp visited Birmingham about this time, and the latter actor, who had secured a theatre at Newcastle, asked Holland to join him. The journey to Newcastle was made by sailing vessel and on the voyage he met Junius Brutus Booth, together with other actors, all having the same destination. It was at Newcastle that Holland's fondness for joking nearly cost him a useful part of his anatomy. Snipping at his nose one evening, to amuse the spectators, he nearly sliced that organ in two. Prompt surgical aid enabled repairs to be made without visible damage and the next day Holland was complimented by his manager on his " spirited and remarkable performance."

In 1825–1826, while playing an engagement at the London Haymarket, Holland received a letter from his friend, Junius Brutus Booth, then stage manager of the Chatham Theatre, New York, offering him an engagement in America. This letter from Booth, with its original spelling and punctuation, gives so interesting and intimate an insight into theatrical conditions as they prevailed in New York at that time that it is worth giving here in full:

NEW YORK, Xmas Eve, 1826.
but direct y'r letter to the Theatre
Baltimore U States.

MY DEAR SIR: Messrs. WALLACK AND FREEMAN, a few days since, shewed me your letter, with the inclosure sent last winter to you at Sheffield.

It is requisite that I inform you Theatricals are not in so flourishing a condition in this Country as they were some two years ago. There are four Theatres in this City each endeavoring to ruin the others, by foul means as well as fair. The reduction of the prices of admission has proved (as I always anticipated from the first suggestion of such a foolish plan) nearly ruinous to the Managers. The Publick here often witness a Performance in every respect equal to what is presented at the Theatres Royal D. L. and C. G. for these prices. Half a dollar to the boxes and a quarter do. to the Pit and Gallery!

The Chatham Theatre of which I am the Stage-Manager, at these low prices one thousand dollars.—Acting is sold too cheap to the Publick and the result will be a general theatrical bankruptcy.

THE THEATRE IN AMERICA

Tragedians are in abundance—MACREADY—CONWAY—HAM-
BLIN—FORREST (now No. 1) COOPER—WALLACK—MAYWOOD [1]
and self with divers others now invest New York. But it won't do;
a diversion to the South must be made—or to Jail three-fourths of
the Great men and managers must go.

Now, sir, I will deal fairly with you. If you will pledge yourself to me for three years, and sacredly promise that no inducement
which may be held out by the unprincipled and daring speculators
which abound in this country shall cause you to leave me, I will, for
ten months in each year, give you thirty dollars per week, and an
annual benefit which you shall divide with me. Beyond this sum
I would not venture, the privilege of your name for Benefits
Extra to be allowed me—and I should expect the terms on
which you would be engaged to remain secret from all but ourselves. Mind this—Wether you play in my Theatres or elsewhere
in the U States, I should look for implicit and faithful performances of your duty toward me or my colleagues! In case I should
require you to travel, when in the United States, which is most
probable, I will defray all the charges of conveyance for you and
your luggage—your living would not be included either by land or
water—Boarding (three meals a day), and your Bed room, may be
had in a very respectable house here, & in Baltimore at from four
to six dollars per week—"Lodgings to let" are very scarce and
expensive, and the customs of this country, in this respect, are essentially different to those of the English.

The M. S. and music of "Paul Pry," with FAUSTUS's music
Do. and Book of the "Pilot." The M. S. and Do. of a piece
played some few years back at Sadler's Wells, called "The Gheber,
or the Fire Worshippers." Two or three of LISTON's new pieces I
should advise you to bring. And particularly the "Gheber" for
me. "The Mogul Tale" here is out of print

In the Exeter Theatre last January were two actresses that I
should like to engage. Miss P——.(not the Miss P. formerly of
Drury Lane) and Miss H. If you will inquire after them—I will
thank you. To each of these ladies a salary of fifteen dollars a

---

[1] Robert Campbell Maywood, tragedian, was born in Scotland in 1786.
He came to America in 1819 and made his début at the Park Theatre as Richard
III. In 1832 he became associate manager of the Walnut and later of the
Chestnut Street Theatre, Philadelphia. In 1834 he was manager of the Chest-
nut and Arch Street Theatres. He died in 1856.

week I can venture offering—15 dollars are upward of three
Guineas and Benefit annually.

Now sir I have offered to you and those ladies as much as I
can in honesty afford to give, their travelling expenses to and from
Theatres in the United States (not including board) I should defray, as I told you respecting your own—and the use of their names
for benefits on Stock nights—Your line of business would be exclusively yours. For the ladies I would not make this guaranty—The
greatest actress in the World I may say is now in this city (Mrs.
D——)² and several very talented women—besides I would en-
deavor to make such arrangements for Miss P—— and Miss
H—— as would not be very repugnant to their ambition.

The reason Mrs. D—— does not go to London is my strenuous
advice to her against it. The passages from Europe I should expect
repaid to me out of the salaries, by weekly deductions of three dollars each. The captain of the ship would call upon the parties or
you might write to them on his visit to you; everything on board
will be furnished that is requisite for comfort, and the expenses I
will settle for her previous to starting. Mind the ship you would
come over in, is one expressly bargained for, and will bring you
where I shall (if living) be ready to welcome you—

Let me recommend you to Economy—see what a number of our
brethren are reduced to Indigence by their obstinate Vanity—I
have here Mr. D—— who was once in London the rival of ELLIS-
TON, and is now a better actor—approaching the age of sixty, and
not a dollar put by for a rainy day—too proud to accept a salary
of twenty dollars per week in a regular engagement—he stars and
starves. Many have been deceived and misled in their calculations
in coming to this country—some have cut their throats, &c., from
disappointment—Mrs. ROMER (once of the Surrey), Mrs. ALSOP,
MR. ENTWISTLE—KIRBY the Clown—are all on the felo de se
list—with others I now forget—

The temptations to Drunkenness here are too common and too
powerful for many weak beings who construe the approval of a
boisterous circle of intoxicated fools as the climax of everything
desirable in their profession—What do they find it, when a weak-
ened shattered brain, with loss of memory and often reason, are

---

² Booth undoubtedly refers here to Mary Duff, who was appearing in New
York about that time. See page 284, Vol. I.

the Result—The hangers on drop astern—and the poor wreck drives down the Gulf despised or pitied, and totally deserted.

If you choose accepting my offer—get for me those ladies. Sims can perhaps tell you where they are, and I will on the first occasion send for you and them, with the articles of agreement to be signed in London and legally ratified on your arrival in America—recollect this—the Passages in Summer, owing to the calms are longer in performing, but they are much safer, and the Newfoundland Bank is an ugly place to cross in Winter, though it is often done, yet still it is a great risk.

The Crisis which left London Docks, last January with all her passengers after being out for 68 days, and being spoken to on the banks by another vessel—is not yet come or will she ever—The icebergs no doubt struck her, as they have many—and the last farewell was echoed by the waves.

Write me soon and glean the information I ask for—The letter bag for United States vessels—from London is kept at the North American Coffee House near the Bank of England. Yours truly,

Booth.

George Holland.

The outlook, as presented, was not very promising, but Holland's love of adventure did not permit of hesitation. He did not accept Booth's offer, but signed a few months later with Manager Gilfert, of the Bowery, and in August, 1827, sailed for America.

He made his American début at the Bowery Theatre, September 12, of the same year, as Jerry in the farce, "A Day After the Fair," in which he impersonated six different characters: a smart servant, a drunken cobbler, an old ballad singer, a drummer, a French songstress and a madman. In this he was inimitable and scored a decided hit. Later, he went to Boston, where he was seen at the newly erected Tremont Theatre. Then he acted at Albany. Following these engagements, began many years of wandering that took him all over the United States. In 1829, he made his first appearance at New Orleans, after which he played at Louisville, Cincinnati, Vicksburg, Montgomery, Mobile and other Western towns. Returning to New York, he settled down at what was known as Holland's Cottage at Yorkville, New York, a snug suburban inn which enjoyed much favor. Later, he went on a joint tour with Thomas Abthorpe Cooper, Hamblin and Barton, Holland's portion of the entertainment being " Whims of a Comedian." In 1832, he joined Ludlow at Louisville, giving entertainments in the principal towns of Kentucky and Tennessee, and two years later became associated with Sol Smith in the management of a theatre at Montgomery, Ala. On leaving Sol Smith, he went, in 1835, to New Orleans and became secretary to J. H. Caldwell, acting also as treasurer of the St. Charles Theatre. He remained in New Orleans until 1843, when he returned to New York and attached himself to Mitchell's Olympic Theatre. In 1849 he returned to New Orleans, appearing at the Varieties, where, says Sol Smith, " he enjoyed a popularity never perhaps equalled by any other actor in that city." In 1853, he was again in New York as a member of Burton's company. Two years later, he joined Wallack's organization, his first appearance under that management being as Chubb in John Brougham's "Game of Love." He remained with Wallack twelve years with the exception of one season, during the panic of 1857, when he joined the Christy Minstrels, playing female characters in black. In 1869, the last year but one of his life, he became a member of Augustin Daly's organization, and made his last appearance at the Fifth Avenue Theatre January 12, 1870, as the Reporter in Olive Logan's comedy, "The Surf." He was given a benefit the following month and died December 20, 1870. Of him William Winter says:

Holland's life was full of strange vicissitudes, but it was animated by honest principle, and characterized by faithful labor and spotless integrity. He was a good man. He attained a high rank in his profession,—largely by reason of his delightful skill as an artist, but more largely by reason of his natural endowments. He was a born humorist, of the eccentric order. To the comedian is accorded the happy privilege of casting the roses of mirth on the pathway of his fellow-men, making glad their hearts with cheerful and kindly feeling and lighting up their minds with the sunshine of innocent pleasure. In the exercise of that privilege George Holland added in no inconsiderable degree to the sum of human happiness.[*]

The story how this good man was refused a Christian burial by a so-called Christian clergyman has been told so often that it scarcely bears repetition here. As a particularly flagrant instance, however, of the narrow-mindedness of certain ministers of the gospel, and of the prejudice that still existed in America against the actor as late as the latter part of the Nineteenth Century, history must record it.

The Holland family had expressed a wish to have the funeral held at the church of the Rev. Dr. William Tufnell Sabine, where Mrs. Holland was an attendant. Edmund M. Holland, the dead actor's son, and Joseph Jefferson, the distinguished comedian, called on Dr. Sabine and asked him to read the burial service. This at first Dr. Sabine agreed to do, but on learning that Holland had been an actor, he

[*]From "The Wallet of Time." Copyright, 1913, by William Winter. Moffat, Yard & Company, Publishers. Reprinted by permission of Jefferson Winter, Esq.

withdrew his consent, and declined to permit the funeral in his church. In this dilemma, Mr. Jefferson exclaimed: "Well, Sir, where can we. go?" To which Dr. Sabine replied: "Oh, there's a little church around the corner where they do that sort of thing," referring to the Church of the Transfiguration in East Twenty-ninth Street. The mourners proceeded there, and the Rev. Dr. George H. Houghton immediately consented to give the dead actor Christian burial in what ever since has been known as "The Little Church Around the Corner."

The elder Holland was survived by three sons— George, Edmund Milton, and Joseph—all of whom were successful actors. George Holland, the eldest, acted with Laura Keene and later became leading comedian at McVicker's Theatre, Chicago. In 1891 he became manager of the Girard Avenue Theatre, Philadelphia, where he organized a stock company. E. M. Holland, a clever comedian of the refined school and a great public favorite, was a member of Wallack's company. Later, he joined the Union Square company and then went to the Madison Square Theatre, where his best-remembered rôles are Captain Redwood in "Jim the Penman," Gibson in "The Private Secretary," and Colonel Moberly in "Alabama." Joseph Holland was long a popular leading man, and, although handicapped by deafness, held a prominent place in his profession.

At the Walnut Street Theatre, Philadelphia, on September 26, 1827, occurred the début of Louisa Lane as the Duke of York to Junius Brutus Booth's Richard III. Louisa Lane, who, as Mrs. John Drew, later became one of the first actress-managers of the

American stage, was born in England, January 10, 1820. Both her parents were players, and she appeared on the stage as a crying baby when only twelve months old. At the age of five, she was playing regular rôles in melodrama. In 1827, Mrs. Lane came to America, and her little daughter made her first bow to the American public, with such success that she was sent to Joe Cowell's Theatre at Baltimore, where she appeared as Albert to Edwin Forrest's William Tell. The following year (March 28, 1828) she made her first appearance in New York at the Bowery as Little Pickle in " The Spoiled Child."

This was the beginning of a remarkable theatrical career which lasted for over seventy years. She acted with nearly all the famous players of her day—Macready, Edwin Forrest, Joseph Jefferson, Tyrone Power, James E. Murdoch, George Holland, Charlotte Cushman. In 1836, she married Henry Blaine Hunt, an English tenor, but the marriage did not prove a happy one, and in 1847 they were separated. The following year she married George Mossop, an Irish comedian. He died a year later. In 1850, while playing at the Albany Museum, she met John Drew, the Irish comedian, and married him. In 1851, Mr. and Mrs. Drew went to Philadelphia and were seen first at the Chestnut Street Theatre and then at the Arch Street Theatre. Two years later, the Arch Street Theatre passed under the management of Wheatley and Drew.

In 1861 Mrs. Drew assumed control of the Arch Street Theatre, the second woman[4] in America to undertake the responsibilities of theatrical manage-

[4] Laura Keene was the first actress-manager in the United States.

ment. During her régime, Philadelphia enjoyed one of the most brilliant periods of its theatrical history. Not only did the most famous players, such as Wallack, E. L. Davenport, Edwin Booth, Charlotte Cushman, Lotta, tread the boards of her theatre, but several of the members of her stock company—Fanny Davenport, Stuart Robson, Louis James—later became stars. For eight years she was very successful, but with the change in theatrical conditions which led to the gradual decline of the stock company in favor of the more commercial combination system, she was forced to follow the example of all the other Philadelphia theatres. " I ceased," she says in her Autobiography, " to have a stock company and called the theatre a ' combination theatre,' but it never did so well as before."

As an actress, Mrs. John Drew was without her equal on the stage. Her versatility was wonderful. During her first season at the Arch Street Theatre she appeared in over forty rôles. Chief among her interpretations were Lady Teazle, Mrs. Malaprop, Peg Woffington, Lady Gay Spanker, Dot, and Lydia Languish. Clara Morris has given us this picture of her:

What a handsome, masterful young creature she must have been in the days when she was playing the dashing Lady Gay, the tormenting Lady Teazle, and all that swarm of arrant coquettes! Her high features, her air of gentle breeding, the touch of hauteur in her manner, must have given the same zest to the admiration of her lovers that the faint nip of frost in the autumn air gives to the torpid blood. And, good heavens! what an amount of work fell to the lot of the stately gentlewoman! . . . She was always a wonderful disciplinarian; hers was said to be the last of those green-rooms that used to be considered schools of good man-

ners. Some women descend to bullying to maintain their authority
—not so Mrs. John Drew. Her armor was a certain chill aus-
terity of manner, her weapon a sharp sarcasm, while her strength lay
in her self-control, her self-respect.[5]

In 1880 she entered into an engagement with
Joseph Jefferson to travel with him and act Mrs.
Malaprop in "The Rivals," and this arrangement
continued until 1892, when she finally gave up active
charge of the Arch Street Theatre. She continued
acting for some time, but she was now ageing.
Her last appearance was May 13, 1897, at the Mon-
tauk Theatre, Brooklyn, for the benefit of Edwin
Knowles. She died in New York, August 31, 1897.

Mrs. Drew had four children, three of whom became players: Georgie (1856–1893), John (born
1853), Sidney White (adopted), Louisa (died 1894).
Georgie Drew made her début at the Arch Street
Theatre, Philadelphia, in 1872. Afterwards, she
joined Augustin Daly's company and later played in
support of Booth, Barrett and other stars. In 1876,
she was married to Maurice Barrymore. Sidney
Drew was for a short time manager for his adopted
mother. He was never conspicuous as an actor until
the popularity of the motion pictures gave him an
opportunity and brought him into prominence. John
Drew, the most successful of the family, made his first
appearance in his mother's stock company at the age
of nineteen. Shortly afterwards he joined Augustin
Daly and later became one of the most prominent of
American stars.

The same year in which George Holland and
Mrs. John Drew came to America, saw also the first

---

[5]Article in *McClure's Magazine* for December, 1903.

appearance here of a French actress who became enormously popular on our stage. This was a dancer named Céline Celeste, who made her début at the Bowery Theatre, June 27, 1827.

Born in Paris in 1814, this talented woman came here with a troupe of French dancers. At first, she knew no English and all her performances were necessarily given in dumb show, but her grace and beauty attracted universal admiration. The year after her arrival, she married an American named Elliott, but continued to be known as Madame Celeste. When, later on, she acquired the language, she soon revealed herself as a melodramatic actress of the first rank. In 1830 she went to England, where she made her first appearance at Liverpool as Fenella in " Masaniello," her London début being made the same year at Drury Lane in the ballet " La Bayadère." She was next seen in " The French Spy " and " The Arab Boy." Later, she visited France, Italy and Germany with equal success. In November, 1834, she was back in New York, where she made a tremendous hit at the Bowery in " The French Spy," and during this season she played some of the most brilliant and successful engagements on record.

Everywhere she went, there was the greatest curiosity to see her performances. " In her prime," says Ireland, " to the greatest elegance and symmetry of person, she added a handsome face and an expressiveness of feature beyond any actress of the age. Every movement was full of grace and every attitude a picture. The power, pathos and effect of her pantomimic acting have never been approached, while her assumption of male attire and heroic characters in such parts as Vanderdecken in 'The Flying Dutchman' and Valentine in 'Valentine and Orson' were marvellous exhibitions of daring ambition and successful achievement. Her success in America has been equalled among women only by Fanny Kemble and Jenny Lind and among the multitude she was undoubtedly the most popular of the trio."[•]

In 1844 she became manager of the London Adelphi and during the next fifteen years produced, and acted in, a great number of plays. In 1851, she returned to America and was seen here in a new play called " The Queen's Secret," and regular repertoire, including Miami in " Green Bushes," " The French Spy," " Mazourka," etc. In November, 1859, she became director of the London Lyceum. She paid a farewell tour to America in 1865, appearing here as Rudiga in " The Woman in Red " and continued acting in London until 1878. She died in 1882.

Another actress of the early Nineteenth Century, who met with almost sensational success, was Clara Fisher, known to a later generation of theatregoers as Mrs. Maeder.

Clara Fisher was born in England on July 14, 1811. Her father was successively a Brighton librarian and London auctioneer. His daughter made her stage début when only six years old at Drury Lane as Lord Flimnap in " Gulliver in Lilliput," introducing an impersonation of Richard III, in which she made a tremendous hit. Immediately, the child was the talk of the town. From Drury Lane, she went to Covent Garden and thence to the provinces. So intense was the curiosity to see the juvenile performer,

[•] Records of the New York Stage, by Joseph N. Ireland.

that applications for her services poured in from all sides and she was soon the sensation of the day. In 1827, she came to America, making her début at the Park Theatre as Albina in " The Will " and the four Mowbrays in " Old and Young." At that time she had not yet reached her seventeenth year. Ireland says of her:

She was one of the most bewitching specimens of feminine creation that eyes had ever looked on. Her person below the middle height and just reaching, but not exceeding, a delicate plumpness, was exquisitely formed; her manners were sprightly and vivacious, yet perfectly natural and artless; her expression arch and intelligent; her cheeks dimpling with smiles. Appearing as she constantly did in the characters of boys and striplings, she had her fine hair closely cut on the back of her head, while on her brow she wore the then fashionable rolls or puffs, a style that was immediately adopted by all fashionable ladies under twenty-five, and by some of more mature age, while an imitation of her delicate but natural lisp was considered equally indispensable. In fact, she belonged to the royal family of lions, and her name was borrowed to give popularity to new fashions and old hotels, slow stages and fast racers, and anything or anybody that could claim the most distant connection with the celebrated Clara Fisher was sure of attracting notice and distinction.[7]

Her best character in tragedy was Ophelia, which she played with grace and simplicity. But she was most effective in the more everyday character of Clari, which she acted with such pathos as always to move the audience to tears. Her formal farewell to the stage took place in November, 1844, but she reappeared in 1851 at Brougham's Lyceum and Niblo's, New York, in opera bouffe. She had married J. G. Maeder, a musician, in 1834.

The year 1827 is also memorable in theatrical

---

[7] Records of the New York Stage, by Joseph N. Ireland.

annals as the date of the building of the Tremont Theatre, the fourth playhouse erected in Boston.

Ever since the Kean riots, the Federal Street house, heretofore known as the Boston Theatre, and then under the management of Finn and Kilner, had been in decline. The house was poorly supported, in spite of the important attractions offered. On October 30, 1826, Macready had made his first appearance in Boston, in the character of Virginius, the demand for seats being so great that the management was compelled to dispose of them at auction. Early the following year (February 5, 1827) Edwin Forrest made his début in Boston, opening in his great rôle Damon, with Mr. Finn as Pythias. But notwithstanding these brilliant engagements, the receipts left much to be desired, and the management was blamed for not catering acceptably to the public taste. Friction had also arisen between William Pelby, the tragedian,[*] and the management, owing to differences of opinion as to salaries. Pelby had asked for a certain increase, which Messrs. Finn and Kilner had declared exorbitant. Pelby retorted that the managers were trying to shut him out, and his adherents were loud in support of a plan to build a new theatre, of which Pelby should be manager. Finally, the new house was determined upon. A site in Tremont (then Common) Street was purchased, and on July 4, 1827, the corner-stone was laid. Inside the box was the following record engraved on a silver plate:

---

[*] William Pelby, an American actor, was born in Boston, Mass., in 1793. He made his début in Philadelphia, November 26, 1821, as Macbeth. He was manager of the Tremont Theatre, Boston, and also built the Warren Theatre in that city. Later he visited England and appeared as Hamlet at Drury Lane. He died in Boston in 1850.

GEORGE HOLLAND, MRS. JOHN DREW

COMMONWEALTH OF MASSACHUSETTS

On the fourth day of July, in the year of our Lord one thousand eight hundred and twenty-seven, and the Independence of the United States of America the fifty-second, this inscription was deposited by the Proprietors of the Tremont Theatre, in token of laying the *Corner Stone.*

Treasurer—W. H. Gardiner.
Secretary—Washington P. Gragg.
Building Committee—Edward H. Robbins, Jr., Oliver Mills, John Redman, Solomon Towne, James Page, James McAllaster, Charles F. Kupfer, Edward D. Clark, Alpheus Cary.
Architect—Isaiah Rogers.
Lessee—William Pelby.
President of the United States—John Quincy Adams.
Governor of Massachusetts—Levi Lincoln.
Mayor of the City of Boston—Josiah Quincy.

The new theatre was opened on September 24, with Mrs. Inchbald's comedy, "Wives as They Were, and Maids as They Are." The special cast included Mr. Herbert, of the New York and Philadelphia theatres; Mr. Webb, of the Philadelphia theatre; Mr. Reed, Mr. Blake, Mr. Doyne, J. Mills Brown, Mrs. Blake, Mrs. Young, Mrs. Pelby. In addition to the foregoing, the company included Mr. Hart, Mr. Field, Mr. Martin, Mrs. Brewster, Mr. Hyall, W. Isherwood, Brewster Kelly, Mr. Collingbourne, Mr. Smith, Mrs. and Miss Riddle, Mrs. Smith, Mrs. Forbes, and Mr. Keene, the vocalist. Leading stars during the first season were Mr. Holland, Mr. and Mrs. Hilson, Mr. Addams, the tragedian, Mr. Horn, Mrs. Knight, Mr. Cooper, Miss Kelly, Mr. and Mrs. Wallack, Mrs. Mestayer and Mme. Hutin, the dancer.

This was the first appearance of Augustus A.

Addams, an American tragedian of uncommon power who was immensely popular with the public of his day. " He was the idol of his audiences," says Lawrence Barrett, " and held an equal place with Forrest for a time in the estimation of playgoers." He died in 1851.

Meantime, the management of the Federal Street house had not been idle. Everything possible was done to counteract the effect of this new and formidable competitor. Mr. Finn was dispatched to Europe for recruits, and for some time Boston theatregoers found the respective merits and prospects of the rival establishments a subject for lively discussion.

The Federal Street house reopened its season, September 17, with " The Rivals," the company consisting chiefly of the recruits from England. These were Thomas Flynn, of the London Haymarket, engaged as principal tragedian; Tom Walton, of the Theatre Royal, York, principal singer, and George Andrews, low comedian. Among others who appeared during the season were Mr. King, Miss Rivers, Miss Rock, Mr. and Mrs. Bernard, Mrs. C. Young, Mr. Finn, Mr. Clarke, Mr. Charnock, Mrs. Finn (née Powell), Mrs. Barnes, Mrs. Papanti, Miss Clarke, Miss McBride, Mr. and Mrs. Duff, Mr. Maywood, Mr. and Mrs. Blake, J. H. Hackett, Edwin Forrest, Clara Fisher and others. But in spite of the excellent bills offered, there was a deficit at the close of the season. The competition was so keen that both houses suffered. " The old house," says Clapp, " carried the day as regards the excellence of the stock company and stars, and the Tremont had superior advantage so far as a new house and a better location was concerned; but neither came out of this first struggle with any decided advantage to themselves." The next season Pelby was induced to sell out his lease of the Tremont Theatre. The company was strengthened and Junius Brutus Booth engaged as acting manager. The house reopened under his direction September 1, 1828, with "Speed the Plough."

On September 1, 1830, Charles Kean, son of the famous tragedian, Edmund Kean, made his first appearance in America at the Park Theatre as Richard III. Educated at Eton, and brought up as a gentleman, he was an entirely different type of man to his father. He lacked the elder Kean's genius, but made a very favorable impression on his first American visit which lasted over two years. Returning to London, he was seen with Edmund Kean at Covent Garden (March 25, 1833), the elder Kean playing Othello and Charles Kean appearing as Iago. In 1839, he again visited America. His third visit to this country was in 1845 when he came with his wife, Ellen Tree, a charming actress whom he had married in 1842 and who was as popular here as in England. It was Ellen Tree who, as Clari in Payne's opera, "Clari the Maid of Milan," popularized the song *Home, Sweet Home.* Charles Kean had many admirers, but as an actor he was only second rate. "No great character either in tragedy or comedy," says J. Ranken Towse, " has been associated with his name." The critic proceeds:

He was the subject of fervent adulation and savage attack, but did not deserve either. Of his father's erratic but brilliant genius he inherited no spark. In stature and carriage he was insignificant;

93

his visage lacked distinction, though he had good eyes and forehead; his voice was deficient in power and range and his utterance was faulty. . . . His wife, Ellen Tree, an actress of uncommon ability, if not of positive genius, and in her prime, before she grew stout and unwieldy, a woman of notable beauty and dignified charm, was his " better half " in more senses than one. They were a devoted couple, and their long wedded life, untouched by scandal, was an example of conjugal happiness and respectability not too common in the profession. She humored his vanity, which was colossal, and held him in complete but unconscious subjection.[*]

On November 22, Master Joseph Burke, the celebrated Irish Roscius, made his first appearance in America at the Park Theatre. This child actor, who came here with an enormous reputation acquired in England, was the son of an Irish physician. The lad early showed extraordinary precocity in music and the power of mimicry, and at the age of five made his stage début at the Dublin Theatre in the characters of Tom Thumb and Lingo. His success in the English provinces was so great that he was at once engaged for the London Haymarket, crowds flocking to see him. " As a prodigy in both music and the drama," says Ireland, " he has been unapproached by any child who has trodden the American stage. His readings were always discriminating and forcible and entirely free from the drilled mannerisms of most child actors. His performance of Richard, Shylock and Sir Giles was so good that none sneered at the absurdity of a child's assuming such parts, while his comedy, especially in Irish parts, was so full of native genuine humor that he never failed to convulse his audience with laughter."

---

[*] Sixty Years of the Theatre. Copyright, 1916, by John Ranken Towse. Funk and Wagnalls Co., Publishers. Reprinted by permission.

GEORGE HOLLAND, MRS. JOHN DREW

On September 21, 1831, at the Bowery Theatre, then under the management of Thomas Hamblin, Miss Josephine Clifton, an American actress, made her first appearance on the stage as Belvidera in " Venice Preserved," supported by Barton as Pierre and Hamblin as Jaffier. Born in New York City in 1813, Miss Clifton was a woman of exceptional beauty and this, together with a fine voice and unusual dramatic gifts, soon gained for her a commanding position on our stage. In 1834, she went to London and appeared at Drury Lane as Belvidera, the first American actress to visit Europe as a star. In 1837 she appeared at the Park Theatre, New York, in the tragedy " Bianca Visconti." At the time of her death, in 1847, says Ireland, no other American actress with the exception of Charlotte Cushman had created so wide a sensation.

CHAPTER XIX

NIBLO'S GARDEN, JEFFERSON, THE KEMBLES

PRODUCTION OF THE FAMOUS "BLACK CROOK." W. J. FLORENCE.
THE RICHMOND HILL THEATRE. ADAH ISAACS MENKEN IN
"MAZEPPA." FIRST ITALIAN OPERA HOUSE BUILT IN NEW YORK.
DÉBUT OF JOHN GILBERT. NEGRO MINSTRELSY. "JIM CROW"
RICE. DÉBUT OF JOSEPH JEFFERSON III. ARRIVAL OF THE
KEMBLES. DÉBUT OF W. E. BURTON IN PHILADELPHIA.

AMONG New York's famous playhouses few have contributed more important chapters to American theatrical history than Niblo's Garden, the home of the ballet spectacle, " The Black Crook." The theatre had a notable career from 1834 to 1895, and during this long span of sixty years almost every artist of consequence identified with the American stage appeared, at one time or another, on its boards.

Situated at the rear of a plot of land at the corner of Broadway and Prince Street—formerly a drill ground—the place was first opened in 1823 under the name Columbia Gardens, summer evening entertainments being given there. Later, William Niblo, a successful coffee house keeper, leased the place and converted it into an ornamental garden for the public. " Large trees," says a writer, " were transplanted from distant woods; choice flowers and plants mingled with rare exotics; fountains gushed and threw their spray on the sunbeams. In the center of the garden a temple was erected and dedicated to music." Niblo also built a theatre with a seating capacity of 1200 persons. In the dramatic company were W. B.

Chapman, Anderson, Stone, George Barrett and Mrs. Jones. George Holland appeared at this house in " Whims of a Comedian."

The experiment being a success, Mr. Niblo in 1830 built a larger theatre which he named Niblo's Garden. William Mitchell, the comedian, opened here June 3, 1834, with a large company, and by 1837 the theatre had become the fashionable resort of the city. A series of popular concerts were given and the Ravel family [1] also appeared with extraordinary success. Writing about the theatre as it appeared at that time, Richard Grant White [2] says:

It was a great New York "institution" in its day—perhaps the greatest and most beneficent one of its sort that New York has ever known. It may be safely said that most of the elder generation of New Yorkers now living (1881) have had at Niblo's Garden the greatest pleasure they have ever enjoyed in public. There were careless fun and easy jollity; there whole families would go at a moment's warning to hear this or that singer, but most of all, year after year, to see the Ravels—a family of pantomimists and dancers upon earth and air, who have given innocent, thoughtless, side-shaking, brain-clearing pleasure to more Americans than ever relaxed their sad, silent faces for any other performers. The price of admission here was fifty cents, no seats reserved; "first come, first served."

The company at that period included such players as Mr. Jefferson, Mr. Thayer, Mr. Thomas, Mr. Lewellen, Mr. Plumer, Mr. Bishop, Henry J. Sefton,

---

[1] The Ravels, a famous French family of rope dancers, acrobats and pantomimists, came to America in 1832. They consisted of ten persons, and made their first appearance in this country at the Park Theatre. They then visited Philadelphia and Boston, after which they toured the South and West. They remained in America many years, their unique performances being very popular everywhere.

[2] Richard Grant White, dramatic and art critic and editor of the *Riverside Shakespeare*, was born in 1821. He died in 1885.

Mrs. Harrison, Mrs. Bailey, Mrs. Knight, Mrs. Maeder and Alexina Fisher.

It was at Niblo's on May 8, 1850, that William J. Florence, the buoyant and droll Irish comedian associated later with Joseph Jefferson, made his first appearance on the New York stage. Mr. Florence was born in Albany, N. Y., in 1831, and after much success as a member of the Murdoch Dramatic Association, made his professional début at the Marshall Theatre, Richmond, Va., as Tobias in "The Stranger." Later, he played Macduff to Booth's Macbeth. In 1852, he was a member of the company at John Brougham's Lyceum, where he appeared for the first time in Irish characters. The following year he was married to Malvina Pray, a *danseuse* at Wallack's. They appeared together at Purdy's National Theatre, June 8, 1853, as the Irish Boy and Yankee Gal, and for many years continued to be billed jointly in Irish plays, in the manner of Mr. and Mrs. Barney Williams, filling engagements everywhere with great success. The song *Bobbing Around,* sung by Mrs. Florence, had a sale of more than 100,000 copies. In 1856, Mr. and Mrs. Florence went to England and appeared at Drury Lane, where Mrs. Florence's performance of The Yankee Girl aroused the greatest enthusiasm. Returning to America, Florence appeared, in 1861, at Wallack's, playing Toodles and Cuttle and other parts made popular by Burton. In 1863, he produced Tom Taylor's play, "Ticket of Leave Man," at the Winter Garden, himself acting the part of Bob Brierly, one of his most successful rôles. A few years later (1867) he presented at the Broadway the comedy " Caste " with an extraordinary array of players, including Mrs. Chanfrau, Mrs. Gilbert, Mrs. Florence, William Davidge, Owen Marlowe, Edward Lamb and Florence himself. His most pronounced hit was as the Hon. Bardwell Slote in Benjamin E. Woolf's play, " The Mighty Dollar," in 1876. Sir Lucius O'Trigger in Mr. Jefferson's production, " The Rivals," and his Zekiel Homespun in " The Heir at Law " are also remembered among his most successful characterizations.

In 1862 William Wheatley secured control of Niblo's and under his direction the theatre achieved some of its greatest successes. The Ravels continued to be a favorite attraction and they were followed at intervals by Edwin Forrest in Shakespearian repertoire; Matilda Heron, in " Camille "; Kate Bateman, in " Leah the Forsaken," " The Hunchback," and other plays; Daniel Bandmann as Shylock; Felicia Vestvali in English drama; Edwin Booth in " The Fool's Revenge "; James H. Hackett as Falstaff; Mr. and Mrs. Barney Williams in Irish plays; Lucille Western, in " The Sea of Ice " and " East Lynne "; Lotta, as Little Nell and the Marchioness, in " The Old Curiosity Shop," and Maggie Mitchell, in " Fanchon."

On February 6, 1865, Jean Davenport Lander made her reappearance at Niblo's in a drama entitled " Mésalliance," and later was seen in "The Lady of Lyons," " The Belle's Stratagem " and other plays of her repertoire. This favorite tragic actress, who had served as a hospital nurse during the Civil War, in which her husband, General Lander, was killed, was born in England in 1827 and made her first appearance in America in 1838 at the National

99

Theatre, New York, under the management of the elder Wallack. In 1842, she went back to Europe, where she won her greatest successes in Shakespearian rôles. Returning to America in 1849, she decided to make this country her home and in 1855 went out to California, repeating her success in such rôles as Juliet, Peg Woffington, Adrienne Lecouvreur, Letitia Hardy, the Countess in " Love," Julia in " The Hunchback," and Camille, Alexander Dumas' idealized courtesan, of whom she was the first representative in this country.

On July 12, 1865, Dion Boucicault's " Arrah Na Pogue " was presented at Niblo's for the first time in America, and the following season saw the production of the spectacular ballet, " The Black Crook," which proved a success unparalleled up to that time in American stage annals.

The production at Niblo's of this sensational spectacle—the fame of which rang round the world—was entirely accidental. The firm, Jarrett and Palmer, who popularized the ballet in this country, had imported from Europe an elaborate ballet with dancers, novel scenic effects and wealth of costume, all of which were to be used in the opera, " La Biche au Bois," at the Academy of Music. At the eleventh hour, the Academy burned down and Jarrett and Palmer found themselves with the ballet on their hands. Shortly before this, an actor named Barras had submitted to Niblo's the manuscript of a spectacular play called " The Black Crook," which Wheatley had contracted to produce. The manager thought the London ballet might be utilized in this piece. The author consented to the necessary changes, agreeing to accept $1,500 for his manuscript, no matter how long or how short the run. When the changes were made, practically nothing remained of the Barras play except the title.

Presented for the first time September 12, 1866, "The Black Crook" took the town by storm. The theatre was packed from pit to dome to witness the première of a piece that created more talk than any piece of its kind before or since. The scenery and costumes were on a scale of magnificence never seen before in this country, but it was the *corps de ballet* which caused the greatest sensation. There were a hundred girl dancers, most of them wearing the scantiest of attire. In fact, "The Black Crook" was the first show of its kind on the American stage to make a feature of the diaphanously draped or semi-nude feminine form. The *première danseuses* were Marie Bonfanti, Rita Sangalli, Betty Rigl and Rose Delval.

The production aroused a storm of controversy. Preachers and moralists thundered against what they denounced as the license of the stage, and the stern pater familias frowned on any member of his home circle seeing the show except himself. But the success of the piece was prodigious. It ran for sixteen consecutive months, during which time four hundred and seventy-five performances were given, to receipts exceeding one million, one hundred thousand dollars!

The success of "The Black Crook" naturally opened the way for a veritable invasion of the American stage by English burlesque dancers, all of them notorious for their generous display of limb. Among the best known and most attractive of these performers were Lydia Thompson, Pauline Markham and

THE THEATRE IN AMERICA

Eliza Weathersby, the last being particularly popular as dancer, actress and singer. Lydia Thompson, a charming and versatile actress, whom the younger Dumas honored to the extent of writing a play especially for her, was born in London in 1836 and made a sensation at the Haymarket by her imitations and dancing. She came to America in 1868 at the head of her own burlesque company and toured the country successfully.

Another playhouse opened in New York in the early thirties was known as the Richmond Hill Theatre. Originally the summer home of Aaron Burr, it was a large, gloomy-looking mansion with a huge, white portico, supported by large wooden columns, and stood at the rear of the lots at the intersection of Varick and Charlton Streets. Converted into a theatre, the place was opened November 14, 1831, with "The Road to Ruin," the company including T. Abthorpe Cooper, Wilson, Finn, Holland, Kilner, Foote, Langton, Judah, C. Thorne, Moreland, Russell, Field, Mestayer, Meer, Moses Phillips, Lenox, Lindsley, Kenny, Wray, and Phillimore, Mrs. Russell, Mrs. Thorne, Mrs. Meer, Mrs. Read and Mrs. Belcour. The famous Mary Duff, who, since her successful début in Boston had appeared frequently in New York, was again seen there at this theatre, April 9, 1832, as Helen Worrett in "Man and Wife."

In the Fall of the same year, the theatre was given over to grand opera, the Montressor company making their appearance October 6 with Rossini's "Cenerentola," already heard at the Park under the title "Cinderella." Other operas were given, but the venture ended in failure.

102

NIBLO'S GARDEN, JEFFERSON, KEMBLES

The second dramatic season began January 1, 1833, with Clara Woodhull in "Lovers' Vows." On April 18 was seen for the first time a highly sensational equestrian drama, "Mazeppa," in which the heroine makes a thrilling flight around the auditorium while bound to the back of a wild horse. Adah Isaacs Menken (1835–1868) was the first performer bold enough to allow herself to be tied to the horse, former Mazeppas having used a dummy. This talented woman, who was a great favorite with audiences in the early sixties, and an intimate friend of Dickens, Swinburne, Dumas the elder and other celebrities, had an adventurous and interesting career. She was born in 1835 in Louisiana, her father being a Presbyterian minister. She received a good education, but, compelled to make a living, she went on the stage as a dancer, first appearing at the French Opera House, New Orleans, in 1855. Soon afterwards, she made her début as an actress in the same city as Bianca in "Fazio," meeting with great success. Subsequently, she supported Booth, Murdoch and Hackett, and later became herself a star, appearing in "Mazeppa," "The French Spy" and "Three Fast Men" to enormous receipts. While acting with the Nashville stock company, she met and married Alexander Isaacs Menken, a musician, and adopted the Jewish faith, in which she died. Her career was spectacular from start to finish. She was in turn dancer, actress, poet, editor, sculptress, teacher of French and Latin. While hunting in Texas, she was captured by Indians and held captive until rescued. She had considerable literary ability and published two volumes of poetry. She died in Paris in 1868.

THE THEATRE IN AMERICA

On June 27, James E. Murdoch made his New York début at the Richmond Hill Theatre in " Venice Preserved."

Although M. Montressor's operatic venture had proved unsuccessful, grand opera was by no means dead in New York. Lorenzo Da Ponte, an aged teacher of Italian literature, inspired by the coming of Garcia and Malibran, which had revived old memories of operatic triumphs in Europe, persuaded a group of wealthy and cultured New Yorkers to build an Italian Opera House. The result was the first opera house erected in New York City. It was situated on the southwest corner of Church and Leonard Streets, and cost $150,000. Under the joint management of the Chevalier Rivafinoli and Da Ponte, it was opened to the public November 18, 1833, with Rossini's opera "La Gazza Ladra." "The new opera house was organized on very much the same social and economic lines," says Henry E. Krehbiel, " as prevail at the Metropolitan Opera House to-day." He continues:

It was the first theatre in the United States which boasted a tier composed exclusively of boxes. This was the second balcony. The parterre was entered from the first balcony, a circumstance which redeemed it from its old plebeian association as " the pit," in which it would have been indecorous for ladies to sit. The seats in the parterre were mahogany chairs upholstered in blue damask. The seats in the first balcony were mahogany sofas similarly upholstered. The box fronts had a white ground, with emblematic medallions, and octagonal panels of crimson, blue, and gold. Blue silk curtains were caught up with gilt cord and tassels. There was a chandelier of great splendor, which threw its light into a dome enriched with pictures of the Muses, painted, like all the rest of the interior, as well as the scenery, by artists specially brought over for the purpose from Europe. The floors were carpeted. The price of the boxes was $6,000 each, and subscribers might own them for a single performance (evidently by arrangement with the owners) or the season.[1]

The first season, which lasted until July 21, 1834, was devoted entirely to Italian opera, among the works produced being Rossini's " Barbiere di Siviglia," " La Donna del Lago," " Il Turco in Italia," " Cenerentola " and " Matilda di Shabran "; Pacini's " Gli Arabi nelli Gallie," Cimarosa's " Il Matrimonio segreto," and " La Casa do Pendere." The receipts for the season were $51,780.89 and the expenses $81,155.98, showing that even in those early days grand opera was an expensive luxury.

The next season the house was leased to Signor Sacchi, the treasurer of Rivafinoli and Da Ponte, but he was no more successful in making both ends meet, and at the end of that engagement the house was taken over by Messrs. Henry Willard and Thomas Flynn, who opened it as the National Theatre, August 29, 1836, with " The Merchant of Venice."

On November 28, 1828, at the Tremont Theatre, Boston, John Gilbert, one of the grand figures of the American stage, made his first appearance on the boards as Jaffier in ' Venice Preserved." He was then only nineteen years of age. He remained in harness, acting continually, for upwards of sixty years, during which time he was seen in an astonishing number of rôles, from Old Norval and Sir Peter Teazle to the Abbé Constantin. Throughout his career, he was identified with old men parts, in which he had no equal. " He was sometimes a great actor; he was always a correct one," says William Winter. " In such characters as Sir Sampson Legend and Sir Anthony Absolute no man of his time approached him, and it is doubtful whether in that line of individuality he was ever equalled." Another critic considers his Sir Anthony Absolute his most notable impersonation. He says:

It is difficult to believe that the choleric old Englishman ever had a better representative. His Sir Peter Teazle is a companion piece of almost equal merit, but is distinctly inferior. It is a little deficient in polish. Take Old Dornton in the " Road to Ruin ": no more perfect picture of probity, benevolence, and tenderness could be imagined. What a wealth of humor he infused into Lord Duberly! His Lord Ogleby is another instance of his wide versatility, as is his Sir Francis Gripe in the " Busybody." Even more striking is the contrast between his Master Walter in the " Hunchback " and his Mr. Hardcastle in " She Stoops to Conquer." His Sir Harcourt Courtly is as finished a modern portrait as any of the old ones just enumerated. Who would suppose this exquisite was identical with the ruffianly McKenna in " Rosedale," the fussy old Brisemouche in " A Scrap of Paper," or the jealous old husband in " The Guv'nor "? [4]

John Gibbs Gilbert was born in Boston in 1810. As a child he played with Charlotte Cushman, his next-door neighbor. After making his début in his native city, he went to New Orleans, where he remained some years. In 1834 he returned East, and spent the next twelve years acting in Boston, New York and Philadelphia. In 1846 he went to London, where he appeared at the Princess Theatre as Sir Robert Bramble. Returning to New York, he was seen at the Park as Sir Anthony Absolute. In 1858 he went to the Arch Street Theatre, Philadelphia, where he remained until engaged by the elder Wal-

[4] J. Ranken Towse in the *Century Magazine.*

lack, in 1862, for his house at Thirteenth Street and Broadway. He remained a member of Wallack's until that organization ceased to exist in 1888 and died in Boston in 1889.

About the time John Gilbert appeared on the stage (1828) a new and peculiarly American form of entertainment was seen for the first time on our boards and soon became very popular. This was negro minstrelsy, which had its origin in the singing and dancing of the slaves on the plantations of the wealthy Southerners. When the master wanted amusement he sent for those among his slaves who could sing and dance. When he sent out invitations for a "small and early," it was the slaves who played the dance music. The entertaining abilities of the despised slave were soon recognized and the white actor began to realize he could make money by imitating the black man.

Thomas D. Rice (Jim Crow Rice), a New Yorker, was one of the first to win fame in this field. Born in 1808, he first appeared in negro character at Ludlow's Amphitheatre, Louisville, Ky. Returning East, he went to Washington, where he made a great hit in his new darkie song and dance, "Jim Crow." He was next seen at the Bowery, New York, the novelty of the entertainment taking the town by storm. "Jim Crow," says Ireland, "attained a popularity unequalled by anything of the kind before or since, and 'wheeled about' its lucky chaunter from poverty to fame and fortune. He probably drew more money to tne Bowery treasury than any American performer in the same period of time. In person, he was tall and slender, and assumed the shambling negro gait and plantation dialect with more amusing accuracy than any other of our African delineators. George W. Dixon led the way in New York with this class of entertainment, but it was reserved for Mr. Rice to naturalize and render it popular, and in consequence he was generally regarded as the father and founder of Ethiopian minstrelsy."[5]

In 1842, E. B. Christy organized the Christy Minstrels, which were enormously successful both here and in England. Later Ethiopian organizations were Buckley's Serenaders, Dan Bryant's, San Francisco Minstrels, Kelly and Leon's, the Callender Minstrels, the Haverly Minstrels, Primrose and West Minstrels and Lew Dockstader. Of late years, the popularity of the negro minstrel has waned. Public taste has changed. The Ethiopian has had to yield the centre of the stage to the girl show. Among our latter-day black-face artists, Al Jolson is perhaps the most successful in keeping alive the tradition of the colored minstrel.

It was with blackened face and in the darkie costume of " Jim Crow " that Joseph Jefferson, our famous Rip (1829-1905), made one of his earliest appearances on the stage. He was then only four years of age, and although he had often been carried on the stage as a property baby, this was his first appearance before the public in a distinct impersonation of his own. Rice had just made his first hit in Washington and baby Jefferson had amused his family and friends with imitations of the negro dialect singer. Rice himself was delighted with the imitation and at once conceived the idea of using little Jefferson in a

_____

[5] Records of the New York Stage, by Joseph N. Ireland.

novel way at his benefit. Blacking the child's face and dressing him so that he was a diminutive counterpart of himself, he put him in a bag which he slung over his shoulder, and thus laden down came down to the footlights and began to sing:

*" Ladies and Gentlemen, I'd have you for to know
That I've got a little darky here that jumps Jim
Crow."*

Turning the bag upside down, he emptied the little boy head first before the eyes of the astonished audience. " Rice," says Joseph Jefferson in his Autobiography, " was considerably over six feet high; I was but four years old, and as we stood there, dressed exactly alike, the audience roared with laughter. Rice and I now sang alternate stanzas and the excitement increased; showers of pennies, sixpences, and shillings were tossed from the pit and thrown from the galleries upon the stage."

With his great-grandfather, grandfather, father and mother players, and himself bred, if not actually born, in the theatre, it would have been strange had Joseph Jefferson III not been a good actor. As we know, he proved the most gifted player of them all. During the seventy-odd years Joseph Jefferson was on the stage, he learned all that can be learned of the art of acting. If most of his gifts—his rich humor as a comedian, his skill as a painter—came to him by right of inheritance, one must also recall that during his earlier years he was a hard and ambitious worker (actually he had over a hundred rôles to his credit), and developed slowly in the bitter school of experience that charm as an actor which endeared him to our public.

THE THEATRE IN AMERICA

He was only eight years old when he and his little sister set out with his father and mother—four strolling players—to explore the still trackless West. In 1838 he was in Chicago—then a mere handful of crudely built frame shacks risen from the wilderness overnight—he and his sister acting children's parts, then pushing on to other towns, now in open wagon, now by sleigh on the frozen rivers, unprotected from the weather, always in peril, not getting enough sleep or food, funds always at the lowest ebb, the father alternating playacting with the painting of scenery or even tradesmen's signs to make both ends meet, the anxious, patient mother undergoing all kinds of privations to help husband and children.

That was Joseph Jefferson's childhood. In 1842 his father died of yellow fever, and Joseph continued touring with mother and sister, acting among others with Macready and Junius Brutus Booth. In 1846 he was in Mexico in the train of the victorious U. S. Army, and opened a saloon in Matamoras, where he served coffee and cake, dodging behind the bar to escape the bullets of the drink-crazed gamblers. Returning to the United States, he made his way to Philadelphia to join his half brother, Charles Burke, who was acting second comedy parts at the Arch Street Theatre, then managed by W. E. Burton. After acting comedy parts in Philadelphia for some time, he quarrelled with Burton and set out for Cumberland, Md., where an opportunity was offered to play a star engagement. His mother's death brought this tour to a close, and later he applied to the manager of the Philadelphia Amphitheatre for an engagement as comedian.

110

"But you don't look like a comedian!" objected the manager. "You have a serious, melancholy expression. You look more like an undertaker."

His first appearance in New York was at the National Theatre, September 10, 1849, as Jack Rackbottle in "Jonathan Bradford," but it was not until 1857, when, as a member of Laura Keene's company, he made a tremendous hit as Asa Trenchard in Tom Taylor's comedy, "Our American Cousin," that his reputation as America's best comedian was firmly established. This part he played for more than one hundred and fifty consecutive performances. "Quaint, easy, natural, perfectly unconscious of his audience," says a writer, "thoroughly imbued with the spirit and meaning of his part, and with a countenance as comically variable and expressive as can well be imagined, Mr. Jefferson attained as high a distinction in broad and eccentric comedy as has ever been awarded to any artist of American birth."

As Dr. Pangloss in "The Heir at Law," Bob Acres in "The Rivals," Caleb Plummer in "The Cricket on the Hearth," Mr. Golightly in "Lend Me Five Shillings," Tobias Shortcut in "The Spitfire," he won his way still further in the affections of American theatregoers.

Rip Van Winkle, acted for the first time in 1866, was the most famous of his impersonations, and the playing of it, which he did periodically to the end of his days, brought him a large fortune. In his Autobiography, Joseph Jefferson says he had not thought of Rip until the summer of 1859 when, one rainy day at a queer old Dutch farmhouse in Paradise Valley at the foot of the Pocono Mountains in Pennsylvania, he happened to pick up the Life of Washington Irving, which suggested the quaint story of Rip Van Winkle. "There was to me magic in the sound of the name as I repeated it. Why, was not this the very character I wanted?"

Several dramatizations of Rip Van Winkle had already been seen on the American boards. As a play, it first came on the stage May 26, 1828, at Albany, N. Y. Jefferson originally appeared in the version used by his half-brother, Charles Burke, but realizing the shortcomings of the piece he commissioned Dion Boucicault to rewrite the drama. The Boucicault version was first produced at the Adelphi Theatre, London, September 4, 1865, and met with instant success. Returning to America the following year, Jefferson opened with the piece at the Olympic Theatre, New York, on September 3, after which he toured the country, attracting enormous audiences and receiving better terms from managers than ever were paid before for a star.

Some critics have charged Joseph Jefferson with being a one-part actor—that he found it easier and more profitable to go on playing the ever-popular "Rip" than studying new parts and risking his money on untried plays. To this charge Jefferson himself has made reply in characteristic fashion:

I have often been taxed with idleness for not studying new parts and adding them to my repertoire. The list of plays that I have acted of late years is certainly a very short one, and the critic who becomes weary of witnessing them over and over again naturally protests against their constant repetition. Setting aside the fact that every one must be the best judge of how to conduct his own affairs, there are other matters connected with the course

112

I have pursued that may have escaped the attention of those who have rated me for my lack of versatility; and reference to a conversation between Charles Mathews and myself on this very subject may serve to illustrate what I mean. We were good-humoredly quizzing each other about our different styles of acting, when he rallied me somewhat after this fashion:

" You call yourself a comedian," said he. " Why, you can only play one part. You are the prince of dramatic carpet-baggers, and carry all·your wardrobe in a gripsack. Look at that huge pile of trunks—mine, sir, mine! Examine my list of parts! Count them —half a hundred, at the very least; you ought to be ashamed of yourself. Where is your versatility? "

" My dear Charlie," said I, " You are confounding wardrobe with talent. What is the value of a long bill of fare if the stuff is badly cooked? You change your hat, and fancy you are playing another character. Believe me, it requires more skill to act one part fifty different ways than to act fifty parts all the same way." And here we ended our rather comical argument.[6]

Is Jefferson entitled to rank among the great actors of history? William Winter replies in the affirmative: " He was not only a great actor, he was a man of noble mind, original character, sympathetic temperament, and lovely spirit; he not only exercised a potential influence upon the dramatic profession, to which his life was devoted, but by virtue of the sweetness and kindness that his genial nature diffused, through the medium of his acting, he deeply affected the lives of thousands who were personally strangers."[7] On the other hand, John Ranken Towse, critic of the New York *Evening Post,* denies to Jefferson the supreme laurels. He says:

None of the parts in which Jefferson delighted his audiences

[6] Autobiography of Joseph Jefferson. Copyright, 1889. Reprinted by permission of the Century Co.

[7] Other Days. Copyright, 1908, by William Winter. Moffat, Yard & Company, Publishers. Reprinted by permission of Jefferson Winter, Esq.

could by any stretch of the imagination be called great. None of them sounded the heights or depths of emotion, lofty flights of imagination or passion, or demanded the exhibition of uncommon intellectual, moral, or dramatic power. They all lay within the limits of the middle register. All of them were played, and often very well played, by actors of no extraordinary capacity. There were many who preferred the Caleb Plummer of John E. Owens—there was certainly more of Dickens in it—and the Acres of George Giddens, to Jefferson's presentment of those characters. It is scarcely an exaggeration to say that Jefferson never really played Acres at all. He did not in the least resemble the unsophisticated British country squire, vainly aping fashionable manners, whom Sheridan sketched. He was delectable, infinitely amusing, utterly unreal—Joseph Jefferson in delicious masquerade. Wherein then—if he was not a creator and could not or did not play great parts, and, therefore, was not, in the true sense, a great actor—is to be found the secret of Jefferson's popularity and fame? The answer is easy. In his consummate artistry and his personal fascination. . . . He was content, throughout the greater part of his long and active life, to play the characters which, in a very special sense, he had made peculiarly his own. In effecting these personifications he employed a technical skill which was as nearly perfect as anything in this imperfect world can be. His most intricate and delicate mechanism worked with flawless accuracy, precision, and smoothness. Everything that he said or did upon the stage appeared to proceed from the impulse of the moment, to be entirely spontaneous. It cost him long years of hard and varied stage work, in his youth, to acquire this mechanical proficiency, but the investment of time and labor brought him an exceedingly rich reward. He earned it and deserved it, but that is no reason why he should be accredited with a genius he did not possess.[8]

Enormous interest was aroused everywhere in the United States in the Fall of 1832 by the coming of Charles Kemble and his daughter Frances Anne, better known as Fanny Kemble. Representatives of the most famous theatrical family in history, the brother

[8] Sixty Years of the Theatre. Copyright, 1916, by John Ranken Towse. Funk & Wagnalls Company, Publishers. Reprinted by permission.

and niece of the celebrated Mrs. Siddons, there was the greatest curiosity to see the distinguished English visitors. Charles Kemble made his American début at the Park Theatre, New York, September 17, as Hamlet, and his daughter was seen the following evening as Bianca in " Fazio." Their success was instantaneous and overwhelming. " The sensation created by their appearance," says Ireland, " had been equalled in kind only in the days of Cooke and Kean and in duration and intensity was altogether unparalleled. The intellectual, the educated, and the refined crowded the theatre when they performed, and during their entire stay their popularity never waned."

The founder of this famous family, Roger Kemble, was originally a strolling player. Later, he became a manager, but the world never heard of him until the growing fame of his children, Mrs. Siddons, John Philip, and Charles, brought his name out of obscurity. Mrs. Siddons, conceded by most critics to be the greatest actress the world has ever seen, was born in 1755. After some experience gained in her father's troupe, she attracted the attention of Garrick, and in 1775 made her début at Drury Lane as Portia. Nervous and awkward, she created no favorable impression on this occasion, and she returned to the provinces full of bitterness and disappointment. Seven years later, she reappeared at Drury Lane as the heroine in " Isabella, or the Fatal Marriage," and won a tremendous triumph. " Her beautiful face and form," says a contemporaneous reviewer, " the exquisite tones of her voice, her deep tenderness, seized upon every heart, and her overwhelming agony thrilled every soul as it had never been thrilled before. Men wept, women fell into hysterics, transports of applause shook the house; the excitement and enthusiasm were almost terrible in their intensity, and the curtain fell amidst such acclamations as perhaps even Garrick had never roused." The following year her brother, John Philip (born 1757), made his first appearance at Drury Lane as Hamlet, surprising all London by his novel and powerful performance. Charles Lamb declared it " difficult for a frequent playgoer to disencumber the idea of Hamlet from the person of John Kemble." Ranked as England's greatest living tragic actor, John Philip Kemble became manager of Drury Lane and from 1803 to 1808 was manager and part owner of Covent Garden.

Charles Kemble, youngest brother of Mrs. Siddons and John Philip, was born in 1775, and made his début at Drury Lane in 1794 as Malcolm in " Macbeth." His reputation rests principally on his Hamlet, Romeo and Pierre in tragedy, and on his Mercutio, Benedick, Falconbridge, Young Mirabel, Petruchio, and Charles Surface in comedy. " His great, unvarying merits," says Ireland, " were his elegance of action, his taste and propriety in costume, his intimate knowledge of his author, and his refinement of manner, which always impressed upon an audience the fact that Mr. Kemble, the high-bred gentleman, stood before them—a fact that he himself never for a moment forgot. There was generally a languor and want of energy about his performances, and his representations of the more violent passions always came tamely off, so that, while he uniformly pleased the scholar and the man of taste, he rarely reached the hearts of the multitude."

His daughter, Fanny Kemble, was born in London in 1809 and made her début at Covent Garden in 1829 as Juliet, with extraordinary success. On her arrival in America her triumphs were repeated. " To the state and dignity of the Kemble school," says Ireland, " she added all the fire and impetuosity of her own original genius, and from her mother she inherited a grace and fascination in her comic delineations that none other of the blood of Kemble ever knew. To her mother, also, she was indebted in her girlhood for a dainty lightness of figure, whose delicacy of outline is completely lost in her maturer years, and for a pair of glorious dark eyes, soft in repose, but able with a single glance to express the intensest shades of every varying passion. No actress that preceded her in America ever held so powerful and deep a sway over the hearts and feelings of her auditors."

While acting in Philadelphia in 1834, Fanny Kemble met and married Pierce Butler, a Southern planter. Incompatibility of taste soon ended in a divorce. She had decided literary skill in addition to her dramatic gift, being the author of several plays and reminiscences of travel. In 1848 she began giving a series of Shakespearian readings. She died in London in 1893.

At the Park, in 1833, appeared for the first time in America Tyrone Power, a distinguished Irish actor, who played Irish character parts with extraordinary success. He made his début August 28 as Sir Peter O'Plenipo in Kenney's comedy, " The Irish Ambassador," and in this and other rôles made an enormous hit, entirely eclipsing all predecessors in the same line.

Born in Ireland in 1797, Tyrone Power made his stage début in the Isle of Wight, in 1815, as Alonzo in "Pizarro." Later he was seen in Dublin as Romeo and Jeremy Diddler. His first London appearance was in 1822, when he played first at the Olympic and subsequently at Covent Garden, where he made his first hit in Irish characters as O'Shaughnessy in Peake's farce, "The £100 Note." "His mercurial temperament," says Ireland, "his genial, refined humor, the merry twinkle of his eye, the rich tones of his voice, his skill in music, the grace and heartiness of his dances, his happy variations of brogue to the different grades of character he represented—in fact, every requisite that nature and art could bestow combined to make him the most perfect comedian ever known to the American stage." After visiting Philadelphia and Boston with equal success, "Paddy" Power toured the United States and Canada, being greeted by audiences everywhere with the greatest enthusiasm. Besides his acting, he was a writer of considerable ability. His "Impressions of America" are a valuable contribution to literature. He was also the author of two novels and several plays. His end was tragic. Sailing from New York March 21, 1841, he was a passenger on the ill-fated steamship *President,* which was never again heard from. His grandson, Tyrone Power, is a well-known tragic actor on our stage to-day.

This year (1833) saw also the first appearance in this country of Mr. and Mrs. Joseph Wood, English opera singers, who made their début at the Park The-

atre, September 9, in Rossini's opera, " Cinderella."
Endowed with a voice of extraordinary compass,
Mrs. Wood (formerly Mary Ann Paton) made a
sensation here almost as great as that made two decades later by Jenny Lind, and was pronounced the
finest English vocalist ever heard in America. Born
in Edinburgh in 1802, she could play the piano at the
age of four and gave public concerts when she was
six. In 1822, she made her début at the London Haymarket with enormous success, and in 1830 appeared
at the Italian Opera as successor of the celebrated
Pasta. It was about this time that she married Mr.
Wood, an exceptionally handsome tenor, who is said
to have begun life as a ploughman. The singers made
a fortune during their American tour and were last
heard here in 1841.

Another theatre was added to New York's constantly growing list of playhouses in 1835. This was
the Franklin Theatre, in Chatham Street, which
opened on September 7 under the management of
William Dinneford with " The School of Reform "
and " The Unfinished Gentleman." The company
included : W. Sefton, stage manager; Jefferson, scenic
artist; John Sefton, J. Mills Brown, Thoman, Senior,
Goodenow, Manley, McDonald, Crane, Parker, Gilbert, Kirkland, Anderson, A. J. Phillips, Williams,
Burke, Madden, Kent, Parkinson, Everard, Mrs.
Duff, Blake, Kent, Alexina Fisher, Mr. and Mrs.
Stevenson, Mr. and Mrs. J. Stickney, Mr. and Mrs.
Lewellen, Amelia Verity, Mary Gannon, and Misses
E. and J. Anderson. Mary Duff made her last New
York appearance at this house. In 1840 George Han-
del Hill (" Yankee " Hill, the comedian) took pos-

THE THEATRE IN AMERICA

session of the house and renamed it Hill's Theatre. The night it opened under the new management, Mrs. Marietta Judah, the " grand old woman of the Western stage," made her New York début. This actress, who was fairly idolized in California, was especially noted for her performance of the nurse in " Romeo and Juliet "—an " impersonation so excellent and unique that Adelaide Neilson confessed her Juliet was dwarfed beside it."

On September 29, 1834, James Sheridan Knowles, author of " Virginius," " William Tell," " The Wife," etc., made his first appearance in America at the Park Theatre as Master Walter in his own play, " The Hunchback." Born at Cork, Ireland, in 1784, Sheridan Knowles was the son of an elocution teacher and a relative of Richard Brinsley Sheridan. After some experience on the provincial stage, he began writing plays, his first attempt, " Caius Gracchus " (1815), making a most favorable impression. Even greater success attended later efforts, " Virginius " (1820) the first of his plays seen in London and " The Hunchback " (1832). In 1831, he made his London début as an actor, appearing as Master Walter, and so poor a representative of his hero was he that Charles Kemble, the original Sir Thomas Clifford, said afterwards that the only person who did not understand the author was the gentleman who played Master Walter. Burly in form, below the middle height, speaking with an Irish brogue, he never attained as a player the rank deservedly accorded to him as a dramatist. He died in 1862.

The Philadelphia season of 1834 was notable for the first appearance in this country of a celebrated comedian who was later to become one of America's most popular and successful theatre managers. Both the Chestnut Street and Arch Street theatres at that time were under the control of Maywood, Rowbotham and Platt. It was on the boards of the latter house, which opened August 23, that W. E. Burton made his American début as Wormwood in " The Lottery Ticket " and Dr. Ollapod in " The Poor Gentleman."

Born in London in 1804, William Evans Burton began life as a printer, succeeding to his father's business. A penchant for amateur theatricals drew his attention to the stage and in 1825 he joined a provincial touring company. Six years later he made his professional début in London at the Pavilion Theatre, as Wormwood, and later he played Marrall to the Overreach of Edmund Kean. His first appearances in Philadelphia were so successful that he stayed in that city until 1837, when he went to New York and made his début at the National Theatre as Guy Goodluck in " John Jones." Four years later found him manager of the National Theatre. Shortly afterwards, the house was destroyed by fire, and, returning to Philadelphia, he leased the Chestnut Street and Arch Street theatres. He also assumed, at the same time, the management of the Washington Theatre and of the Front Street Theatre, Baltimore. In 1848, he was back in New York as manager of Palmo's Opera House, henceforth known as Burton's Theatre. Here he held sway until September, 1856, laying the main foundation of his celebrity as actor and manager. At this house he revived " A Midsummer Night's Dream," " Twelfth Night," " The Merry Wives of

Windsor," "The Winter's Tale," "The Tempest," himself playing Bottom, Sir Toby Belch, Falstaff, Autolycus, and Caliban. He produced dramatizations of Dombey and Son, David Copperfield, Oliver Twist, Nicholas Nickleby, and Pickwick, himself appearing as Captain Cuttle, Bumble, Micawber, Squeers and Sam Weller. "His pictures from Dickens," says W. L. Keese, "were careful studies, revealing fine sympathy and appreciation; his Shakespearian delineations were felicitous interpretations of the master's spirit. In the extravagance of farce it was impossible to be funnier than he was. Mirth came from him in exhalations. . . . Other qualities of his acting were a simple and natural pathos, and an earnestness in the expression of homely feeling, blent with dignity."[*]

Under his enterprising management, the theatre reached its highest point of prosperity and in a few years Burton was estimated a millionaire. "For several years," says Ireland, "Burton's Theatre was the resort of the most intelligent class of pleasure-seekers, and there beauty, wit, and fashion loved to congregate, without the formality or etiquette of attire, once deemed necessary at the Park. But trade and commerce encroached on his location, and fashion, ever fickle, finally fancied that it saw a dash of vulgarity about the place, and began to turn its errant footsteps elsewhere, when the manager, fired with an ambition for a theatre in Broadway, where he could more successfully cope with his most formidable rival, Wallack, and in hopes of extinguishing entirely the light of Laura Keene, a new competitor in management,

[*] William Burton—Actor, Author and Manager. By W. L. Keese.

disposed of his downtown establishment, and succeeded in gaining possession of the theatre then under
the direction of that lady, which he opened September, 1856, under the name of Burton's New Theatre."

It was during Burton's administration of the
National Theatre, New York, in 1841, that Josephine
Shaw, a beautiful and accomplished actress, better
known to a later generation of theatregoers as Mrs.
John Hoey, made her début in " The Naiad Queen."
Born in England in 1824, this actress came to America with her father, a musician and poet, and made
her first stage appearance in this country at the
Museum, Baltimore, in 1839, as Eliza in " Nature
and Philosophy." While acting at Burton's Theatre,
she was married to John Hoey, of the Adams Express
Company, and shortly afterwards announced her retirement from the stage. But when Wallack opened
at Broome Street and Broadway, she was induced to
change her mind and she became leading lady in the
Wallack company, a position she maintained until
1865. She was noted for her excellent taste in dress,
and her gowns were the talk of the town. More fortunate than most actresses, she was able, owing to her
husband's means, to gratify her every whim. She is
said to have originated the present extravagant style
of stage costuming, her wardrobe being the largest
and most expensive of any actress of her day.

CHAPTER XX

CHARLOTTE CUSHMAN

AMERICA'S GREATEST TRAGEDIENNE. MITCHELL'S OLYMPIC. F. S. CHANFRAU AS MOSE. DÉBUT OF EDWARD L. DAVENPORT. WALLACK SECURES THE NATIONAL THEATRE. DECLINE OF THE OLD PARK. ARRIVALS OF THE VANDENHOFFS. BENEDICT DE BAR. GEORGE L. FOX IN " HUMPTY DUMPTY." THE CHATHAM STREET THEATRE. COMING OF CHARLES J. MATHEWS, JR., AND MME. VESTRIS. FANNY ELSSLER'S GREAT SUCCESS. ARRIVAL OF JOHN BROUGHAM. JOHN E. OWENS MAKES HIS DÉBUT.

ALTHOUGH several actors of American birth had already won laurels on our boards, no native-born actress of the first rank had appeared until the coming of Charlotte Cushman.

This great tragedienne, who dominated our stage in the middle of the last century, came of genuine Puritan stock, her original ancestor in America, Roger Cushman, having delivered, within a year of the landing at Plymouth, the first sermon in this country extant. Born in Boston in 1816, the eldest of five children and compelled by the death of her father to earn a livelihood, she began her professional career as a vocalist, making her first appearance on any stage April 8, 1835, as the Countess Almaviva in the opera " The Marriage of Figaro." She had previously sung at concerts, when her fine contralto voice attracted the attention of Mrs. Joseph Wood, who advised her to go on the stage. Her first appearance was successful enough to bring an offer of engagement as " leading singing lady " at the St. Charles Theatre, New Orleans. But her singing career did

not last long. In her anxiety to please, she so strained
her voice that it was soon ruined for operatic purposes, and in this dilemma, she was ready enough to
follow the suggestion of Mr. Barton, the tragedian,[1]
that she devote herself henceforth to acting. Under
his guidance, she made her first appearance as a tragedienne in New Orleans in the character of Lady
Macbeth with such success that she was encouraged
to continue. Proceeding to New York, she approached the Park Theatre management, but, receiving little or no encouragement, she signed an engagement with Thomas Hamblin, manager of the Bowery
Theatre, for three years at $25 a week, and made
her début at that house September 12, 1836, as Lady
Macbeth to the Macbeth of Hamblin. The following
night she was seen as Helen McGregor in " Rob
Roy," and for her benefit on September 17 she acted
Alicia in " Jane Shore." Three days later, the Bowery Theatre was destroyed by fire, and Miss Cushman was not seen again in New York until the following April when she appeared at the National
Theatre, then under the management of J. H. Hackett, as the Count in " The Devil's Bridge." The following month she was seen as Lady Macbeth, Romeo
and Meg Merrilies (her most famous part). On the
close of that season, she went to Boston and repeated
her successes at the Tremont Street Theatre, then
under the management of Thomas Barry, astonishing
everyone by her performance.

By this time, the management of the New York
theatre realized her importance, and that same fall

---

[1] Mr. Barton, an English tragedian, made his first appearance on the
American stage in 1832 at the Park Theatre, New York, as Hamlet. He was
acting manager at the St. Charles Theatre, New Orleans, for several seasons.

she was engaged as leading stock actress. She remained at the Park until 1840, acting during those years such rôles as Romeo, Goneril in " Lear," the Queen in " Hamlet," Emilia in " Othello," Belvidera in " Venice Preserved " and Julia in " The Hunchback," but her most conspicuous success was always as Meg Merrilies and Nancy Sykes in "Oliver Twist." She had already been joined at the Park by her sister Susan, "who," says Mrs. Clement, her biographer, "made an unfortunate marriage, and, by the desertion of her husband, was left in destitute circumstances with a child. Through the influence of Charlotte, she was led to cultivate her talent for the stage, and was engaged at a small price by the managers with whom her sister made contracts."

On August 30, 1841, Charlotte appeared in " A Midsummer Night's Dream," as Oberon to Susan's Helena. The following October, Charlotte played Lady Gay Spanker in the first American performance of Dion Boucicault's comedy of fashionable life, " London Assurance." In 1842, she began a season as " directress-star " at the Walnut Street Theatre, Philadelphia. When Macready paid his last visit to America, Miss Cushman supported him in leading parts, and on his advice she went to London, appearing at the Princess Theatre, February 13, 1845, as Bianca in Milman's tragedy, " Fazio," and making a profound impression on press and public. In December, she opened at the Haymarket as Romeo to her sister's Juliet, with such success that the play had a run of eighty nights.

In October, 1849, Charlotte Cushman was again in America, appearing at the Broadway Theatre,

CHARLOTTE CUSHMAN

New York, as Mrs. Haller in "The Stranger." On May 15, 1852, the actress took a benefit at the Broadway, announcing it as her "farewell to the American stage," and the same year she made the first of many visits to Italy. After another visit to England, she again toured the United States. Early in the summer of 1858 she began a series of "farewell" performances at Niblo's Garden, New York. At Burton's, the year before, she had given for the first time her impersonation of Cardinal Wolsey, the only time the character has been played by a woman. Other "farewells" followed until Oct. 1, 1860, when she was seen at the New York Winter Garden. She appeared for the last time in New York Nov. 7, 1874, at Booth's Theatre, when she played Lady Macbeth to the Macbeth of George Vandenhoff. Her powers now began to fail, owing to the inroads of cancer, from which she had been suffering for some years. In 1870 she reappeared on the stage as a Shakespearian reader. Her last appearance was in Boston May 15, 1875, as Lady Macbeth. She died of pneumonia February 18, 1876.

Concerning Charlotte Cushman's rank as an actress, there is little diversity of opinion. All critics concede the originality of her genius, although some are more reserved than others in their praise. William Winter, the warmest of her admirers, says:

No woman in the theatre of this period (1908) shows the inspirational fire, the opulent intellect, the dominant character and the abounding genius—rising to great heights and satisfying the utmost demand of great occasions—that were victorious and imperial in Charlotte Cushman. . . . The attributes of Miss Cushman's performance as Meg Merrilies were romance, tenderness, pathos, profound knowledge of grief, and the authentic royalty of innate power. It was a creation of wild excitement, wavering reason and physical misery, incident upon frequent famine and years of habitual hardship, the compulsory recollection of a terrible crime committed by others, lonely communing with the haunting mysteries of Nature, and a rooted devotion to one purpose of sacred duty and love. At the moment, in the play, when Meg Merrilies encounters Bertram in the gipsy camp, at night, Miss Cushman made an entrance of felicitous dexterity and startling effect,—thrusting back the folds of a tent and suddenly projecting herself from the aperture, but doing this in such a manner that she occupied exactly her right place in the dusky, romantic stage picture before any except an expert observer could discern whence she came or how she got there; and the figure that she then presented,—gaunt, haggard, dishevelled, piteous and yet majestic, a veritable incarnation of all that is ominous, fateful and strangely beautiful,—was a vision to register itself at once in the memory and there to remain forever. It was in that scene that she crooned the lullaby of the Bertrams of Ellangowan; and human ears have not heard a more touching cadence than when her voice trembled and broke in that simple, tender, fitful melody.[2]

James E. Murdoch considered her lacking in imagination. He writes:

Her acting possessed in a remarkable degree the elements of force; she grasped the intellectual body of the poet's conception without mastering its more subtle spirit; she caught the facts of a character, but its conceits were beyond her reach. Her understanding was never at fault; it was keen and penetrating. But that glow of feeling which springs from the centre of emotional elements was not a prominent constituent of her organization. She was intensely prosaic, definitely practical, and hence her perfect identity with what may be termed the materialism of Lady Macbeth, and the still more fierce personality of that dramatic nondescript, Meg Merrilies, neither of which characters was of " imagination all compact," but rather of imperious wilfulness.[3]

John Ranken Towse did not care for her Lady Macbeth. He says:

[2] Other Days. Copyright, 1908, by William Winter. Moffat, Yard & Company, Publishers. Reprinted by permission of Jefferson Winter, Esq.
[3] The Stage. By James E. Murdoch.

CHARLOTTE CUSHMAN

I do not believe that her conception was the right one, but the power with which she realized it compelled admiration and wonder. It was melodrama "in excelsis." Founded upon the pattern left by Mrs. Siddons—which, doubtless, has lost many of its true outlines in the course of several generations of stage reproduction—it exhibited no characteristic trait of feminine nature except its occasional physical weakness. This Lady Macbeth was a splendid virago, more than masculine in ambition, courage, and will, more bloody, bold, and resolute than she wished her husband to be. She was the source and mainspring of the whole tragedy. She was inhuman, terrible, incredible, and horribly fascinating.[4]

Joseph N. Ireland found her too masculine to be entirely satisfying in all the rôles she portrayed:

Her masculine personal appearance entirely unfitted her for many parts in which those ladies excelled, and it was as impossible for her to properly portray Juliet, Ophelia, Pauline, or Viola, as it was for her to look them. Not that she could not fully understand and appreciate them, but that she was denied the absolutely necessary physical requirements to render them satisfactory. Miss Cushman is tall and commanding in person, but somewhat ungraceful and awkward in her movements; her hair and complexion are fair; her chin is projecting and her nose retroussé; her expressive eyes of bluish gray are her finest features, and give an air of refinement to an otherwise plain and unattractive face. Her voice, originally deep and powerful, has become painfully weak and husky, and is now beyond her control in expressing the various shades of feeling with delicacy and distinctness. Her true forte is the character of a woman where most of the softer traits of womanhood are wanting, or if not extinct, where they are only apparent in fitful gleams; or in characters where, roused by passion or incited by some earnest and long cherished determination, the woman, for the time being, assumes all the power and energy of manhood. Such, for instance, are Nancy Sykes, Meg Merrilies, Katharine, "the shrew." . . . Topsy never was born; Miss Cushman no doubt was; that she was ever young, however, is a supposition difficult to be made. Not a particle of girlishness was ever seen in her

[4] Sixty Years of the Theatre. Copyright, 1916, by John Ranken Towse. Funk & Wagnalls Company, Publishers. Reprinted by permission.

face or displayed in her manners and deportment. She was always a grave, earnest, self-reliant woman, and her indomitable force of character is what has carried her through her difficult path, in spite of physical disadvantages and disheartening discouragements, to the topmost round of triumph.[5]

On the failure of New York's new Italian Opera House, in Leonard Street, that establishment, it will be recalled, was reopened as the National Theatre on August 29, 1836, with "The Merchant of Venice." In the shorter piece which followed, " The Man with the Carpet Bag," William Mitchell, the popular low comedian and later proprietor of one of New York's most successful resorts, made his first appearance before an American public.

Born in England in 1798, William Mitchell began his career as a clerk. After some experience in amateur theatricals, he made his début on the professional stage at Newcastle-on-Tyne as one of the country boys in " The Recruiting Officer." Later, he secured a hearing in London, but made little or no impression until he scored a hit as Jim Baggs. He came to New York, but attracted no particular attention until 1839, when he assumed the direction of the Olympic, a theatre originally built for Willard and Blake at 442 Broadway, and which from now on, was known as Mitchell's Olympic. Under the new management, the house quickly became one of the most popular places of amusement New York had ever known.

"The auditorium," T. Allston Brown tells us, " was small. The pit, wholly devoted to the male sex, was entered by a subterranean passageway running

[5] Records of the New York Stage. By J. N. Ireland.

beneath the boxes and furnished with distinct ticket venders and doorkeepers. The first and second tiers of boxes, shut off from the lobby by a series of doors, were set aside for ladies and the gentlemen who accompanied them. A bar room on the second tier was liberally supplied with liquors and other refreshments. When the house opened, the prices were 75c to the boxes and 37 1-2 c to the pit." [•]

On the boards of this theatre William Mitchell at once established himself as a warm local favorite, his inimitable personations of Dickens' characters, Crummles and Squeers, raising him to the very summit of popular favor and insuring for him an extraordinary patronage for several years. " His superior judgment," says Ireland, " led him to hit exactly the taste of the town, and his wonderful tact in discovering and developing incipient talent, by which he produced several excellent performers, male and female, was undoubtedly a principal cause of his continued success." A novel feature of the theatre was the unique character of the announcements. The following is characteristic of them all:

GRAND COMPLIMENTARY BENEFIT
Given by Mr. Mitchell to Himself.

The seats of the pit will be covered with people—(Perhaps).

The dress circle will be full if enough tickets are sold to fill it, and the upper boxes will positively be above the dress circle.

The arrangements will *not* be under the direction of a committee of gentlemen at the Astor House.

The prices will be, for this night only (being the last night of the season), the same as usual.

_____

[•] A History of the New York Stage, by T. Allston Brown. Copyright, 1902, by Dodd, Mead & Co., Publishers.

Observe that all pipe laying is finished opposite the theatre—drivers will, therefore, to prevent confusion, set their company down with the horses' heads in front and their tails behind.

On arriving at the doors of the theatre the audience will purchase their tickets (if not provided with them previously), and proceed at once in a grand cavalcade to the interior, where they will seat themselves as comfortably as possible, and laugh and applaud incessantly. It is particularly requested that those who cannot get front seats will sit on the back ones, and those who cannot get any will stand at ease and pay attention.

This sort of thing delighted the hoi polloi, and the theatre was so prosperous that it weathered the bad times of 1840–41 triumphantly, attaining a popularity which kept it in a prosperous condition when other theatres were causing the bankruptcy of their managers. Says T. Allston Brown:

When Mr. Mitchell resolved on lowering the prices to a democratic standard, his associate, Wardle Corbyn, stoutly opposed it, remarking that the weather having been so *foul*, the place had not had a *fair* chance. However, the prices were reduced from twenty-five cents to twelve and a half cents for admission. On that night every newsboy in New York was snugly ensconced in the pit, and the "Little Olympic" was on the top wave. For each succeeding Saturday the pit was the exclusive property of the newsboys and the Centre Market butcher boys. Mitchell had them under excellent control, however, and if they became uproarious, he would step forward and say in the blandest tone and manner: "Boys, if you misbehave yourselves I shall raise the prices." The house soon became the nightly resort of James T. Brady, the Belmonts, Fitz Greene Halleck, J. Prescott Hall, Dr. James Quinn, the Costars, Livingstons, Dandy Marks, and many other notables.[7]

It was at Mitchell's Olympic on February 15, 1848, that F. S. Chanfrau made his great hit as the

---

[7] A History of the New York Stage, by T. Allston Brown. Copyright, 1902, by Dodd, Mead & Co., Publishers.

fireman Mose in " A Glance at New York "—" a performance," says Ireland, " that carried him as a star triumphantly throughout every theatrical town in the Union." A prominent figure in the history of the American theatre, Francis S. Chanfrau was born in New York in 1824, and although he received a good education, went out West working as a ship carpenter. Returning to New York, he began to interest himself in amateur theatricals and finally secured a job as super at the Bowery. Here he made a hit with his imitations of Edwin Forrest. Later, he joined the company at Mitchell's Olympic, where as Jeremiah Clip, in " The Widow's Victim," he gave imitations of every actor of note. His great hit as Mose followed. In 1858, he married Miss Henrietta Baker, whom he presented at Wallack's the same year as Jane Chatterly in the farce " The Widow's Victim." One of the most natural actresses on the stage, Mrs. Chanfrau was the original representative in America of Esther Eccles (" Caste "), May Edwards ("Ticket of Leave Man ") and Dora in Charles Reade's play. She played Ophelia during the hundred-night run of " Hamlet " at Booth's Theatre, New York.

At this house also, on September 18, 1848, Mary Gannon, the well-known comic actress at Wallack's, made her first appearance since reaching womanhood. Born of Irish parentage in 1829, she had made her first appearance on any stage at the Richmond Hill Theatre at the age of three, her real début occurring at the Walnut Street Theatre, Philadelphia, January 18, 1838, in Garrick's farce, " Lilliput," when she was known as the " Lilliputian

THE THEATRE IN AMERICA

Wonder." When Wallack began his fourth season
at the Brougham Lyceum, Mary Gannon joined the
company and soon became an acknowledged favorite
of the Wallack audiences. " Entirely original in
style," says Ireland, " with a truthfulness to nature
almost unparalleled and a fund of quiet humor appa-
rently inexhaustible, she has in some characters never
been approached."

A native-born tragedian of considerable distinction made his first appearance on our stage in the
year 1836. This was Edward L. Davenport, one of
the most prominent and popular of American players
and the founder of the well-known theatrical family
of that name.

Edward Loomis Davenport was born at Boston
in 1815. His father, a business man, had a horror of
the stage and would have nothing to do with playgoing. But some forebear must have entertained
quite different sentiments toward the theatre, for
the succeeding generations of Davenports were all
successful histrions. Edward began his career as
assistant in a dry-goods establishment. Mercantile
life palling on him, he sought recreation in amateur
theatricals and soon discovered that acting was his
true vocation. He made his professional début in
1836 at Providence, Rhode Island, as Wellborn in
Massinger's " A New Way to Pay Old Debts," and
with such success that he was invited to become a
member of the Tremont Theatre, Boston, stock company. This was followed by appearances at the Park
Theatre, New York, and the Arch Street Theatre,
Philadelphia, in such rôles as Romeo, Benedick,
Fazio, St. Pierre, etc. In 1845, he appeared at

CHARLOTTE CUSHMAN

Niblo's Garden in "The Lady of Lyons," as Beauseant to the Pauline of Anna Cora Mowatt, and soon afterward he became leading man in that actress' company. In 1846, he played Romeo to Mrs. Mowatt's Juliet at the Park Theatre, and the following year appeared as Armand in Mrs. Mowatt's play of that name. A few months later, the company sailed for England, Mr. Davenport, in support of Mrs. Mowatt, making his début at Manchester and later at the Princess Theatre, London. He remained in England seven years, returning to America in 1854. After some time spent in starring, he appeared in 1856 at Burton's, New York, as Hamlet. " Second only to Booth's," says Mr. Towse, " his Hamlet was an exceedingly able performance, princely, thoughtful, tender, gravely humorous, sympathetic, and, in the crises, finely passionate." The critic continues:

The text he read with scholarly and eloquent discrimination. His Othello revealed a much larger insight than McCullough's and was stronger in the elemental passions than Booth's. Of the mystery of Macbeth he exhibited a firm psychological grasp. His Lear I never saw; but once, when by a happy chance he supported Booth in that character, he proved an incomparable Edgar. . . . His Bill Sykes was one of the most terrific exhibitions of savage blackguardism ever witnessed on the stage, while only Booth could excel him in the craft and finesse of Richelieu. His Sir Giles Overreach was generally admitted to be the best upon the stage. In the final act it reached a pitch of passion that was maniacal. In " Julius Caesar " he was a splendidly dignified and magnanimous Brutus. He was a sterling actor and artist who, in these later days, would be considered a paragon, but it was his ill-fortune to be somewhat overshadowed, the fates were not always propitious to him, and he never won the full recognition that he deserved.[8]

[8] Sixty Years of the Theatre. Copyright, 1916, by John Ranken Towse. Funk & Wagnalls, Publishers. Reprinted by permission.

In 1857, he became joint lessee of the American Theatre, New York. In 1859, he was manager of the Boston Athenæum; in 1865, joint lessee of the Old Washington Theatre, and, in 1870, lessee of the Chestnut Street Theatre, Philadelphia. He was last seen in New York in 1876 and made his last public appearance at Cumberland, Md., April, 1877.

He had nine children, seven of whom became players. The one who achieved the most conspicuous success was his daughter Fanny, of whom an account will be found elsewhere.

Charles Burke, the comedian and half brother of Joseph Jefferson III, made his début at the National Theatre, September 3, 1836. A fine mimic and superb dancer, Burke was an immense favorite with his audiences. Jefferson used to say of him: " We get as near Burke as we can and he who gets nearest succeeds best." The parts in which he was especially popular were: Rip Van Winkle, Paul Pry, Solon Shingle, Seth Slick, etc.

Later that same year the theatre was sold to Mr. Mauran, a New York merchant, and James H. Hackett, and they leased the house to James W. Wallack. The new management marked the beginning of an important epoch in the history of the New York stage. " It was," says Ireland, " the first opposition to the Park that had not been quickly overcome, and though it may not have proved a profitable speculation to its projectors, it resulted in so dividing the patronage of the public and in showing what improvements could be made in the general mounting and getting up of even old standard plays, that the hitherto proudly styled Old Drury of America lost

CHARLOTTE CUSHMAN

its supremacy as the leading theatre and never again
fully recovered that position. Young America took
a fancy to new managers, new actors, and new stage
fashions, and the glory of the old Park gradually
vanished."

On January 20, 1837, James W. Wallack, Jr.,
eldest son of Henry Wallack, made his professional
début as the Corporal in " My Husband's Ghost."
Handsome in face and person, like all of Wallack
blood, and capable, like most of the name, of appearing to the best possible advantage where elegance of
mien, picturesqueness of attitude and spirited decla-
mation produce the most telling effect, " he was," says
Ireland, " extremely popular with a certain class of
theatregoers and in a minor class of theatres was
recognized as a star of the first brilliancy." His
greatest popular successes were achieved in melodramatic rôles, such as Leon de Bourbon in " The Man
with the Iron Mask " and Fagin in " Oliver Twist."

J. W. Wallack opened his first regular season
September 4, 1837, with " The Rivals " and " The
Day After the Wedding." His remarkably full and
effective stock company included Messrs. Wallack,
H. Wallack, J. W. Wallack, Jr., James Browne, Mr.
Barnes, George Stanley, Mr. Morley, T. Matthews,
Mr. Gann, John Woodhull,, Mr. Rogers, Mr. Bal-
dock, Mr. Russell, William Vandenhoff, J. H. Hack-
ett, Henry Horncastle, W. H. Williams, Ben de Bar,
Mr. Gilbert, Mr. Percival, Mr. Caines, Mr. Hatton,
Mr. Jones, Mesdames Turpin, Flynn, Kemble,
Emma Wheatley, Rogers, Carter, Hautonville, W.
Sefton, Ayres, Russell, Fletcher, Baldock, Everard,
Sands.

William Vandenhoff, who made his début September 11 as Coriolanus, ranked as one of the most distinguished tragedians of his time. Born at Salisbury, England, in 1790, he was educated for the priesthood. The stage, however, proved an irresistible attraction, and, in 1808, he made his first appearance in the provinces as Earl Osmond in " The Castle Spectre." He continued acting in the provinces for many years and in such parts as Virginius, Rolla, etc., became a decided favorite. In 1820 he appeared for the first time at Covent Garden as Lear, meeting with brilliant success, and this triumph was duplicated a few years later when he was first seen as Coriolanus. His style of acting has been described as lofty, grand and heroic. A distinguished English critic ranks him in intellect and power next to Macready, and adds that " in grandeur of presence and heroic dignity, he is not surpassed by an actor of the age." His son, George Vandenhoff, later became a great favorite with American audiences and made his permanent home here. He was first seen at the Park, September 21, 1842, as Hamlet, and at once showed himself an accomplished and versatile actor, with a strong predilection for the more difficult Shakespearian rôles. His Hamlet was long considered a model of elocution, and in Claude Melnotte, Falconbridge, Mercutio, Benedick, Doricourt and similar parts demanding a fine stage presence and impeccable manners, he ranked with the best actors yet seen on our stage. Mr. Vandenhoff was also very popular as a dramatic reader. In 1858, he took to the bar, for which his earlier training fitted him, and was admitted to practice in the courts of Massachusetts.

Benedict de Bar, another prominent member of the Wallack company, was born in London of French descent and had appeared on the New Orleans stage two years previously. He remained in New York only one season and then returned West, where he became a great favorite as actor and manager. In 1843, he was again in New York as manager of the New Chatham Theatre.

James Browne was the original Robert Macaire in this country. A tall, handsome man, he was in his day one of the most popular actors of light and eccentric comedy ever seen here. He made his début May 23, 1839, as Gratiano in " The Merchant of Venice."

In the fall of the same year the National was destroyed by fire and Wallack removed temporarily to Niblo's. The house was rebuilt later, when it was known as Purdy's National Theatre, and it was here that George L. Fox, the famous pantomimist, was seen for the first time in New York (October 25, 1850) as Christopher Strap. This popular performer had made his first appearance on any stage in 1830 as one of the children in " The Hunter of the Alps " at the Tremont Theatre, Boston. After serving as a volunteer in the Civil War, he became manager of the old Bowery. Later, he was stage manager of the Olympic, New York, where he made a big hit in the pantomime " Humpty Dumpty," an impersonation acted by him 1268 times in New York alone.

The year 1839 also saw the opening of the Chatham Theatre, one of the most popular of New York's playhouses in its day. Situated in Chatham

Street, between Roosevelt and James Streets, the house was opened September 11 under the management of Thomas Flynn with "A New Way to Pay Old Debts." The company included Charles R. Thorne, Emily Mestayer, Mrs. Judah, Mrs. Blake, J. Hudson Kirby, Mr. Stevens and C. Mestayer.

Mr. Kirby was born at sea in 1819, while his parents were en route from England to America, and made his stage début in 1837 at the Chestnut Street Theatre, Philadelphia. His strong point as a tragedian was in his dying scenes, which gave rise to the well-known saying of the galleryite who often slept during the tame passages of the play: "Wake me up when Kirby dies."

Later, C. R. Thorne secured control of the house and conducted it with considerable success, such stars as the elder Booth, Mme. Celeste, Henry Placide, Mrs. Duff, Edwin Forrest, appearing there under his direction.

In the Fall of 1838, Charles J. Mathews, Jr., son of the English comedian whom American audiences had found so much to their liking fifteen years previously, made his first appearance in America at the Park Theatre as Charles Swiftly in "One Hour." The comedian was accompanied by his wife (formerly the famous Mme. Vestris).

Although suffering by comparison with his celebrated father, Mr. Mathews made a distinct hit, and his success was even more pronounced at the time of his second and third visits in 1857 and 1871. He was then sixty-eight years of age, "and yet," says Henry Austin Clapp, "he seemed to me then, and seems to me now, an unequaled incarnation of the spirit of youth and jollity." The critic continues:

As a producer of mirth of the volatile, effervescent variety I have never seen his equal. Nothing happier, wholesomer, or sweeter in this light kind can be imagined, and the receptive spectator of the comedian's playing often found himself affected with a delicious cerebral intoxication, which passed away with the fall of the curtain, and left naught that was racking behind. The laugh cure is the only mode which is accepted by physicians of every school, and Mr. Mathews must have been a potent therapeutic and prophylactic agent in the health of Great Britain. He inherited his histrionic talent, and had been finely trained in the old methods. Even in France his style was considered admirable in grace, finesse, and dexterity.[9]

Mme. Vestris, who had passed the meridian of her powers at the time of her visit here and whose reputation in England was not of the best, was received coldly by American audiences, and it was probably for this reason that the stay of herself and Mr. Mathews in this country was exceedingly brief. Lucy Eliza Bartolozzi-Vestris was born in London in 1797 and at the age of fourteen made her stage début under the guidance of the famous ballet master, Armand Vestris, whom she married two years later. In 1815, she made her début at the King's Theatre, as Proserpina in the opera " Il Ratle Proserpina," her charming voice and graceful figure taking London by storm. For several years she was enormously popular both in England and on the continent. Later, she became manager on her own account, making beautiful and costly productions that were the talk of the town. In 1838, she married

[9] Reminiscences of a Dramatic Critic. Copyright, 1902, by Henry Austin Clapp. Reprinted by permission of the publishers, Houghton, Mifflin & Co.

Charles Mathews. After their visit to America she succeeded Macready as manager of Covent Garden, gathering about her an admirable company, of which her husband (Mr. Mathews) was a member. Caring nothing for money, stopping at no expense, her Shakespearian and other productions were always on the most lavish scale, her extravagance naturally resulting in a deficit which lost her the theatre. " She was," says H. Barton Baker, " one of the most extravagant of women, to whom the most costly luxuries had become necessities of life. In such a small item as gloves, for instance, she would sometimes use up a box in a single night; if a pair, or half a dozen pairs in succession, fitted with the slightest crease, they were cast aside, and for every scene a fresh pair was put on. When lace curtains were required upon the stage they were real lace, and everything else was on the same scale; while so minutely particular was she in small matters, that she would pass a white laced handkerchief over the furniture of the green-room, and even the balusters of the staircases leading to the dressing-rooms, and woe to the cleaners if the delicate cambric was soiled. All that this meant can, perhaps, only be appreciated by those who are acquainted with that temple of dust—behind the scenes of a theatre." [10] She died in 1856.

In the year 1840, a world-famous dancer, Fanny Elssler, was seen at the Park Theatre, New York, for the first time on the American stage, and in a pas seul called " La Cracovienne " and a ballet, " La Tarantale " took the town by storm.

Fanny Elssler was born in Germany and made

[10] History of the London Stage. By H. Barton Baker.

her début at the age of ten. The sensation her dancing made in America was prodigious. " Nightly,"
says T. Allston Brown, " the largest theatres of our
principal cities were crowded to study every attitude,
watch every motion, and applaud to the echo every
exertion of ' the Elssler.' When she danced in America at the Park, all other theatres in the city were
deserted. Her reception was something never before
or since equalled in this country. The whole house
rose and gave a shout such as is seldom heard in a
theatre. Parsons preached, old maids talked, moralists shook their heads, but nothing would abate the
excitement of the public."

In Baltimore her arrival created such a furore
that the people cut the traces of her carriage and
dragged the dancer from the theatre to her hotel.
When she reached Richmond she was met by a dele-
gation of prominent citizens who escorted her to her
hotel headed by a brass band. She remained in
America two years, realizing from her numerous
engagements over $85,000.

In 1842, a distinguished player arrived from
England in the person of John Brougham, an admirable comedian and playwright, who at once won the
hearts of American audiences, and remained a favorite with this public, both as actor and manager, for
over thirty years.

John Brougham was born in Ireland in 1810 and
educated at Trinity College. His first appearance
as an actor was at the Tottenham Theatre, London,
in " Tom and Jerry," in which he enacted some twelve
or fourteen parts. In 1831, Mme. Vestris engaged
him for the Olympic and took him with her later to

Covent Garden. Management next claimed his attention, and the year 1840 found him joint director of the London Lyceum, where he also made his first bow as author. His second wife, Emma Williams, a woman without any marked gifts as an actress, but of great personal beauty, accompanied him to America. They opened at the Park Theatre, October 4— Brougham as O'Callaghan in the farce " His Last Legs " and Mrs. Brougham as Lady Teazle. A few nights later he was seen as Sir Lucius in "The Rivals" and as Dazzle in " London Assurance." Shortly afterwards, he joined Burton's company in New York and for that manager wrote " Bunsby's Wedding," " The Confidence Man," " Don Cæsar de Bassoon," " Vanity Fair," " The Irish Yankee," " Benjamin Franklin," " All's Fair in Love," " The Irish Emigrant," and a play on " Dombey and Son." Later, he assumed control of Niblo's and produced there his fairy tale entitled " Home," and the play " Ambrose Germain," written for Mlle. Blangy.

In 1850, a theatre known as Brougham's Lyceum (afterwards Wallack's) was built for him on Broadway, but the venture did not prove successful and he joined Wallack's company, being a valued member of that organization and also of Burton's for the next ten years. In 1869, he opened a second Brougham's Theatre on the site of the Madison Square Theatre, but retired from its control a few months later, and remained connected with stock companies to the time of his death, his last appearance taking place at Booth's Theatre in 1879.

His rank among actors it is difficult to assign. William Winter says: " Brougham excelled in humor rather than in pathos or sentiment, and was at his best in the expression of comically eccentric character." The critic continues:

Among the parts that memory associates with his name are Stout in "Money," Dennis Brulgruddery in "John Bull," Sir Lucius O'Trigger in "The Rivals," Cuttle, Micawber, Bagstock, O'Grady in "Arrah-na-Pogue;" Dazzle in "London Assurance;" Captain Murphy Maguire in "The Serious Family," and O'Callaghan in "His Last Legs." His animal spirits, dash, vigor, and brilliancy, in those parts, were great; he entered deeply into their spirit; he could be consciously joyous or unconsciously droll; he was never for an instant out of the stage picture; and he spoke the language with delicious purity.[11]

It was at Brougham's Lyceum, December 23, 1850, that John E. Owens, the great comedian, appeared for the first time in New York, in the character of Mr. Fright in the farce "Crimson Crimes."

John Edmond Owens, who has been aptly described as "one of the most comical men that have graced and cheered the stage," was born in Liverpool in 1823. His father, a Welshman, came to America when the boy was only three years old and settled in Baltimore. In 1840, the son went to Philadelphia with a view to going on the stage, and was fortunate enough to become associated with that other great comedian, W. E. Burton, at the National Theatre. Successful as an actor from the start, he soon entered the managerial field, securing control of theatres in Baltimore and New Orleans. After acting he sailed for Europe, and made an extensive Continental tour, including an ascent of Mount Blanc. Returning to America, he gave his Mount Blanc

[11] The Wallet of Time. Copyright, 1913, by William Winter. Moffat, Yard & Co., Publishers. Reprinted by permission of Jefferson Winter, Esq.

entertainment with panoramic illustrations. In 1864, he began at the Broadway Theatre, New York, one of the most brilliant engagements on record, and made almost sensational hits with his Solon Shingle, the country teamster in " The People's Lawyer," and Caleb Plummer in " The Cricket on the Hearth "— two impersonations, says Winter, which " marked him as a great comedian and established his rank beyond question." The same critic continues:

Owens was born to be a comic actor. He was intrinsically funny. His personality was comic and at the same time lovable. . . . His humorous vitality was prodigious. It sparkled in his bright brown eyes; it rippled in the music of his rich, sonorous, flexible voice; it exulted in the bounteous health of his vigorous constitution; it rejoiced in his alert demeanor, his elastic step, his beaming smile, his exuberant and incessant glee. He was, when acting, too truly an artist ever to intercept with his personality the spectator's view of the character he had assumed; but, when playing a humorous part, he invariably conveyed the impression of joyous ease and personal relish. His cheeriness overflowed. His comic acting was rosy with health and redolent of enjoyment.[12]

Among other rôles of his repertoire in which he excelled were Uriah Heep, Dr. Pangloss, John Unit in " Self," Paul Pry, Graves in " Money," and Grimaldi in " The Life of an Actress."

[12] The Wallet of Time. Copyright, 1913, by William Winter. Moffat, Yard & Co., Publishers. Reprinted by permission of Jefferson Winter, Esq.

CHAPTER XXI

NEW THEATRES IN BOSTON

BOSTON, in the early forties, added materially to
her places of amusement, and this notwithstanding
that the old Puritanical opposition to plays and playacting persisted even among the intelligent classes.
A large number of Bostonians, in spite of the fact that
the old restraining municipal ordinances had long
been repealed, still refused to patronize the existing
theatres, not because they saw anything really immoral or objectionable in the dramatic entertainment
offered, but because they had been born and bred in
the tradition that the theatre was the house of Satan.
This belief, too deeply rooted to be easily eradicated,
meant that amusement enterprises lost the financial
support, otherwise to be depended upon, of a large
and well-to-do class of potential theatre-goers.

Finally, a way was found to conciliate the views
and win the patronage of this particular part of the
population. In June, 1841, an establishment known
as " The Boston Museum and Gallery of Fine Arts,"
exhibiting a collection of stuffed animals, wax figures,
etc., was opened by Mr. Moses Kimball at the corner
of Tremont and Bromfeld Streets. Over the Museum

proper was a spacious music saloon with a seating capacity of 1200 persons. The suggestion was made that this be turned into an auditorium in which dramatic performances might be given without the place being designated or known as a theatre. This subterfuge, it was shrewdly thought, might be welcomed by Bostonians as enabling them to attend without doing violence to their time-honored convictions.

In 1843, John Sefton and Mrs. Maeder were engaged to produce operettas and on February 6 of that year " The Masque Ball " was given. This was the first of the dramatic performances at the Boston Museum.

In the Fall of the same year, a well-rounded stock company was organized under the direction of W. H. Smith, with such success that the place soon became too small to accommodate the attending throngs. In 1846, a new Museum was built on Tremont Street, between School and Court Streets, and from that time on the Boston Museum ranked as one of the leading theatres in the country, a position it retained for nearly fifty years. Henry Austin Clapp, the well-known critic, writing in the year 1900, gives the following interesting description of this famous old theatre:

The Boston Museum was in a distinctive and peculiar sense the theatre of the capital of Massachusetts: partly because of its age and unbroken record as a place of amusement, even more because of the steady merit of its performances and the celebrity of many of its performers. At the outset, as every Bostonian knows, this establishment was conducted on the plan of Barnum's, of New York. The word " theatre " was not visible on any of its bills, programmes or advertisements. It was a museum, and justified its title by an edifying exhibit of stuffed animals, bones, mummies,

148

minerals, wax figures and other curios; making, through these
" branches of learning," and its long continued obeisance to Puritan
tradition—after that tradition had ceased from the Municipal
Ordinances—by closing its doors on Saturday nights, an eloquent
appeal to the patronage of sober persons, affected with scruples
against the godless theatre. The appeal was as successful as it was
shrewd. To this day, I doubt not there are citizens of Boston who
patronize no other place of theatrical amusement than its Museum,
though the stuffed beasts and observance of the eve of the Lord's
Day are things of the past.[1]

At the Museum appeared for many years W. H.
Smith, an admirable actor-manager of the old school;
Mrs. Thoman, a charming interpreter of light comedy; Mr. Finn, a droll comedian; J. Davies, a heavy
villain; J. A. Smith, celebrated for his fops; Kate
Reignolds, a sterling player; Charles Barron, popular leading man, Annie Clarke, dear old Mrs. Vincent, and last, but by no means least, William Warren,
Jr., a warm favorite with Boston theatregoers for the
better part of half a century.

A native of Philadelphia and son of the late manager of the Chestnut Street Theatre, William Warren, Jr., made his first appearance on the stage at the
Arch Street Theatre, as Young Norval in " Douglas."
He was first seen in New York at the Park, in 1841,
as Gregory Grizzle in " My Young Wife and Old
Umbrella." In 1845, he went to England and acted
at the Strand. On his return here, in 1847, he joined
the Boston Museum stock company, of which organization he was the dominating spirit for a great number of years. " In him," says Clapp, " Boston had a
Théâtre Français, as long as he lived and played. His
career as an actor covered exactly fifty years, from

---

[1] Reminiscences of a Dramatic Critic. Copyright, 1902, by Henry Austin
Clapp. Reprinted by permission of the publishers, Houghton, Mifflin & Co.

1832 to 1882, and during that period he gave 13,345 performances and appeared in 577 characters." The critic continues:

His art touched life, as life is presented in the drama, at ten thousand points. His plays were in every mode and mood of the Comic Muse, and ranged in quality from the best of Shakespeare to the worst of Dr. Jones. In old-fashioned farces, with their strong, sometimes vulgar, often noisy, usually vital fun; in tawdry patriotic or emotional melodramas; in standard old English comedies; in cheap local pieces, narrow and petty in their appeal; in delicate French comediettas, whose colors are laid on with a brush like Meissonier's; in English versions of the best Parisian dramas, subtle, sophisticated, exigent of *finesse* and *adresse* in the player—in each and all of these Mr. Warren was easily chief among many good actors.

The Tremont, unable to meet the competition of such young and lusty rivals as the National, the Howard Athenæum, and the Boston Museum, had at last reached the end of its interesting career. On June 23, 1843, the final performance took place, the entire company, headed by John Gilbert, assembling on the stage to say farewell to the public they had served so long. Later, the building was altered into a church, known as the Tremont Temple.

The old Boston Theatre, on Federal Street, for many years used as a lecture room, was reopened in 1846 for dramatic purposes. A strong stock company was organized, including Mr. and Mrs. Gilbert, and with Henry Placide, J. W. Wallack, Mr. and Mrs. Charles Kean, Edwin Forrest and Charlotte Cushman as " guest " stars, but the house had lost its hold on the public, and on April 13, 1852, the old theatre—originally opened Feb. 3, 1794, and rich in historical associations—was offered at public sale.

NEW THEATRES IN BOSTON

The National Theatre—the fifth theatre to be built in the city of Boston—was originally known as the American Amphitheatre, and was opened by William and Thomas L. Stewart, for equestrian purposes, on February 27, 1832. That same year the house was acquired by William Pelby, former manager of the Tremont, and opened July 3, 1832, as the Warren Theatre. In 1836, Mr. Pelby made elaborate improvements and reopened the house under the higher sounding name of National Theatre. With a strong company and plays produced in a manner even superior to their production at the Tremont, this house enjoyed the favor and patronage of the Boston public for many years. On September 10, 1838, Thomas Abthorpe Cooper, the veteran actor, after an absence from the stage of six years, reappeared at the National as Sir William Dorillon to his daughter's Miss Dorillon in Mrs. Inchbald's comedy, " Wives as They Were." The house was only fairly well filled, and that interest in the once-famous star had waned may be inferred from the fact that the receipts amounted to only $131, whereas in former times Cooper seldom drew less than $1000 a night. In April, 1852, the house was destroyed by fire. Rebuilt the same year, as the New National, it was opened with " The Heir at Law," the company including W. M. Fleming, W. H. Curtis, Douglass Stewart, Mr. and Mrs. J. J. Prior, J. Munroe, Mr. and Mrs. Buxton, S. D. Johnson, Fanny Howard, Cornelia Jefferson, Bertha Lewis, Julia Pelby and Mrs. Vickery, the tragic actress.

It was on the stage of the National Theatre that Edwin Adams, best remembered as the personator of Enoch Arden in the play of that name, made his first appearance on any stage. Born in Medford, Mass., in 1833, he made his début in Boston August 29, 1853, as Stephen in " The Hunchback." The original in America of Robert Landry in " The Dead Heart," and of Ivan Khorvitch in " The Serf," he was also for one year supporting star at Booth's Theatre, New York, his repertory including all the chief rôles of tragedy. Although an actor of the second rate only, his fine voice, dash and commanding bearing made him a favorite with the million. Joseph Jefferson, in his Autobiography, says of him:

The animation of his face, the grace of his person, and, above all, the melody of his voice well fitted him for the stage. While he could not be fairly called a great artist, he was something often more highly prized—a born actor, a child of nature if not of art, swayed by warm impulse rather than by premeditation. His Enoch Arden, so far as the character is related to the stage, was a creation entirely his own, and one, too, that touched the sympathy of his audience.[2]

Another new Boston playhouse of the thirties was the Lion Theatre. Built in 1835, for equestrian and dramatic purposes, this house was opened January 11, 1836, a feature of the entertainments being elaborate spectacular effects rendered possible by its circus-like construction. In the popular spectacular drama " The Jewess " the entire circus stud of horses, elephants, camels and dromedaries was drawn upon to give fine effect to the procession.

The disappearance of the Tremont and the closing of the Boston Theatre had made the want of another leading theatre severely felt. In 1845, the

[2] Autobiography of Joseph Jefferson. Copyright, 1889. The Century Co., Publishers.

NEW THEATRES IN BOSTON

Boston Museum and the National were the only leading playhouses of Massachusetts' capital. At this time there was, in Howard Street, a Tabernacle which had formerly been the meeting-place of the Millerites.[*] After the subsiding of the Millerite sensation of 1843–44 the Tabernacle was abandoned. A syndicate of theatrical men, headed by W. F. Johnson, W. L. Ayling, Thomas Ford and Leonard Brayley, thought the building would make a good theatre, and they approached the Millerites, who, after considerable opposition, finally granted a lease. Extensive alterations were made in the old Tabernacle, a handsome front erected, and the house formally opened October 13, 1845, as the Howard Athenæum, with the following stock company:

Mesdames Maeder, H. Cramer, W. L. Ayling, W. H. Chippendale, C. W. Hunt, Walcott, Judah, G. Howard, William Jones, W. H. Smith; Misses Drake, Booth, Mace, De Luce; Messrs. W. F. Johnson, W. L. Ayling, G. W. Jamieson, J. A. Neafie, A. J. Phillips, D. Whiting, C. M. Walcot, G. Howard, Sullivan, Booth, Barker, Munroe, Russell, Binnie, Taylor, Davis, Jones, Adams, Resor, Gilbert and Master Fox. The theatre was destroyed by fire February 25, 1846, and rebuilt the same year and opened with a performance of " The Rivals."

The Adelphi was another Boston theatre very popular in the forties. It was opened April 5, 1847, by Messrs. Brougham and Bland, and was the favorite resort of lovers of fun, " Brougham," says Clapp, " being the life of the place."

---

[*] The followers of William Miller (1781-1849) who predicted the second coming of Christ in the year 1843.

153

THE THEATRE IN AMERICA

Although Boston now had three playhouses of the first class, it was felt there was still room for another, and in 1852 a committee of prominent citizens was appointed to select a site and solicit subscriptions. On May 15, 1852, the Boston Theatre Company was incorporated with a capital stock of $200,000, and a site purchased on Washington Street. The new house, with Thomas Barry as lessee and manager, and surpassing in convenience and elegance of appointments any theatre yet built in America, was opened September 11, 1854, with " The Rivals."

At the Walnut Street Theatre, Philadelphia, on October 7, 1850, Mme. Ponisi, an Englishwoman who later became one of the best all-round actresses on the American stage, made her first appearance in this country as Marianna in " The Wife." A native of Huddersfield, this actress had made her London début in 1848 at the Surrey Theatre as Lady Walsingham in " The Secretary." She was first seen in New York November 11, 1850, as Lady Teazle. " She was," says Mr. Towse, " an invaluable member of the Wallack Company."

In stage knowledge she was almost the equal of Gilbert himself, though far behind him in special ability. If seldom brilliant, she was always thoroughly intelligent and competent. In her time she had played many of the principal tragic and comic characters of Shakespeare. She was a sound and impressive Lady Macbeth, was admirable in the old women of artificial comedy, as the aristocratic dames of modern social drama, in domestic plays, farce or melodrama.[4]

Another attempt to introduce Italian opera in New York was made in 1844 by Ferdinand Palmo,

---

[4] Sixty Years of the Theatre. Copyright, 1913, by J. Ranken Towse.

proprietor of a popular restaurant known as the Café
des Milles Colonnes. Securing the premises on
Chambers Street, formerly occupied by Stoppani's
Arcade Baths—a relic of the time when New Yorkers
had no running water in their houses and were forced
to perform their ablutions in public establishments
—he opened the place February 3 as Palmo's Opera
House. The venture was no more successful than its
predecessors and four years later the house was taken
over by W. E. Burton.

An interesting sidelight on some of the problems
that confronted the New York theatregoer of that
time, especially as regards transit facilities and street
rowdyism, difficulties which the modern playgoer
happily has not to contend with, is found in a notice
on the Palmo Opera House programme, which reads:

Arrangements have been made by the management with the
Railroad Company (the Harlem R. R. Company, the only one then
running a city line) for the accommodation of ladies and gentlemen living uptown so that a large car, well lighted and warmed,
will start after the Theatre closes, and Police officers will be in
attendance to prevent disorder.

Among New York's early theatres one which
enjoyed great popularity was the establishment
known as Castle Garden. As a playhouse it did not
have a very long or very distinguished career, but
it is interesting as the stage on which Jenny Lind, the
famous Swedish nightingale, made her first bow to an
American public.

The theatre, now used as an Aquarium, was a
circular building at the south end of Battery Park,
and was erected originally for a fort. In 1845, it was
given over to amusement purposes, a troupe of min-

strels, headed by Charles White, appearing there. The same year, the Garden was opened as a regular theatre with a company that included such well-known players as George Holland, Charles M. Walcot, Herr John Cline, a remarkable slack-wire performer, Miss Clarke, Mrs. W. Isherwood and others. Later, grand opera was given there by a company of singers from Havana.

The engagement extraordinary was that of Jenny Lind, which began September 11, 1850, under the management of Phineas T. Barnum, the world-famous showman. The coming of the celebrated songstress had been loudly heralded for months with all the refinements of the advertising art that Barnum knew so well how to employ, and the curiosity to see the Swedish singer was tremendous.

Jenny Lind was born in Stockholm in 1820 and received her first lessons in singing from Berg and others at the Court Theatre. In 1841, when she went to Paris to study with Garcia, great triumphs were predicted for her by Meyerbeer. In 1847, she was in London and Meyerbeer's prophecy came true. Vast crowds flocked to hear her, and prices at Her Majesty's soared to fabulous heights. An English critic describes her voice at that time as follows:

> It is a pure soprano of the fullest compass of voice belonging to this class and of such evenness of tone that the nicest ear can discover no difference of quality from the bottom to the summit of the scale. Her lowest notes come out as clear and ringing as the highest, and her highest are as soft and sweet as the lowest; mellow roundness distinguishes every sound she utters. Much of the effect of this unrivalled voice is derived from the physical beauty of its sound, but still more from the exquisite skill and taste with which it is managed and the intelligence and sensibility of which it is the organ.

NEW THEATRES IN BOSTON

When the singer arrived in New York great crowds met her at the dock, which was decorated with flags and had two triumphal arches bearing the inscriptions: WELCOME, JENNY LIND—WELCOME TO AMERICA. On the night of the first concert, five thousand persons crowded into Castle Garden, the gross receipts being $17,864. The ticket speculator made his appearance for the first time on this occasion. The rush to hear the singer was so great that people were willing to pay almost any price for seats, which afforded the speculator his inspiration and opportunity.

After giving six concerts in New York Jenny Lind toured the country, giving in the various cities ninety-five concerts, which netted $712,000. In 1852, the singer was married in Boston to Otto Goldschmidt, a musician. She died in England in 1887, one of the few stage artistes to be honored with a tablet in Westminster Abbey.

It was on the stage of Niblo's, early in 1835, that Phineas T. Barnum, Jenny Lind's manager, had made his first bid for public patronage. This singular genius of the circus business was born in 1810 at Danbury, Conn., where his father ran a livery stable. Phineas tried all sorts of occupations before he found his true vocation, being in turn clerk, storekeeper, agent for a lottery, book auctioneer, newspaper editor and boarding-house keeper. In 1835, he happened to stumble across a decrepit old negress—the celebrated Joice Heth whom he purchased for $1000 and introduced to the gullible public as the nurse of General Washington. How old the woman really was or where she came from, Barnum himself never knew.

157

She was totally blind and her eyes were so deeply sunken in their sockets that they had disappeared altogether. Her left arm lay across her breast with no power to move it. Her fingernails were four inches long and on her left hand, always closed, extended above her wrist, while the nails on her large toes were nearly a quarter of an inch in thickness. She insisted that she raised " dear little Georgie," and bills of sale were exhibited to show that she was once owned by the Washington family.

Barnum's next investment was the purchase of a steamboat on which he navigated the Mississippi, visiting the principal towns with a theatrical company. Later, he was back in New York selling Bibles and serving as press-agent. In 1841, he secured control of Scudder's Museum and removed to the building at the corner of Ann Street and Broadway, afterwards known as Barnum's Museum, the whole valuable collection of stuffed animals and curiosities, to which he proceeded to make large additions.

This step was the beginning of his successful career as a showman. In 1842, he introduced to the public Charles S. Stratton, a dwarf he rechristened Tom Thumb, who proved such an extraordinary attraction that Barnum decided to exhibit him in Europe. A triumphal tour was made through England, Scotland, Ireland, France and Belgium, returning to America in 1847.

Meantime, the Museum in New York had prospered greatly. In addition to the Museum proper there were dramatic performances in what was known as the " Moral Lecture Room," the company including such well-known players as Caroline Chap-

man, Mrs. Phillips, George Chapman, Maria Barton, Great Western, John Dunn, Barney Williams,
Billy Whitlock, Luke West, the Martinetti family
and others. The performances were practically continuous, as many as twelve being given in one day to
as many audiences, so that Barnum may be said to
have originated the continuous programme which
has proved so attractive a feature of vaudeville in
recent years. " In those early days, as throughout his
whole career as a showman," says A. H. Branigan,
" Barnum was a profound believer in advertising—
not only by a liberal use of printer's ink but by turning every circumstance to account in drawing the
attention of the public to his enterprise." The writer
continues:

It was not long before Barnum's Museum was the most talked
about and popular resort in America. It was here that the famous
woolly horse, the Albino family, the white negress, Robert Houdin's
ingenious automaton writer, Faber's automaton speaker, the Japanese mermaid, the white whales, and other curiosities were exhibited. Here Mr. Sothern, Barney Williams, Mary Gannon and
a host of actors and actresses who afterwards attained fame began
their professional careers. Here first appeared those celebrated
midgets Tom Thumb, Commodore Nutt, Minnie Warren and her
sister Lavinia, who was eventually married to Tom Thumb.[5]

Jenny Lind's American engagement brought
Barnum a fortune, which he lost in unfortunate speculation. After a temporary retirement from public life,
he again reappeared as organizer of the famous travelling menagerie and circus which to-day bears his
name. He died in 1891.

On September 6, 1852, there took place at Castle
Garden what was called a " great dramatic festival

---

[5] A. H. Branigan in an article in the *Theatre Magazine*, July, 1910.

in commemoration of the introduction of the drama to America September 6, 1752." The bill on this occasion was " The Merchant of Venice," followed by Garrick's farce, " Lethe " (erroneously supposed to be Hallam's original Williamsburg bill), some of the most prominent players in the country taking part. Seeing that the drama had been introduced here at least thirty years earlier than the date celebrated, this " centennial " performance was decidedly in the nature of an anticlimax. Although laboring under a delusion, the promoters meant well, and seeing that the occasion helped to swell the coffers of a worthy charity—the American Dramatic Fund —their efforts cannot be said to have been entirely in vain.

The same year that brought Jenny Lind to America also introduced to our stage a new and successful comedy of manners, entitled " Fashion," written by Anna Cora Mowatt, an American author-actress of much social prominence.

Mrs. Mowatt was the daughter of Samuel Ogden, of New York, and a great-granddaughter of Francis Lewis, one of the signers of the Declaration of Independence. Born in 1823, at Bordeaux, France, where her parents were residing temporarily, the young girl married at the age of fifteen Mr. James Mowatt, a lawyer. Her husband becoming bankrupt, she was forced to work for a livelihood and took to literature, turning her attention later to dramatic writing and public readings. Finally, she went on the stage, making her début at the Park Theatre, June 13, 1845, as Pauline in " The Lady of Lyons." A few months earlier she had completed her comedy, " Fashion."

a satire on the social foibles of the day, which was produced at the Park with great success. Although faulty in construction and lacking in literary quality, the play is one of the few pieces of native workmanship which has stood the test of time and only recently was revived by the Drama League. Another play by Mrs. Mowatt, a drama entitled " Armand," produced later, with E. L. Davenport in the title rôle, was less favorably received. In 1847, Mrs. Mowatt went to England with Mr. Davenport, and after acting some time in the provinces made her début at the London Princess', being received with great favor. " Delicacy," says Ireland, " was Mrs. Mowatt's most marked characteristic. A subdued earnestness of manner, a soft, musical voice, a winning witchery of enunciation, and indeed an almost perfect combination of beauty, grace and refinement fitted her for the very class of characters in which Miss Cushman was incapable of excelling."

In the Fall of 1847, New Yorkers acquired a new place of amusement in the playhouse now generally referred to as the Old Broadway. Situated on the east side of Broadway between Pearl and Anthony (now Worth) Streets, the house was modelled after the Haymarket Theatre, London, and had a seating capacity of 4000 with an immense pit to which only men and boys were admitted. Edwin Forrest and W. C. Macready won some of their greatest triumphs on the boards of this theatre, which was first opened to the public September 27, 1847, with a performance of " The School for Scandal," Henry Wallack playing Sir Peter and George Barrett appearing as Charles Surface. The company included the following players: Fanny Wallack, Rose Telbin, Miss Winstanley, Miss Carman, Mrs. Heild, Helen Matthews, Henry Wallack, John Lester (Wallack), Thomas Lynne, J. M. Dawson, Thomas Vache, Henry Hunt, C. W. Hunt, Mesdames Watts, Bernard, Sargeant and Chapman, the Misses Gordon, Fitzjames, George Vandenhoff, G. Chapman, H. Bernard, J. Everard, Dennison, William Fredericks, E. Shaw, J. Bernard, J. Kingsley, J. Walters, Thompson Allen, Mlles. St. Clair and Céleste.

A number of distinguished players made their first appearance on the stage of this theatre, among them being Lester Wallack, Charles W. Couldock and William Davidge.

Mr. Couldock, who for many years was one of the most popular actors on the American stage, was born in London in 1815 and began his professional career in 1835. After making his New York début October 8, 1849, as Othello, he went to Philadelphia, where for a few seasons he was leading man at the Walnut Street Theatre. He also toured in support of Charlotte Cushman. In 1858 he joined Laura Keene's company. Iago and Hamlet ranked as his best performances fifty years ago, but his greatest success was as Louis XI. Later in life, Mr. Couldock leaned more toward the domestic drama. In 1880, he originated the character of Dunstan Kirke in the highly popular "Hazel Kirke," and he continued to act the part at the Madison Square Theatre until the piece was finally withdrawn May, 1881, after its long run of 486 performances. He died in 1898.

William Davidge was first seen in this country at the Broadway Theatre, August 19, 1850, as Sir

NEW THEATRES IN BOSTON

Peter Teazle. Born in London in 1814, he began his career as a chorister, making his début as an actor at Nottingham as Adam Winterton in "The Iron Chest." He stayed at the Old Broadway for five years, playing "leading comedy" and "old men" in all the standard repertory. In 1869, he joined the company of Augustin Daly, with whom he remained until 1877, undertaking such characters as Sleek in "The Serious Family," Sir John Vesey in "Money," Sir Harcourt Harkaway and Meddle in "London Assurance," Jesse Rural in "Old Men and Young Hearts," etc., etc. In 1879, he was the first American representative of Dick Deadeye in "H. M. S. Pinafore." In 1888, he joined the company of the Madison Square Theatre with which he was associated when he died.

A sensational première at the Old Broadway occurred December 29, 1851, when a woman whose escapades for years had furnished scandal at tea tables all over the world, made her first appearance before the American public. This was Lola Montez, notorious rather than famous as the actress who had ruled a kingdom.

Eliza Gilbert, or, as she called herself, Lola Montez, was born in Ireland in 1818, her father being a British officer and her mother a beautiful Irish woman claiming descent from a Spanish grandee. When Lola was nineteen, her mother planned to marry her to a rich old Indian judge, but the high-spirited girl rebelled and eloped with a young Irish officer with whom she went to Dublin, where the couple were received at the Vice-regal court. With her youth, beauty and vivaciousness Lola became a great

163

favorite and carried on flirtations right and left, until, her reputation irretrievably compromised, she became an outcast from London society. She immediately went on the stage, securing an engagement at Her Majesty's as a dancer. The critics were loud in praise of her performance, but a *cabale* organized against her by friends of her husband compelled her to leave London. She travelled all over Europe, visiting Brussels, Paris, Warsaw and St. Petersburg, in which last city began a platonic intimacy with Czar Nicholas I. From Russia, she went to Germany, where she met Franz Liszt, then at the height of his fame and living with the Countess d'Agoult who had borne him three children. It was a case of love at first sight on both sides and the Countess was forgotten. But her most extraordinary adventure was to come. In Munich she danced before King Ludwig, and that monarch, hopelessly infatuated, at once made her his intimate friend, councillor and adviser. His ministers, scandalized, threatened to resign *en masse,* but he insisted. They resigned and Lola appointed their successors. The King created her Countess of Lansfeld and Baroness Rosenthal and granted her a large annuity. Finally, the opposition became too strong and the King was induced to sign a warrant for her exile. After more scandalous escapades in England and Spain she came to America, making her début as Betty in " The Tyrolean." Later, she was seen in a dramatization based on incidents in her own life called " Lola Montez in Bavaria," in which she played herself the *danseuse,* the politician, the revolutionist and the fugitive. For a time, she was the sensation of the day and made a great deal of money, squandered as rapidly as it came in. After leaving New York she appeared in most of the principal cities of the country. In 1860, she was stricken with paralysis and died the following year. To-day her grave in Greenwood Cemetery is one of those, among other celebrities, pointed out to curious visitors.

CHAPTER XXII

NEW THEATRES IN NEW YORK

THE middle of the Nineteenth Century saw a marked increase in the number of theatres and concert halls opened in New York. Already the Empire City had gained the position she has ever since maintained as the most important theatrical centre in the United States. Most of the new places of amusement were of mushroom growth, predestined to short and inglorious careers, but some were popular in their day and deserve brief mention, if only as a matter of record.

Of the historic Park Theatre, destroyed by fire in 1848, nothing remained but a memory. The leading theatres now were Burton's, in Chambers Street; Wallack's, at the corner of Broome Street and Broadway; Niblo's, near Prince Street and Broadway; the Broadway, near Worth Street; the Bowery, near Canal Street; the National, in Chatham Street, and Tripler Hall, later known as the Metropolitan, on Broadway near Bond Street. There were also theatrical performances in the " lecture room " of Bar-

NEW THEATRES IN NEW YORK

num's Museum for those whose religious or moral scruples did not permit them to patronize a regular theatre.

For this prejudice against the playhouse, which still persisted in some quarters of New York, as it did even more strongly in other cities, the peculiar conditions surrounding the theatres and players of that day were largely to blame. It is difficult for the present generation of American playgoers, accustomed as they are to the most luxurious and comfortable theatres in the world, with their perfect seating arrangements, their polite and well disciplined attendants, their orderly, well-mannered audiences, to visualize the theatres which our forefathers frequented half a century ago. What the famous Park Theatre looked like in 1845, after twenty-five years of service, Richard Grant White, the well-known Shakespearian editor, who, doubtless, was a frequent patron, tells us:

Its boxes were like pens for beasts. Across them were stretched benches consisting of a mere board covered with faded red moreen, a narrower board, shoulder high, being stretched behind to serve for a back. But one seat on each of the three or four benches was without even this luxury in order that the seat itself might be raised upon its hinges for people to pass in. These sybaritic inclosures were kept under lock and key by a fee-expecting creature who was always half drunk, except when he was wholly drunk. The pit, which has in our modern theatre become the parterre (or, as it is often strangely called, the parquet) the most desirable part of the house, was in the Park Theatre hardly superior to that in which the Jacquerie of old stood upon the bare ground (*par terre*) and thus gave the place its French name. The floor was dirty and broken into holes; the seats were bare, backless benches. Women were never seen in the pit, and, although the excellence of the position (the best in the house) and the cheapness of admission (half

167

a dollar) took gentlemen there, few went there who could afford to study comfort and luxury in their amusements. The place was pervaded with evil smells; and not uncommonly, in the midst of a performance, rats ran out of the holes in the floor and across into the orchestra. This delectable place was approached by a long underground passage with bare whitewashed walls, dimly lighted except at a sort of booth, at which vile fluids and viler solids were sold. As to the house itself, it was the dingy abode of dreariness. The gallery was occupied by howling roughs, who might have taken lessons from the negroes who occupied a part of this tier, which was railed off for their particular use.

Little wonder that the playhouse had a bad name among respectable people. Another grave objection was the opportunity the theatres afforded for indulgence in drink and rubbing shoulders with dissolute characters. "The playhouse," says Judge Daly, "deserved the hard things that were said about it." He continues:

In every theatre there was an upper tier with a bar, where strong drinks were supplied and (in some houses) where the profligate of both sexes resorted. To be sure, there was no necessity for the patrons of the family circle or the boxes to come in contact with such visitors, as the bad company was confined to the upper and cheaper parts of the house—the "shilling gallery," admission to which was twelve and a half cents (there was a coin of that value in those days); but it was natural to fear that to that part of the house young men bent upon seeing life would be tempted, for access to it was open. The actor shared the uncertainties of the manager; salaries were small and sometimes irregular. And the player too often was more convivial than ambitious. After the performance he resorted to taverns and coffee houses (all well known and respectable enough) and entertained the patrons of the theatre (all well known and respected, too), and there until the early hours he discussed the glories of the stage and many tobies of strong ale. He was not then the conservative and prosperous capitalist that he is today. Several causes combined to lower his self-respect, and it was not increased by the public sentiment which condoned his failings and tolerated the upper circle of the play-house with its bar.[1]

Among the minor New York theatres of the early fifties may be mentioned Fellow's Opera House, situated at 444 Broadway, and later known as Christy and Woods Minstrel Hall. In 1860, the house was reopened as Mrs. Brougham's Theatre, with a performance of " The Rivals," Mrs. Brougham being seen for the first time in New York as Mrs. Malaprop. A few months later, Robert W. Butler took control of the house, reopening it as the American, but the place was always known and acquired considerable popularity as Butler's " 444."

Another favorite resort at that time was Buckley's Minstrel Hall, situated at 539 Broadway, near Spring Street, which later acquired considerable notoriety as the Melodeon Concert Hall. Burlesque operas were a feature of this establishment, and later " Tom and Jerry," and specialties were presented. In 1863, P. T. Barnum took a lease of the building, opening it as Barnum's New Museum.

A more select *clientèle* frequented Niblo's Saloon, a small auditorium situated in the same building as Niblo's Garden and opened in 1852. For a long time this stage served for the appearances of visiting musical artists. Adelina Patti sang here September 1, 1853, at a benefit concert, and on May 24, 1856, Felicita Vestvali made her first appearance in concert at this house. Beginning in 1859, the Hooley and Christy and other minstrel organizations took a lease of the house, remaining in control until 1862, when

---

[1] "The Life of Augustin Daly." By Joseph Francis Daly. Copyright, 1917, the Macmillan Co.

THE THEATRE IN AMERICA

Paul Juignet began his first French comedy season. It was on this stage that Lotta, " the California pet," made her first bow to a New York audience.

Lotta Crabtree, from 1865 to 1885 one of the most popular and successful of American comediennes and who made more money on the stage than any other American actress of her day, was an interesting figure in the early development of the drama in the West. Her father, a Scotsman, emigrated to California during the gold rush, taking with him his wife and daughter, the latter a bright little girl with bright red hair, aged six. The child had a good voice and, being a clever dancer and banjo player, her parents took her from camp to camp to entertain the miners. In this way Lotta soon became popular all along the coast, the rough miners showing their appreciation by showering the stage with gold coins. In 1858, the young girl made her début as an actress as Gertrude in " Loan of a Lover " at Petaluma, California, this appearance being followed by others in plays especially written for her—crude melodramas showing her as a waif of the mining camps, in ragged dress, the guardian angel of good-hearted but drink-crazed miners, who, thanks to her, are finally redeemed, strike a rich vein of gold and find themselves millionaires. Other plays in which she had great success were " Zip," " Musette," " The Little Detective," " Mam'sell Nitouche," and " Little Nell and the Marchioness," her most ambitious effort. For twenty years Lotta was an immense favorite with American audiences, especially in the West, where she was idolized. Her earnings were enormous, a conservative estimate of her fortune being $4,000,000.

NEW THEATRES IN NEW YORK

In San Francisco, the scene of her first triumph, the City Council passed a resolution accepting an offer by Lotta to present to the city a fountain to be placed on Market Street, in the heart of the town. This fountain—still known as Lotta's Fountain—is one of the few city landmarks which survived the great earthquake and fire.

White's Varieties was the name of a theatre situated at 17–19 Bowery, which was opened in 1852 with Frank S. Chanfrau as manager. The dramatic company included John Dunn, A. H. Davenport, Jerry Merrifield, Mr. Keeler, Mlle. Albertine (who had played Lize to Chanfrau's Mose in California), Rose Merrifield, Miss Isherwood, Mr. and Mrs. France and William R. Floyd. The following year the house was altered and reopened as the St. Charles Theatre.

A great novelty in America was Franconi's Hippodrome, opened during the winter of 1853. A syndicate of showmen secured a plot of land at the corner of 23rd Street and Broadway and erected a large structure in which chariot races and gladiatorial contests took place. In 1858, the Hippodrome was torn down, and the Fifth Avenue Hotel erected on its site.

Another novelty was the Crystal Palace, situated at 42nd Street and 6th Avenue, on the site of Bryant Park. Modelled after the plan of its famous prototype in London, the sides of the building were of glass, supported by iron girders. It was two stories high, the first in the form of an octagon, the second in that of a Greek cross. The centre of this was a dome 145 feet high. " Viewed at a distance," says T. Allston Brown, " its burnished dome resembled a half-disclosed balloon, as large as a cathedral but light, brilliant and seemingly ready to burst its bands and soar aloft." Fairs were held in the Palace, and there were military bands, a grand chorus and an immense organ. It was destroyed by fire in 1858.

Buckley's Hall, at 585 Broadway, was famous in 1856 as the home of the Buckley Serenaders, opera, burlesques and minstrelsy being the entertainment offered. The following year the house was opened as a regular theatre under the name of the New Olympic, the company including F. S. Chanfrau, Kate Pennoyer, the popular dancer and pantomimist, Mrs. Stephens, A. F. Blake and other favorites. The house changed its name as often as it did lessees, and had an unsavory reputation until 1875 when Tony Pastor turned it into a variety theatre, and first introduced to the public several performers who later became famous on our stage, among others Nat Goodwin, Evans and Hoey, May and Flo Irwin, Francis Wilson and Lillian Russell.

The most important event of that period, however, was the opening, in 1854, of the Academy of Music, at the corner of 14th Street and Irving Place.

Although four distinct attempts had been made to give New Yorkers the costly luxury of grand opera, all such enterprises had thus far met with disaster. Palmo, the ex-restaurateur, returned to his pots and pans when, in 1845, his box-office receipts were seized by the sheriff to satisfy clamoring creditors, while the more pretentious Astor Place Opera House, the fashionable home of opera from 1847 to 1852, having also proved unsuccessful, was eventually turned into a public library.

But there still remained wealthy music lovers willing to finance further ventures of the kind. As Henry E. Krehbiel, the well-known music critic, puts it, " in the opinion of the upper classes, it was not Italian opera that had succumbed, but only the building that housed it." The critic adds:

The Academy of Music had its birth in the expiring throes of the Astor Place Opera House. The spirit of which it was the material expression seems to have been admirable. To this the name of the establishment bears witness. It was not alone the official title of the French institution, popularly spoken of as the Grand Opera, which was in the minds of the promoters of the New York enterprise—the new opera house was to be a veritable academy of music, an educational institution. Not only was fashionable society to have a place in which to display and disport itself, but popular taste and popular knowledge were to be cultivated. To this end, the auditorium was to be three times as commodious as that of the Astor Place Opera House, and the low prices which had been prevalent only at Niblo's, Burton's, and Castle Garden were to be the rule at the new establishment.[2]

The new opera house seated 4600 persons, the auditorium and stage being one of the largest in America. Max Maretzek, the first lessee, was a Hebrew, educated in Vienna, who had come here from London to conduct at the Astor Place Opera House. He sublet the house to J. H. Hackett, who opened the first season, October 2, 1854, with a performance of " Norma," sung by a company engaged to support the famous stars Mario and Grisi, who had already been heard at Castle Garden.

Mario, Cavalieri da Candia, the greatest operatic tenor of his time, was of an old and noble family. He made his début at the Paris Opera House in 1838 in

---

[2] Chapters of Opera. Copyright, 1908, by Henry Edward Krehbiel. Henry Holt & Company, Publishers. Reprinted by permission.

the rôle of Robert le Diable with instantaneous success. The following year he was heard in London, where he was considered the greatest stage lover ever seen. For a quarter of a century Mario sang in Paris and London, always associated with Mme. Grisi, whom he eventually married. Giulia Grisi, one of the world's most famous operatic singers, made her first appearance in public as Emma in Rossini's "Zelmira." In 1832, she made her début in Paris with tremendous success, and for sixteen consecutive years was supreme at the Théâtre des Italiens.

Expecting a tremendous rush to hear these eminent artistes, the management charged three dollars for parquet seats, a price then considered exorbitant. It proved a fatal policy, for the public showed its resentment by staying away, business remaining poor to the close of the season, which ended December 29 with a deficit of $8000.

Ole Bull, the celebrated Norwegian violinist, was the next lessee. His régime was very brief, the stockholders then assuming the management and showing a loss on the year of $50,000.

The new management began the season February 19, 1855, with "Rigoletto." On April 30 of the same year "Trovatore" was heard for the first time in America with the popular Felicita Vestvali, Steffanone, Brignoli and Amodio in the cast. Max Maretzek was the next impresario, he being succeeded in turn by Maurice Strakosch and Bernard Ullmann, who, with occasional intermissions, continued to give opera until 1878, when Colonel James H. Mapleson assumed the management.

The Academy of Music continued to be the home

174

of grand opera in this country until 1883, when a conflict between the old Knickerbocker box holders and the younger generation of *nouveaux riches* which the rapidly increasing prosperity of the country had brought to New York, resulted in the secession of the new subscribers and the building of another opera house further up town.

Grand Opera in its early beginnings in this country, as now, was largely a social function; a rendezvous of the wealthy, a place for the ostentatious display of beautiful toilettes and priceless jewels, and the furthering of social ambitions. When the Academy of Music opened its doors in 1854, the house was considered large enough for the old Knickerbocker society. But as the country grew in prosperity, with almost daily accessions to the ranks of newly made millionaires, eager, above all, for social prestige and ready to spend anything to secure it, the size of the Academy of Music was found inadequate. "It marked," says Mr. Krehbiel, "the decay of the old Knickerbocker régime, and its amalgamation with the new order of society." The critic continues:

It had become plain that the Academy of Music could not accommodate all the representatives of the two elements in fashionable society, who, for one reason or another, wished to own or occupy the boxes which were the visible sign of wealth and social position. There was no manifest dissatisfaction, either, with the Academy of Music, or with the performances under the direction of Colonel Mapleson, though these were conventional enough and the dress of the operas looked particularly shabby in contrast with the new scenery and costumes at the new theatre when once the rivalry had begun. The house being satisfactory, popular taste contented with the representations, and there being no evidences of insufficient room in any part of the audience room except the private boxes, it seems obvious to the merest observer from without

175

THE THEATRE IN AMERICA

that social, and not artistic, impulses led to the enterprise which produced the new establishment.[3]

The new temple of music, situated at 39th Street and Broadway, and known as the Metropolitan Opera House, cost nearly two million dollars. It was an ugly structure without, but of vast size and splendidly decorated in rich red and gold within, the house being modelled after some of the most famous opera houses in Europe. The first season began October 22, 1883, under the direction of Henry E. Abbey.[4]

The opening bill was " Faust," with this cast: Marguerite, Christine Nilsson; Siebel, Mme. Scalchi; Martha, Mlle. Lablanche; Faust, Signor Campanini; Valentine, Signor Del Puente; Mephistopheles, Signor Novara. The season was not a success, and, Mr. Abbey declining further responsibility, the directors accepted a proposition from Dr. Leopold Damrosch to give opera in German. The first German performance took place November 17, 1884, the opera being Richard Wagner's " Tannhäuser." German opera continued to be given at the Metropolitan for seven years, after which Italian opera was again restored to favor under the management of Henry E. Abbey and Maurice Grau. Mr. Abbey

[3] Chapters of Opera. Copyright, 1908, by Henry Edward Krehbiel. Henry Holt & Company, Publishers. Reprinted by permission.

[4] Henry E. Abbey (1846-1896), one of the most important figures in the American managerial field, was born at Akron, O. His first vocation, that of a cornet player in his native town, early indicated his taste for music. Later, theatricals claimed his attention, and he became manager of the Akron Theatre. In 1876 he joined forces with John B. Schoeffel, a Rochester theatrical man, and with him gradually developed several theatrical enterprises. He secured control of the Park Theatre, corner of Broadway and 22nd Street, New York, opening the house as Abbey's Park Theatre. Later, he became manager of the Park and Tremont Theatres, Boston, and was active in a number of important enterprises, notably in organizing American tours of celebrated foreign stars, including Bernhardt, Henry Irving, Coquelin, Mounet Sully and others.

176

NEW THEATRES IN NEW YORK

died in 1896 and Maurice Grau, under whose able direction grand opera prospered as never before, continued in control until 1903. Heinrich Conried, formerly manager of the German Theatre in Irving Place, was the next director. He caused an international sensation by producing, December 24, 1903, Wagner's opera " Parsifal," without the consent and despite the protests of the Wagner family. Conried's régime, noted for its sensational features and exploitation of Signor Caruso and other famous singers, came to an end in 1909 when Signor Gatti-Casazza assumed control.[5] A crisis in America's operatic affairs was reached in 1906 when Oscar Hammerstein, a former cigarmaker who had become prominent in amusement circles as producer and theatre-builder, challenged the supremacy of the aristocratic Metropolitan by building the Manhattan Opera House on West 34th Street, and presenting there such modern operas as " Thaïs," " Louise," " Le Jongleur de Notre Dame," etc., works that had hitherto been excluded from the strictly classic repertoire of the Metropolitan, and introducing to our public such fine vocal artists as Mary Garden, Tetrazzini, Bonci, Dalmores, and Renaud, none of which singers the Metropolitan had afforded a hearing. Encouraged by his success, Hammerstein built a splendid Opera House in Philadelphia, and keen rivalry with the Metropolitan followed, with heavy losses to both, until finally Hammerstein capitulated and withdrew from the operatic field.

[5] The above is, of course, only the barest outline of the history of grand opera in the United States. The reader is referred to "Early Opera in America," by Oscar G. Sonneck, G. Schirmer, Publisher, and to "Chapters of Opera," by Henry Edward Krehbiel, Henry Holt & Company, Publishers.

In the intervals between operatic seasons, dramatic performances were given on the Academy stage. On May 29, 1855, a testimonial benefit was tendered to James W. Wallack, Sr., in which Edwin Forrest, E. L. Davenport, John Brougham, William Davidge and other favorites took part.

On November 24, 1859, Adelina Patti, who had already been heard at concerts, made her first appearance in opera at the Academy of Music as Lucia in " Lucia da Lammermoor." Born in Madrid in 1843, this celebrated singer was the youngest daughter of Salvatore Patti, an Italian singer, who later came to America and for a time was director of the Italian Opera at New York. After her New York operatic début, Adelina Patti went to London, appearing at the Royal Italian Opera as Amina with tremendous success. Similar triumphs as Lucia, Violetta, Zerlina, Martha and Rosina followed and from that time on Patti was world famous. In 1884, she revisited New York and sang at the Academy under Mapleson.

In 1861, Professor Herrmann, the well-known prestidigitator, whose favorite feat of shooting a single card from a pack in his hand to the top gallery by a quick twist of his powerful wrist, and other tricks, delighted and mystified thousands, made his first appearance in America at the Academy.

Until about this period the old Bowery Theatre had enjoyed what was practically a monopoly of East Side theatrical patronage, but in 1859 George L. Fox, the pantomimist, and James W. Lingard, the actor, opened a new theatre between New Canal and Hester Streets, which they called the New Bowery. The house was opened September 5, with " The Orange

Girl of Venice " and " The Four Lovers." On October 31, " Uncle Tom's Cabin " was given, and the following month Fanny Herring, for several years a great favorite at the old Bowery, made her first appearance at this house, acting seven characters in a piece called " Fast Women of a Modern Time, or Life in the City and Suburbs." The bills were mostly of this sensational order, but occasionally Shakespeare was presented. The house was totally destroyed by fire December 18, 1866.

A place of amusement known as Wood's Minstrel Hall, situated at 514 Broadway, below Spring Street, was opened to the New York public in 1862. At first the new house was devoted to Ethiopian minstrelsy, but in 1866 it was converted into a regular theatre, and reopened as Wood's Theatre. A number of favorite performers played engagements, including F. S. Chanfrau, Tony Pastor, Lucille Western, Barton Hill and the famous Worrell sisters, who appeared in an extravaganza called " The Three Sisters," in which each sister took the part of six different characters. The Hanlon Brothers—famous gymnasts—were the next lessees, after which followed a short interlude, when the house was devoted to German drama. After that it was reopened as the Theatre Comique, Harrigan and Hart, the well-known Irish comedians, taking a lease in 1876. Harrigan's amusing sketches of Irish-American life, "The Mulligan Guards " and " The Mulligan Guards' Ball," etc., etc., were produced here in 1879.

Instances of a theatre being turned into a place of worship are rare—although not unknown—but churches have often been converted into theatres.

The Church of the Messiah, a gray stone edifice erected in 1838, at 724 Broadway, dismantled as a place of prayer in 1865, was opened as a place of entertainment that same year by James H. Hackett. It was called the Broadway Athenæum, the programme consisting of readings, recitations and concerts. A few months later, Lucy Rushton, the actress, took a lease of the place and reopened it as Lucy Rushton's Theatre with a performance of "The School for Scandal," the cast including C. M. Walcot as Sir Peter Teazle, J. K. Mortimer as Charles, D. W. Waller as Joseph, W. A. Mestayer as Sir Benjamin Backbite, Mrs. Mark Smith as Lady Sneerwell, Lucy Rushton as Lady Teazle and Clara Maeder as Mrs. Candour. The receipts not coming up to expectations, Miss Rushton soon gave up the venture, and the following year the house was reopened by John Lewis Baker and Mark Smith with a good company, including: Mark Smith, John Lewis Baker, A. H. Davenport, McKee Rankin, W. Gomersal, Humphrey Bland, George Metkiff, F. Percy, H. Vernon, Farley, King, Chapman, Newton, Williams, Mrs. W. Gomersal, Mrs. H. H. Wall, Mrs. Marie Wilkins, Mrs. H. Bland, Alicia Mandeville, Sadie Cole, Solado.

The following year Baker and Smith, the lessees, retired, and the Worrell Sisters—Sophie, Irene and Jennie—took a lease of the house, which they reopened as the Worrell Sisters' New York Theatre. It was during their tenancy that Augustin Daly's drama, "Under the Gaslight," was seen for the first time.

In 1873, Mr. Daly, driven by fire from his Twenty-fourth Street Theatre, took a lease, reopening it as Daly's Fifth Avenue Theatre. He stayed only one season, when the place was taken over by George L. Fox. The house, from now on, had almost as many lessees and different names as it had years still to exist, being successively known as the Globe, the National and the New Theatre Comique. Destroyed by fire in 1884, the skeleton building for a time was used for exhibition purposes. It was finally demolished in 1902.

The French drama in New York, energetically fostered for many years by Paul Juignet and other enterprising citizens of French descent, found another and more imposing home, in the year 1866, in the fine new playhouse erected in Fourteenth Street, near Sixth Avenue, on the site of the Cremorne Garden. Opened May 26, as the Théâtre Français, an interesting season of French plays and opera was given. The same year Jacob Grau took a lease of the house, presenting Italian opera.

On September 26, under Grau's management, Adelaide Ristori made her first appearance in America at this theatre in the character of Medea. This celebrated Italian tragedienne was born in 1822, her parents being strolling players. She made her début at an early age, and before she was twenty had attained a commanding position on the Italian stage. For many years she toured with great success throughout Italy and France, rivalling the famous Rachel in the grandeur of her classic portrayals. Her most famous rôles were Medea, Schiller's Mary Stuart, Giacometti's Queen Elizabeth, and Lady Macbeth. "Her Elizabeth," says John Ranken Towse, "was generally acknowledged to be her masterpiece, and, beyond question, it was a wonderful feat of impersonation, embodying the popular ideal of England's Virgin Queen with extraordinary felicity. The haughty carriage, imperious address, fierce temper, blunt humor, masculine sagacity, petty vanity, and feminine jealousy, were all indicated with surpassing skill and blended into a consistent whole with finished artistry. The performance was a very fine one, but there was nothing in it significant of phenomenal capacity." *

At first, Ristori's American tours made a great deal of money, but the actress' later visits were less successful, owing to her attempts to act in English.

In October, 1867, there began another season of French opera, Mlle. Tostee, a very popular French singer, being heard for the first time in Offenbach's " Grande Duchesse."

On September 22, 1871, Maria Seebach, the celebrated German actress, made her American début at this house as Gretchen in " Faust." Although a fine artist, and a great favorite with those playgoers whose knowledge of German permitted them to follow her performances intelligently, Seebach's American tour was not a financial success. That same year the theatre was taken over by new lessees, Messrs. Snyder and Wheatleigh, who reopened it as the Fourteenth Street Theatre.

Another important new theatre built in New York about this time was the Grand Opera House, a million-dollar structure situated at the corner of Eighth Avenue and 23rd Street. The house opened Janu-

* Sixty Years of the Theatre. Copyright, 1916, by John Ranken Towse. Funk & Wagnalls Company, Publishers. Reprinted by permission.

ary 9, 1868, with Italian opera under the direction of Max Strakosch. The following year James Fisk, Jr., and Jay Gould secured control of the theatre, and from now on dramatic performances alternated with seasons of English and French light opera. On March 31, " The Tempest " was presented with great splendor of *mise en scène,* and a company that included E. L. Davenport, Frank Mayo (his first appearance in New York) and William Davidge. Here also was seen George C. Boniface in " Twelve Temptations," a spectacle as famous in its day as the " Black Crook."

On May 24, Sardou's " Patrie " was seen at this theatre for the first time in America. In 1870, a strong opera comique and opera bouffe company was organized with Signor Carlo Patti as musical director. Marie Aimée, the French comic opera star and one of the most popular singers ever seen in this country, appeared on January 12, 1871, as Boulotte in "Barbe Bleu." Later, she sang the title rôle in " La Périchole," her acting in the drinking song taking the house by storm.

In 1872, control of the house was assumed by Augustin Daly, who opened it August 26 with this company: Mrs. John Wood, Rose Hersee, Emma Howson, the Majiltons, Annie Deland, Ella Dietz, Miss C. Bronte, Helen Strange, Mary Stuart, Blanche Hayden, Annie Yeamans, John Brougham, Robert Craig, Stuart Robson, Lauri Family, J. W. Jennings, G. F. Ketchum, J. G. Peakes, Martin Golden, Julian Cross, J. A. Meade and J. A. Mackay.

CHAPTER XXIII

WALLACK'S—1852–1887

THE date 1852 is an important one in the annals of the American stage, for in that year the first theatre bearing the name " Wallack's " over its portals was opened to the New York public.

The first playhouse controlled by Wallack was the National, at the corner of Church and Leonard Streets, in 1836. That house, it will be remembered, was destroyed by fire and Wallack went temporarily to Niblo's, as already recorded. In 1850, John Brougham built a theatre at the corner of Broome Street and Broadway, but the venture was not successful. Two years later, the elder Wallack secured possession of the house, completely renovated it and reopened it September 8, 1852, as Wallack's Lyceum.

The bill on the opening night comprised " The Way to Get Married," followed by the farce " The Boarding School," the company engaged including the following players: Mr. Seguin, W. R. Blake, Mr. Lester (Lester Wallack), Charles Hale, Mr. Reynolds, Mr. Lyster, C. Bernard, Mr. Baker, Mr. Hunt,

D. Thompson, Mr. Stuart (E. A. Sothern), John Brougham, C. K. Mason, A. Baker, F. A. Vincent, H. B. Phillips, Frank Rea, F. Chippendale, Jr., Mr. Trevor, George F. Browne, Mr. Burke, Mr. Durant, James Wallack, Laura Keene, Kate Horn (Mrs. Buckland), Mrs. W. R. Blake, Mrs. John Brougham, Julia Gould, Mrs. Stephens, Fanny Cramer, Mrs. McGill, Mrs. Tayleure, Mrs. Osborne, Mrs. Deane, Mrs. Charles Hale, Mrs. F. Rea, Miss Cramer, Miss Malvina Pray (Mrs. W. J. Florence), Mrs. Hughes, Mrs. Barton and Mrs. Scott.

Once fairly settled in his new house, Wallack soon succeeded in rivalling Burton's Theatre in the favor of the playgoing public. " The hand of a master," says Ireland, " was visible in every production, and the taste, elegance and propriety displayed about the whole establishment gave it a position of respectability never hitherto enjoyed in New York except at the old Park Theatre. The ascendancy Wallack's then secured was maintained and for many years it remained the leading theatre of the city."

On September 20, a performance at Wallack's of " The Will " served for the American début, in the character of Albina Mandeville, of Miss Laura Keene, a young London actress and protégée of the famous Mme. Vestris. The newcomer made a most favorable impression and soon became one of the most popular stars on our stage.

The first actress in this country to enter the managerial field,[1] Laura Keene was born in London in 1826. After studying with Mme. Vestris, she made

---

[1] Mrs. John Drew, that other famous actress-manager, did not assume control of the Arch Street Theatre, Philadelphia, until 1861.

her début at the London Olympic in 1851 as Pauline in " The Lady of Lyons " with such success that she was immediately engaged by Wallack for his New York theatre. After remaining at Wallack's a short time, she went to Baltimore where she opened a theatre, and later started on a tour that took her round the world. After acting in Australia and California, she returned to New York and opened her own theatre, where she produced a number of light comedies and dramas, and began her successful career as actress manager.

It was also at Wallack's, in the Fall of 1854, that Edward A. Sothern, the famous Dundreary of a few years later, made his first bow to New York audiences.

Edward Askew Sothern was born in 1826 in Liverpool, where his father was engaged in the shipping business. The boy was well educated with a view to his becoming a surgeon, but his own inclination led him toward the stage, and, after some experience in amateur theatricals, he made his professional début as Othello, using the stage name " Douglas Stuart." He continued acting in the provinces and, after playing juvenile and light comedy rôles for some time, was advised to come to America. He arrived here in 1852 and made his first appearance in this country at the National Theatre, Boston, on November 1 of that year, as Dr. Pangloss. The American début of the young English comedian, who was described as " tall, willowy and lithe with a clear red and white complexion," received little or no attention, and, greatly discouraged, Sothern accepted an offer from Barnum's to play comedy parts at his New York theatre at a salary of $20 a week.

WALLACK'S—1852-1887

The engagement at Wallack's followed, his first real opportunity to show his ability coming in 1853, when he played Armand to the Camille of Matilda Heron, play and players being applauded by crowded houses for forty consecutive nights. Soon after this he joined Laura Keene, whose production in 1858 of Tom Taylor's comedy, "Our American Cousin," brought him fame and fortune. When the play was first read to the members of the company Sothern looked very glum, he seeing nothing in the piece to suit him. Joseph Jefferson was cast for the shrewd, keen Yankee boy, Asa Trenchard, and Mr. Couldock was to play Abel Murcott. There was nothing left but the English fop, Lord Dundreary, and Sothern saw nothing in the part. Indeed, it was owing mainly to an accident that he made his extraordinary hit in the rôle. How this came about Joseph Jefferson tells us in his charming Autobiography:

Sothern was much dejected at being compelled to play the part. He said he could do nothing with it, and certainly for the first two weeks it was a dull effort, and produced but little effect. So in despair he began to introduce extravagant business into his character, skipping about the stage, stammering and sneezing, and, in short, doing all he could to attract and distract the attention of the audience. To the surprise of every one, himself included, these antics, intended by him to injure the character, were received by the audience with delight. He was a shrewd man as well as an effective actor, and he saw at a glance that accident had revealed to him a golden opportunity. He took advantage of it, and with cautious steps increased his speed, feeling the ground well under him as he proceeded. Before the first month was over he stood side by side with any other character in the play; and at the end of the run he was, in my opinion, considerably in advance of us all. And his success in London, in the same character, fully attests,

187

whatever may be said to the contrary, that as an extravagant, eccentric comedian in the modern range of comedy he was quite without a rival.[2]

Later, Sothern went to England, where his success was repeated. " Dundreary " ran for nearly two hundred nights in London. The public went wild over the character. Men wore Dundreary coats and sported Dundreary whiskers. By the end of 1861 the play had been acted in America over a hundred and fifty times, and it continued to hold the boards successfully for many years. Sothern is identified with several other rôles, but in none did he meet with as much success as in Dundreary.

A notable première at Wallack's, December 24, 1855, was that of Brougham's celebrated extravaganza, " Pocahontas, or the Gentle Savage," one of the most successful burlesques of its kind ever seen on the American stage. On this occasion, John Brougham was seen as Powhatan, J. H. Stoddart as Gol-o-gog, Charles M. Walcot as Capt. John Smith, and Georgina Hodson as Pocahontas. The following year, Agnes Robertson appeared in " The Phantom," by Dion Boucicault, and in other plays.

On January 22, 1857, Matilda Heron, an actress very popular with American theatregoers, made a tremendous hit at Wallack's as Dumas' heroine, Camille. Born in Ireland in 1830, Matilda Heron came to America at a very early age. Her stage début was made at the Walnut Street Theatre, Philadelphia, in 1851, as Bianca in Milman's tragedy, " Fazio." Later, she went to California, where she

---

[2] Autobiography of Joseph Jefferson. Copyright, 1899. Reprinted by permission.

became an immense favorite. She was first seen in
New York at the Bowery Theatre, August 23, 1852,
when she appeared in the support of Thomas S.
Hamblin in " Macbeth." Later, she appeared with
great success in such parts as Juliet, Mrs. Haller,
Pauline, Ophelia and Parthenia. Her success at
Wallack's as Camille was the sensation of that season, her impersonation being noted for its repulsive
naturalness. William Winter wrote of her:

She had a wildness of emotion, a force of brain, a vitality in
embodiment and many indefinable magnetic qualities, that combined to make her exceptional among human creatures. . . .
She appeared in other parts, but Camille was the part she always
acted best. It afforded the agonized and agonizing situation which
alone could serve for the utterance of her tempestuous nature.[3]

On December 3, 1860, the production at Wallack's of " The Model Hypocrite " served for the first
appearance on any stage of Madeleine Henriques, a
young amateur actress who was very popular with
Wallack audiences, and later became leading woman
of that organization.

After nine successful seasons, Wallack, in 1861,
relinquished control of the theatre and moved further
north, up Broadway to Thirteenth Street, where a
new theatre had been built for him.

In this new Wallack's, for more than twenty years
the most famous playhouse in America, some of the
greatest triumphs connected with the name of Wallack were achieved. For the lavishness of its productions and the brilliancy of its casts, this theatre
has never been equalled in this country. During its

[3] From an article by William Winter in the *New York Tribune*, March
12, 1877. Reprinted by permission.

remarkable career of two decades, the following distinguished players appeared on its boards: Charles Fisher, John Sefton, Mark Smith, John Gilbert, James Williamson, J. W. Wallack, Jr., E. L. Davenport, Wm. Holston, Frederic Robinson, J. B. Polk, J. H. Stoddart, Owen Marlowe, George Clarke, Chas. Mathews, George Boniface, Sr., Harry Becket, E. M. Holland, Edward Arnot, Eben Plympton, H. J. Montague, Dion Boucicault, Steele Mackaye, Charles Coghlan, Charles Barron, Harry Edwards, Maurice Barrymore, Gerald Eyre, Osmond Tearle, William Elton, Harry Pitt, Fanny Morant, Mrs. John Sefton, Mary Gannon, Mrs. John Hoey, Ione Burke, Marie Wilkins, Jane Coombs, Lotta, Mrs. Clara Jennings, Rose Eytinge, Emily Mestayer, Effie Germon, Mrs. Thomas Barry, Helen Tracy, Katharine Rogers, Rose Coghlan, Mme. Ponisi, Jeffreys Lewis, Ada Dyas, Rose Wood, Stella Boniface, Maud Granger, Adelaide Detchon, Mrs. Vernon and Madeleine Henriques.

The elder Wallack himself never acted in this house, and while he was ostensibly the manager, his son, Lester Wallack, had virtual control of the artistic direction, assisted at the business end by Theodore Moss.

John Lester, the only one of James W. Wallack's four sons to become an actor, was born in New York City in 1819 at the time of his parents' first visit to this country. He was educated in England and made his first appearance on the professional stage as Angelo in "Tortesa the Usurer" in support of his father, who was then touring the English provinces. Later, he appeared at Rochester, playing the Earl of

190

Rochester in John Howard Payne's " Charles II," and on this occasion for the first time he was billed as " Mr. Lester." His London début was made at the Haymarket, where he appeared in " The Little Devil " with such success that shortly afterwards he received an offer from New York. Sailing at once for America, the young man made his début at the Old Broadway, September 27, 1847, as Sir Charles Cold-stream in the farce " Used Up." The following year, at the Chatham Theatre, he had much success as Don Cesar de Bazan and as Edmond Dantes in " Monte Christo." In 1849, he produced two of his own plays, " The Three Guardsmen " and " The Four Mus-keteers." In 1850, he was associated with Burton's Theatre, where he was seen as Charles Surface, and two years later he acted leading parts at his father's theatre at Broadway and Broome Street, in addition to performing the duties of stage manager. Describing his appearance at that time, Ireland wrote:

For many years the handsomest man on our stage, the most graceful and gallant in his carriage and bearing, and we had almost added the most careful and correct in costume, he is nevertheless rather slender in person, and his fine features are somewhat deficient in variableness of expression. With the highest capabilities otherwise for his profession and with undoubted merit as the general juvenile hero of all modern comedies he has had but one rival and no superior, and we know of no one who can be justly called his peer. His worst faults are a tendency to turn legitimate comedy into farce and a habit of being too familiar with his audience.

During his professional career of half a century, Lester Wallack acted no fewer than 291 rôles, among the most successful being Hugh Chalcote in " Ours," Henry Beauclerc in " Diplomacy," Prosper Coura-mont in " A Scrap of Paper," Viscount de Ligny in

191

Planché's " Captain of the Watch," Manuel in " The Romance of a Poor Young Man," Young Dornton in " The Road to Ruin," Don Felix in " The Wonder," Benedick in " Much Ado," Rover in " Wild Oats," Evelyn in " Money," Christopher Marlow in " She Stoops to Conquer," Charles Surface in " The School for Scandal," Jack Wilding in " The Liar," and John Garth in the melodrama of that name.

For forty years Lester Wallack, both as actor and manager, was one of the most conspicuous figures of the American stage. " He was essentially a romantic actor," says John Ranken Towse, " as well as an accomplished comedian." The critic goes on to say:

I should hesitate to place him among the " great " actors, for his range was not wide and he had no eloquence in the profounder emotions, but what he did do, in his own proper sphere of romance and comedy, he did preëminently well. Nature had been very bounteous to him. With his raven locks and flashing dark eyes, his fine figure and superb carriage, he was one of the handsomest men of his time, and naturally he was adored by the fair sex. There was no suspicion of effeminate dandyism about him. His temperament was indisputably virile and all his embodiments had a most attractive manliness. He could be a fervent and fascinating but not a passionate lover. He could never have given a good performance of Romeo, Armand Duval, or Claude Melnotte; nor could he express profound pathos, although he could upon occasion be sympathetic and affecting, but as the man of cool resource and prompt action, in all the lighter moods of gayety and cynical levity, and in the attributes of the man of the world, he was brilliantly efficient, acting with authoritative ease, grace and spontaneity.[4]

The new Wallack's Theatre at Thirteenth Street and Broadway was opened September 25, 1861, with Tom Taylor's comedy, "The New President," the cast

---

[4] Sixty Years of the Theatre. Copyright, 1916, by John Ranken Towse. Funk & Wagnalls Company, Publishers. Reprinted by permission.

including Lester Wallack, Charles Fisher, W. R. Blake, W. H. Norton, Charles Parsloe, Mrs. Vernon, Madeleine Henriques, Mary Gannon, W. R. Floyd and Mrs. John Hoey. Before the play began, James W. Wallack came before the curtain and made an address to the audience. This was the elder Wallack's last appearance on any stage.

The opening piece, a modern comedy, not proving profitable, was quickly withdrawn and Wallack fell back upon the old comedies with success. Interesting bills of the first two seasons included " The King of the Mountains," " The Magic Marriage," Tom Taylor's drama " Up at the Hills," " She Stoops to Conquer," with Lester Wallack as Young Marlow, Mrs. Hoey as Mrs. Hardcastle and George Holland as Tony Lumpkin, " The Love Chase," " London Assurance," " The Wonder," " The School for Scandal " (in which John Gilbert made his début at this house as Sir Peter), " Money," " Bosom Friends " (an adaptation of Sardou's " Nos Intimes "), " The Jealous Wife," " Speed the Plough," and Lester Wallack's own comedy, " Central Park."

On January 1, 1862, " The School for Scandal " was presented with this interesting cast: Lester Wallack as Charles, Mr. Blake as Sir Peter, Mr. Norton as Oliver, Charles Fisher as Joseph, George Holland as Moses, Mrs. Hoey as Lady Teazle, Madeleine Henriques as Maria, Mrs. Sloan as Lady Sneerwell and Mrs. Vernon as Mrs. Candour.

The season of 1863 opened September 30 with the first performance on any stage of Lester Wallack's play, " Rosedale." The piece proved a great success and had a hundred and twenty-five performances during the season.

THE THEATRE IN AMERICA

On the death of the elder Wallack the following year, Lester Wallack became sole proprietor of Wallack's. He gathered about him a most brilliant stock company and until the year 1887, when he finally retired, succeeded in sustaining the great reputation of the house. He himself acted in the old-time comedies and assumed the leading rôle in many of the new plays.

In 1867, profiting by the renewed interest in Dickensonia, aroused by the visit of Charles Dickens, " Oliver Twist " was presented December 27 of that year with this remarkable cast: James W. Wallack, Jr., as Fagin, Edward L. Davenport as Bill Sykes, Rose Eytinge as Nancy and George Holland as Bumble.

It was at Wallack's early in the season of 1872–73 that Rose Coghlan, sister of Charles Coghlan, and one of the best Lady Teazles ever seen on our stage, made her first appearance in America. Born at Peterborough, England, in 1852, this actress first appeared at the Theatre Royal, Greenock, as one of the witches in " Macbeth." After considerable success in London burlesque, she came to America in 1872, and made her début at Wallack's, September 2, as Jupiter in " Ixion." She remained at Wallack's on and off until 1888, appearing as Magdalen in " False Shame," Zicka in " Diplomacy," Clarissa in " Clarissa Harlowe," Lady Gay Spanker in " London Assurance," also in " The School for Scandal," " Our Club," " My Son at Last," " Spellbound," " A Scrap of Paper," etc., Rosalind in " As You Like It," Stephanie in " Forget Me Not," " La Belle Russe," " Caste," " Money," etc., etc. Later, she starred with considerable success.

194

WALLACK'S—1852-1887

During the season of 1874-5, H. J. Montague, a clever and attractive English light comedian, joined the Wallack organization, making a big hit as Manuel in " The Romance of a Poor Young Man." Harry Montague at once became immensely popular with theatregoers. He was the matinee idol of the middle seventies, and a special favorite of Wallack, who surrendered to the young actor some of his best parts. His career unfortunately was not destined to be a long one. He was in very delicate health and soon died in California of consumption.

That same year (1874) Wallack produced Dion Boucicault's Irish drama, " The Shaughraun." The play was an enormous success and broke the record up to that time as a theatrical moneymaker. The cast included: H. J. Montague as Captain Molineux, Ada Dyas as the patriotic heroine, John Gilbert as the Parish priest, J. B. Polk as Robert Ffolliott, Harry Becket as Harvey Duff, the traitor, Mme. Ponisi as Mrs. O'Kelly, E. M. Holland as Reilly, and Boucicault himself as Conn, the humorous, mischievous scapegrace.

Following this came a series of delightful old comedy revivals in which the splendid stock company was seen at its best: Holcroft's " Road to Ruin," with Harry Montague playing the part of Young Dornton, one of Lester Wallack's most successful rôles, John Gilbert as Old Dornton and Mme. Ponisi as the Widow Warren; " The Rivals," with John Gilbert as Sir Anthony Absolute, Edward Arnott as Jack Absolute, W. R. Ford as Sir Lucius, Mme. Ponisi as Mrs. Malaprop and Ada Dyas as Lydia Languish; Mrs. Centlivre's old comedy, " The Wonder," in

THE THEATRE IN AMERICA

which Wallack appeared in his old rôle, Don Felix, John Gilbert as Don Pedro and Ada Dyas as Violante; O'Keefe's "Wild Oats," with Wallack as Rover, John Gilbert as Thunder, Effie Germon as Johnny Gammon and Harry Becket as Ephraim Smooth; Bulwer Lytton's "Money" with Wallack as Evelyn, John Gilbert as Sir John Vesey, John Brougham as Stout, Mme. Ponisi as Lady Franklin and Rose Coghlan as Clara Douglas, and "The School for Scandal," in which Charles Coghlan, a most versatile and popular actor, made a great hit as Charles Surface. Mme. Ponisi played Mrs. Candour on this occasion and Rose Coghlan was the Lady Teazle.

Charles Coghlan, an English actor, had already been seen the previous season at Daly's, where he made his début on the American stage, September 12, 1876, as Evelyn in "Money." A handsome, well-built man with a fine voice and engaging personality, Coghlan's success with American audiences was immediate, and he remained prominently before the public for a number of years, his most successful rôles being those of Clarence in his own adaptation from the French, entitled "The Royal Box" (produced at the Fifth Avenue December 21, 1897), and the title part in his own drama, "Citizen Pierre," seen at the same theatre, April 12, 1899.

In the Spring of 1880, Wallack revived Foote's comedy, "The Liar," he playing his old part, Jack Wilding, one of his most successful rôles. The same season saw a splendid revival of "As You Like It," with Osmond Tearle, an English actor, as Jacques and Rose Coghlan as Rosalind. A few seasons later,

1884, came a revival of "She Stoops to Conquer," with Wallack in his rôle of Young Marlow.

Between these revivals Wallack produced a number of modern plays. In 1875, he gave " Caste," with George Honey as Eccles and Ada Dyas as Esther, Charles A. Stevenson as Hawtree, H. J. Montague as D'Alroy and Mme. Ponisi as the Marchioness. This was followed by the Planché comedietta, " The Captain of the Watch," one of Wallack's best parts; " John Garth," in which he was also very successful, " Diplomacy " and " A Scrap of Paper." The production of " Our Girls " November 6, 1879, served for the American début of Maurice Barrymore, a handsome young English actor of the romantic type, in the rôle of Tony Judson. His real name was Blythe and he was born in India in 1847. After studying at Harrow and Oxford he went on the stage, coming to this country in 1875 with Charles Vandenhoff and making his American début at the Boston Theatre in 1875 in " Under the Gaslight." Later, he was seen as Captain Molineux in " The Shaughraun." In 1876, he married Georgiana Drew, daughter of Mrs. John Drew, and in this way these two prominent theatrical families became related. In 1875, Barrymore made his first New York appearance at the Fifth Avenue Theatre in " The Big Bonanza." He remained with Mr. Daly two seasons and left him to act in support of Fanny Davenport. At Wallack's he was very successful in leading rôles, and in 1882 joined Mme. Modjeska. He was the author of several plays, notably a drama of Polish life, called " Nadjeska," which Modjeska produced. Afterwards, he was leading man in A. M. Palmer's stock company. He had three children, all of whom have since become very popular on our stage—Lionel, Ethel and John Barrymore.

By the year 1880, Wallack began to consider a change of location. A very decided uptown movement had been in progress in New York for some time, and Thirteenth Street was soon considered an inconvenient position by the class of theatregoers to whom Wallack's appealed. The following year, therefore, Wallack built a new theatre at the corner of Thirtieth Street and Broadway, and opened there on January 4, 1882, with a splendid revival of "The School of Scandal." Rose Coghlan appeared as Lady Teazle, John Gilbert as Sir Peter, Mme. Ponisi as Mrs. Candour and Osmond Tearle as Charles. Other interesting bills followed, including "The Money Spinner," by A. W. Pinero; "Youth," an English spectacular piece, and "La Belle Russe," by David Belasco, but the new house failed to maintain the prestige of the old establishment. Melodrama and other sensational attractions were allowed to invade the glorious stage of Wallack's, and inevitably the work of the stock company deteriorated. On November 6, Mrs. Langtry, the English professional beauty, made her American début in "An Unequal Match," supported by her own English company. Later, she was seen as Rosalind in "As You Like It." Lester Wallack made his reappearance January 3, 1883, in "Ours" and two weeks later was seen as Young Marlow in "She Stoops to Conquer." On January 27, "The Silver King" was acted for the first time in America, and the following Spring saw the first performance in this country of George Ohnet's drama,

"Le Maitre de Forges," with Rose Coghlan as Lady Clare and Osmond Tearle as the ironmaster.

In the Fall of 1884, Mme. Théo, a popular French singing comedienne, was seen for the first time at Wallack's, and the following year, Mme. Judic, another famous French light opera singer, was heard in "Nitouche." That same season (1885) Kyrle Bellew, a picturesque looking and talented actor who won great popularity in romantic rôles, and later toured in association with Mrs. James Brown Potter, made his American début in "In His Power." A few nights later he was seen as Captain Absolute in "The Rivals."

Lester Wallack was seen again in "A Scrap of Paper," "London Assurance," "Impulse," "Diplomacy," "Valerie," "Home" and "Central Park." These were the last appearances of the famous actor-manager. When he had last acted "Young" Marlow (December 8, 1884) he was already sixty-four years old. His last appearance at Wallack's took place on April 19, 1886, as Viscount de Ligny in "The Captain of the Watch." He did not act again, but remained in control of the theatre until October, 1887, when he retired from the management. His last appearance on any stage was at the Grand Opera House, on May 29, 1886, when he was again seen as Young Marlow in "She Stoops to Conquer." On May 21, 1881, he was tendered a benefit at the Metropolitan Opera House, which, for the prominence of the actors and actresses taking part, will ever remain one of the most famous affairs of the kind ever organized. "Hamlet" was the play given, the remarkable cast being as follows:

THE THEATRE IN AMERICA

Hamlet, Edwin Booth; Ghost of Hamlet's father, Lawrence Barrett; King Claudius, Frank Mayo; Polonius, John Gilbert; Laertes, Eben Plympton; Horatio, John A. Lane; Rosencranz, Charles Hanford; Guildenstern, Lawrence Hanley; Osric, Charles Koehler; Marcellus, Edwin H. Vanderfelt; Bernardo, Herbert Kelcey; Francisco, Frank Mordaunt; First Actor, Joseph Wheelock; Second Actor, Milnes Levick; First Gravedigger, Joseph Jefferson; Second Gravedigger, W. J. Florence; Priest, Harry Edwards; Ophelia, Helena Modjeska; The Queen, Gertrude Kellogg; the Player Queen, Rose Coghlan.

Lester Wallack died September 6, 1888.

CHAPTER XXIV

DION BOUCICAULT, RACHEL AND FECHTER

COMING OF AGNES ROBERTSON. BOUCICAULT'S IRISH PLAYS. ANEC-
DOTES OF THE PLAYWRIGHT. FIRST PRODUCTION OF " THE OCTO-
ROON." RACHEL'S TOUR DISAPPOINTING. LAURA KEENE'S
VARIETIES. BURTON'S. MATILDA HERON AS NANCY SYKES. THE
CELEBRATED " COUNT " JOANNES. WINTER GARDEN DESTROYED
BY FIRE.

AFTER Wallack left Brougham's Lyceum in 1861
to go further uptown, the house was reopened as the
Broadway Music Hall. Tony Pastor, New York's
pioneer variety manager, made one of his earliest
appearances at this theatre. The enterprise was not
a success, and from now on the house frequently
changed hands. On March 1, 1862, it was opened as
the New York Athenæum, and after a few weeks' poor
business was closed and reopened as Mary Prevost's
Theatre. Wilkes Booth appeared here as Richard III.
Later, George L. Fox, the pantomimist, took a lease,
opening the house as George L. Fox's Olympic. The
place had varying fortunes until 1864, when George
Wood, the Cincinnati manager, leased the house,
made alterations and reopened it as the Broadway.

Under the new management, the theatre regained
much of its former prestige, and many prominent
stars appeared on its boards, among others the Keans,
Edwin Forrest in " Virginius," with Barton Hill in
his support, Mrs. Jean Davenport Lander in " Elizabeth, Queen of England," F. S. Chanfrau in " Sam,"

THE THEATRE IN AMERICA

Mr. and Mrs. W. J. Florence, Madame Celeste in " The Woman in Red," Maggie Mitchell in " Fanchon," J. H. Hackett as Falstaff, E. L. Davenport as Damon, Julia Dean in " The Hunchback," Lotta in " Little Nell," John E. Owens as Solon Shingle and Adah Isaacs Menken in " Mazeppa." It is also interesting to note that when Helen Western presented " Satan in Paris," at this house April 28, 1866, James A. Herne, the author of " Shore Acres," was in her support.

On August 5, 1867, Robertson's play " Caste " was performed at this house for the first time in America, with this distribution of the parts:

Hon. George D'Alroy ....W. J. Florence
Captain Hawtree ....Owen Marlowe
Eccles ....William Davidge
Sam Gerridge ....Edward Lamb
Marquise St. Maur ....Mrs. G. H. Gilbert
Esther Eccles ....Mrs. F. S. Chanfrau
Polly Eccles ....Mrs. W. J. Florence

The last performance here took place April 28, 1869, with a benefit performance for the business manager, William A. Moore. The bill included Mr. and Mrs. Barney Williams in " Ireland As It Was," followed by a *pas de deux* by the dancers Signor Novissimo and Marie Bonfanti. Soon afterwards the theatre was torn down.

Burton's popular Chambers Street Theatre, although feeling the formidable rivalry of Wallack's, introduced to the New York stage some interesting artists about this time. The season of 1852 opened on August 23 with " The King's Gardener," W. H. Norton, an English actor, who was later a favorite

DION BOUCICAULT, RACHEL, FECHTER

with Wallack audiences, making his début as Captain Popham in " The Eton Boy," Mr. Burton appearing as Toodle.

On the 30th, Charles Fisher, another English comedian who became a great favorite both at Wallack's and Daly's, made his first appearance in this country as Ferment in " The School of Reform." Later, he was seen as Mantalini in " Nicholas Nickleby." The next season began August 10, 1853, with a triple bill—" A Capital Match," " A Duel in the Dark " and " The Secret "—Mr. Holland appearing in the last piece as Thomas, a part he played over five hundred times.

It was at this house, on October 22, that Agnes Robertson, a young Scotch actress, remarkable for her beauty and charming simplicity, made her first appearance in America as Maria in " The Young Actress," a musical interlude written by her husband, Dion Boucicault.

Born in Edinburgh in 1833, Agnes Robertson was a protégée of Mr. and Mrs. Charles Kean. She had joined them in 1851, playing Nerissa in their production of " The Merchant of Venice," and was a member of their company at the Princess', where Boucicault was employed as adaptor and translator of plays. The brilliant, witty Irish dramatist at once won her heart, and although the Keans strenuously opposed the match the young couple were married and came to America together in the Fall of 1853.

A most sympathetic and graceful comedienne, Agnes Robertson quickly established herself in the affections of American theatregoers. In Boston, her popularity was so great that seats were sold at a premium, and later she visited the principal cities South and West with equal success. In after seasons, she played the leading feminine rôles in most of her husband's plays. She was the Jessie Brown in his drama, "Jessie Brown, or the Relief of Lucknow," produced at Wallack's February 22, 1858; played Dot in his dramatization of "The Cricket on the Hearth"; Smike in his stage version of "Nicholas Nickleby," and Jennie Deans in his dramatization of "The Heart of Midlothian," produced at Laura Keene's Theatre in 1860. She also originated the rôles of Zoe in "The Octoroon" (1859) and Eily O'Connor in "The Colleen Bawn" (1860).

Dion Boucicault, whose fame rests chiefly on his romantic Irish plays, made his American début at the Old Broadway Theatre, November 10, 1854, as Sir Charles Coldstream in his own farce, "Used Up." This was the beginning of the career in this country of a remarkably brilliant man, an actor-playwright with an extraordinary instinct for the stage, who from that time up to the day of his death dominated the American theatre.

Dion Boucicault was born in Dublin about 1822, the family being of French descent. He was educated as a civil engineer, but, finding that vocation little to his taste, he began to dabble in playwriting. His first piece, "A Lover by Proxy," was refused by the management of Covent Garden, but his next attempt, "London Assurance," produced May 4, 1841, proved a great success and established Boucicault's reputation as a dramatist to be reckoned with. Other plays written at this period were "The Irish Heiress," "Alma Mater," "Woman," "Old Heads

204

and Young Hearts," "A School for Scheming,"
" Confidence," " The Knight of Arva," " The Broken
Vow," " The Queen of Spades," and "The Vampire."
In America, he acted in several of his own plays.
In " Smike," he appeared as Mantalini, and in " The
Octoroon " he played the Indian Wah-no-Tee. In
" The Shaughraun " he was seen as Conn. His great-
est hit was as the romantic peasant Myles-na-Coppa-
leen in " The Colleen Bawn." But it was as a drama-
tist that he attracted most attention. He wrote in all
over 400 plays and adaptations, some of them being:
" Love in a Maze," " The Dublin Boy," " Grimaldi,"
" Used Up," " The Willow Copse," " Janet Pride,"
" How She Loved Him," " The Fox Hunt," " The
Old Guard," " Arrah na Pogue," " Rip Van Win-
kle," " The Long Strike," " Louis XI," " The Flying
Scud," " Foul Play," " The Corsican Brothers,"
" The Streets of New York," " Omoo," " To Parents
and Guardians," " Presumptive Evidence," " The
Cherry Tree Inn," " After Dark," " Hunted Down,"
" A Dark Night's Work," " Jezabel," " Led Astray,"
" Mora," " Mimi," " Belle Lamar," " The Man of
Honor," " Rescued," " A Bridal Tour," " The Jilt,"
" Robert Emmet," " Ninety Nine."
Most of these and his other plays were adaptations
from French originals. With a thorough knowledge
of French, speaking and writing the language flu-
ently, he gathered his materials from many French
sources, never hesitating to appropriate freely whatever served his purpose. " Like Shakespeare and
Molière," said Charles Reade, " the beggar steals
everything he can lay his hands on; but he does it so
deftly, so cleverly, that I can't help condoning the

theft. He picks up a pebble by the shore and polishes it into a jewel. Occasionally, too, he writes divine lines, and knows more about the grammar of the stage than all the rest of them put together."

" Boucicault's supreme talent," says William Winter, " was a felicitous dexterity in making a story tell itself in action rather than in words. . . . His equivoke was clever, and his writing, like his talk,— and, indeed, like his personality,—was colored with a dry, droll humor." The critic goes on:

In drama Boucicault's supreme achievements are the ticking of the telegraph, in " The Long Strike "; the midnight farewell of the schoolmaster, in " The Parish Clerk "; the incident of Jessie's concealment of the broken floor, in " Jessie Brown "; the heroic self-sacrifice of Shaun, in " Arrah-na-Pogue "; the sentinels in the opening scene of " Belle Lamar "; and the pathetic situation wherein the poor old father learns that his son's honor has been vindicated, in " Daddy O'Dowd." As an actor Boucicault will be remembered chiefly for his impersonation of Conn, in " The Shaughraun." That play was original with him, in every respect. The best performance that he ever gave was that of Daddy O'Dowd,—a performance that completely illuminated the entire method of his acting. He was himself as cold as steel, but he knew the emotions by sight, and he mingled them as a chemist mingles chemicals; generally, with success.[1]

In personal appearance Boucicault was not unlike Shakespeare, a fact on which he rather prided himself. His head was bald, his face oval, while his eyes, shrewd and alert, gave to his countenance a crafty expression. He made large fortunes with his plays, but lived in a style of the greatest extravagance. John Coleman, the actor, has given us some idea of the dramatist's manner of living:

[1] Other Days. Copyright, 1908, by William Winter. Moffat, Yard & Company, Publishers. Reprinted by permission of Jefferson Winter, Esq.

DION BOUCICAULT, RACHEL, FECHTER

This distinguished actor and author had (so he himself told me) left England under a cloud, but had " cast his nighted color off " in America, and returned to triumph. When we first met he was living " en grand seigneur " in the famous mansion at Kensington Gore, which had formerly been the home of the Countess of Blessington. He was then making a fortune one moment and spending it the next. . . . His accomplishments were many and varied. He knew something about everything, and what he didn't know about the popular drama (which to some extent he incarnated in himself) wasn't worth knowing. Although no longer young, his mind was alert as a boy's, and I can well believe what Charles Mathews, Walter Lacey and John Brougham often told me—that in his juvenilia he was the most fascinating young scapegoat that ever baffled or bamboozled a bailiff. He was still handsome. His head, though perfectly bald, was shaped like the dome of a temple, and was superbly, I may say, Shakespeareanly, beautiful. His face was a perfect oval, his eyes brilliant, his figure elegant.[2]

Not content with his numerous activities as a playwright, Boucicault also lectured on theatrical art, and went into management on his own account. In 1859, he joined William Stuart in presenting Jefferson in repertoire at the Winter Garden, and in London he took a lease of Astley's.

He was only seventy when he died, but he had lived the lives of two men. Up to the time of his death, he remained in harness, striving to turn out a new play that might refill his badly depleted coffers. Only a few weeks before the end, A. M. Palmer asked him for a play for the Madison Square Theatre. The veteran dramatist set to work and submitted a scenario, but it no longer had the old Boucicault quality. The once sparkling wit was dulled, the keen mentality no longer there. Palmer, to his

[2] Plays and Playwrights I Have Known. By John Coleman.

regret, was compelled to decline the play. Meantime, the dramatist's health was rapidly failing. The end came quickly and he died at his New York residence September 18, 1890.

A New York theatre which had an unusually eventful history during its comparatively brief existence was " Tripler Hall," situated on the West side of Broadway, nearly opposite Bond Street, and built originally for a music hall to serve for the début of Jenny Lind. Not being ready in time for that event, it was opened October 17, 1850, by Mme. Anna Bishop, that popular vocalist being followed by Henrietta Sontag and Alboni. A few years later, the concert hall was damaged by fire and when repairs had been made the place was reopened as the Metropolitan.

Here, on September 3, 1855, Madame Rachel, the greatest tragic actress France has ever produced, made her first appearance before an American public as Camille in Corneille's tragedy, " Les Horaces." The great French tragedienne at this period was thirty-four years old, well past the zenith of her fame and already bore within her the germs of the malady which, three years later, carried her to the grave. The American tour had been undertaken at the urgent prompting of her brother, who, fascinated by the reports of Jenny Lind's large earnings, promised receipts equally satisfactory. The results disappointed expectations. Listening to a singer whose trills one can enjoy without having to know the language in which she sings, is a very different matter to trying to follow an actress in a rôle acted in a tongue with which one is not familiar. The French colony was small, and, as only about one in twenty of the Americans present understood French, the severely classic tragedy, with its long and tedious speeches, proved too much for the patience of the audience. Public support was not forthcoming, and this in spite of the critics who did not spare their praise. The *Tribune's* reviewer wrote:

There was but one feeling; she surpassed expectation, and the enthusiasm of shout and flowers in which it found expression evidently convinced her that the American people know how to appreciate and reward true genius.

Figures, however, spoke more eloquently than words. The first night's receipts were only $5016, not a third of the amount taken in by Jenny Lind, and the second night when she appeared as Phédre, her finest rôle, they fell still lower. If her health had not given way, compelling her return to France, it is probable that the actress would have had to cancel her tour, confessing it to be a failure. Yet twenty years later, another famous French tragedienne, Sarah Bernhardt, an actress endowed with far less genius, made a triumphant tour of America and went back to Paris with a million!

While playing in Philadelphia, Rachel contracted a cold which aggravated her malady. Returning to France, she died there, January 5, 1858.

On the termination of the Rachel season, Laura Keene took a lease of the house, which she rechristened "Laura Keene's Varieties" and opened December 27, 1855, with Boucicault's "Old Heads and Young Hearts." The following year, owing to a flaw in the lease, she was compelled to surrender the theatre to W. E. Burton, and John W. Trimble, the architect, built her another theatre on the east side of Broadway above Houston Street, which she also called " Laura Keene's Varieties " and opened November 18, 1856, with " As You Like It." This famous playhouse, after a long and prosperous career, passed into the hands of Mrs. John Wood, the popular English burlesque actress, who reopened it as Mrs. John Wood's Olympic. It was at this house, on March 10, 1868, that George L. Fox, the popular clown, presented his successful pantomime, "Humpty Dumpty," which had an extraordinary run of four hundred and eighty-three performances.

Burton's opened September 8, 1856, with a performance of " The Rivals." Burton continued in control for two years, but at the end of that time, having lost both money and patronage, he withdrew and the house was reopened in 1859 as the New Metropolitan. Later that same year it again changed hands, the new lessees being William Stuart and Dion Boucicault, who made extensive alterations and reopened the place September 14, 1859, as the Winter Garden, the bill being " The Cricket on the Hearth," with Agnes Robertson as Dot.

On December 5, Boucicault's famous anti-slavery drama, " The Octoroon," was seen there for the first time, Agnes Robertson appearing as Zoe and Boucicault himself as Wah-no-tee. A few days after the première, Mr. and Mrs. Boucicault withdrew from the Winter Garden, owing to a misunderstanding as to the division of the receipts.

On February 2, " Oliver Twist " was seen for the first time, Matilda Heron appearing as Nancy Sykes and J. W. Wallack, Jr., making his big hit as Fagin.

210

DION BOUCICAULT, RACHEL, FECHTER

Later in the spring, Mareztek's opera company began an engagement, and on April 30 Halévy's opera, " La Juive," was sung at this house for the first time in America.

Many players who were very popular on the American stage appeared at the Winter Garden about this time. Among them were Mrs. John Wood; Julia Dean Hayne, daughter of the well-known Western actress and herself long a great favorite both in California and the East; Avonia Jones, sister of the celebrated " Count " Joannes ' and herself a distinguished tragedienne; Fanny Herring, a great favorite at the Old Bowery; J. H. Stoddart, famous for his old men; Mr. and Mrs. Barney Williams, who starred together in Irish plays; Charles R. Thorne, Jr., son of the old-time actor-manager and destined to become leading man of the famous Union Square Theatre; John Dyott, a well-known and popular actor whose wife, Ireland tells us, was a very useful actress " in countesses and chambermaids "; Kate Reignolds, very popular at Burton's Chambers Street Theatre and for a long time the reigning favorite at Laura Keene's Theatre; Mrs. D. P. Bowers, a Shakespearian manager and actress who was an immense favorite in Philadelphia; John Sleeper Clarke, the eminent American comedian and brother-in-law of Edwin Booth; Kate Bateman, her first appearance since childhood; Charles Walcot, later leading man at Laura Keene's Theatre; Cecile Rush, a popular actress who

---

' "Count Joannes," or George Jones, was an eccentric figure of the American stage. Born in England in 1810, he made his first appearance as an actor in Philadelphia in 1831. Later, he went into management and built the Avon Theatre at Norfolk, Va. After a tour in Europe he returned to this country and, assuming the title of "count," showed himself so eccentric that theatre audiences guyed him unmercifully.

had made her début in Philadelphia as Bianca in
" Fazio " in 1856 and later became a successful star;
Mrs. Sedley Brown, known as Mrs. Sol Smith; and
Maggie Mitchell.

This last actress, a prime favorite with American
theatre audiences in the sixties, in " Fanchon " and
other pieces, was born in New York in 1837. In 1857
she was applauded at Burton's as Julia in " The Soldier's Daughter," and shortly afterwards toured in
the South and West in such plays as " The Young
Prince," " The Spy," etc. Her greatest success was
in " Fanchon the Cricket," a play adapted from the
French of George Sand. She was first seen in the
piece at the St. Charles Theatre, New Orleans, in
1860, and two years later (June 9, 1862) she repeated
her success at Laura Keene's Theatre, New York.

The Winter Garden was completely destroyed by
fire on March 23, 1867.

On January 10, 1870, at Niblo's, Charles Fechter
made his first appearance in this country as Ruy Blas
in Hugo's tragedy of that title.

This famous French artiste, who made America
his home during the early seventies and was prominently connected with our stage both as manager and
actor, was born in London in 1824. His father was
a Frenchman of German descent, and his mother an
Italian. After being educated in France and studying dramatic art at the Conservatoire, he made his
début at the Théâtre Français in 1844, and from that
time until 1860 he was a great favorite with the Paris
public, particularly as Armand Duval, which he
played to the Marguerite Gauthier of Eugenie Doche
in the first production of " La Dame aux Camélias."

DION BOUCICAULT, RACHEL, FECHTER

In 1860, he went to England and acted in English at the Princess Theatre such rôles as Ruy Blas, the Corsican Brothers, Don Cæsar de Bazan, Othello and Hamlet, which last rôle he played in a blonde flowing wig. John Coleman has written this description of Fechter as he appeared at that time:

He was of middle height; figure more sturdy than elegant; features distinctly Hebraic, vivacious, expressive, powerful, changeful as the colour of a chameleon's skin; olive-complexioned; piercing but penetrating eyes, now melting with the languor of love, now ablaze with the lurid light of hell; firm, well-cut mouth, which opened and shut like the jaws of a bulldog; massive head with a thatch of dark brown hair; bull neck splendidly poised, but a little too short. Such was Fechter when first I beheld him. He was then a man of forty, but, had I not known it, I should have guessed him five and twenty at the outside. At first the voice seemed guttural, the French accent unendurable, but it was only at first. After a few moments the voice made music and I forgot all about the accent.[4]

Later, he went into management, securing a lease of the Lyceum, which he opened with " The Duke's Motto." A man of new ideas, he began his managerial régime by abolishing back of the curtain many of the traditions heretofore sacred to the theatre. Baker, in his " History of the London Stage," says:

Fechter inaugurated a new idea in English histrionic art that led to the great theatrical revival of the nineteenth century. He began by revolutionizing the stage. The ancient grooves, trapdoors and sticky flats were abolished; the flooring so constructed that it could be taken to pieces like a child's puzzle; scenery could be raised or sunk bodily and all the shifting was done on the mezzanine stage beneath; ceilings were no longer represented by hanging cloths, or the walls of a room by open wings, but were solidly built.

---

[4] Players and Playwrights I Have Known. By John Coleman.

THE THEATRE IN AMERICA

After appearing for a few weeks in New York, Fechter went to Boston, where he opened in March at the Boston Theatre. His success in Boston was immediate. The critics disapproved of his Hamlet, but the fascination of the man and his polished style of acting were undeniable. " With the appearance of Fechter," says H. A. Clapp, " American audiences first came in contact with an actor of great natural gifts and Continental training, who used the English language at his performances." The critic continues:

In many ways the experience was a revelation. Here was the culture of the Comédie Française, conveyed through the vernacular, and not under the immense disadvantage of exposition in a foreign tongue. One could see, as Fechter played, the potency of abundant but perfectly appropriate gesture, the action fitted to the very word, the word to the action, according to Hamlet's prescript; the trained aptitude for rapid transitions of feeling; the large freedom of movement; the ease and force of style which seemed spontaneous and unstudied, when most refined. After an experience of Fechter in tragedy or romance, one returned to our great native artists, and found them, by contrast, rather cool and starchy.[1]

For a time Fechter was manager of the Globe Theatre, Boston, and later he was connected with the Park Theatre, corner of Broadway and Twenty-second Street, New York. Failure, however, persistently attended all his American managerial ventures and after final appearances at the Broadway Theatre in 1877, when he was seen as Monte Christo, Hamlet, and Ruy Blas, he retired permanently from the stage.

Carlotta Leclercq, who supported Mr. Fechter in this country, afterwards undertook a starring tour and proved very popular both in comedy and tragedy.

[1] Reminiscences of a Dramatic Critic. Copyright, 1902, by Henry Austin Clapp. Houghton, Mifflin Co., Publishers.

CHAPTER XXV

THE RISE OF EDWIN BOOTH

FIRST OPPORTUNITY. TRIUMPHS IN CALIFORNIA. VISIT TO LONDON. ASSASSINATION OF LINCOLN BY JOHN WILKES BOOTH. RETURN TO THE STAGE. BUILDING OF BOOTH'S THEATRE. ASSOCIATION WITH LAWRENCE BARRETT. GIFT OF THE PLAYERS CLUB. CRITICAL OPINION AS TO HIS RANK AS A PLAYER. LAWRENCE BARRETT AND JOHN M'CULLOUGH.

THAT erratic stage genius, Junius Brutus Booth, when he died in 1852, left behind him four sons, three of whom became actors—Junius Brutus Booth, Jr., who never achieved fame on the stage; John Wilkes Booth, who inherited his father's fiery temperament and came to a shameful end as the assassin of President Lincoln, and Edwin Booth, the most popular, if not the greatest, actor America has yet produced.

Edwin Booth was born on his father's farm, Harford County, Maryland, November 13, 1833. He probably had but a superficial education, for at an early age we find him accompanying his famous father on tour, nominally as attendant and dresser, but in fact as the " chosen monitor and guardian of that wild genius."[1] His first appearance upon any stage was at the Boston Museum, September 10, 1849, in the minor part of Tressel in " Richard III." For the next two years he continued to act with his father, serving his apprenticeship in a large number of minor rôles, and advancing steadily in his profession. In

[1] The Elder and Younger Booth. By Asia Booth Clarke.

215

1851 came the great opportunity which is said to knock at every man's door at least once in a lifetime. His father had been billed to appear as Richard III at the National Theatre, New York, but at the eleventh hour was unable to appear. It was thought afterwards that he had feigned illness to permit of Edwin substituting him. No announcement was made and a large audience had gathered, eager to see a famous tragedian in his best part. At first, the new Gloster was received with coldness, but as the play proceeded and the young actor revealed unexpected powers, the house gradually forgot its first disappointment and finally broke into hearty applause.

Soon after this, Edwin went out to California, joining his brother, Junius Brutus, Jr., at the Jenny Lind Theatre, San Francisco. Later, he accompanied his father to Sacramento, Edwin playing Jaffier to the elder Booth's Pierre in " Venice Preserved." It was on seeing himself in the sable trappings of Jaffier that the young actor was first fired with the ambition to one day attempt Hamlet, a rôle which in after years was to bring him fame and fortune. A few months later, in San Francisco, he appeared as Richard III, taking the town by storm. This triumph was followed by performances of Sir Giles Overreach and Macbeth, crowds pouring into the theatre to see and applaud him.

Returning East, he first appeared at Baltimore, where he enacted Richard. Then followed a tour of the South. At Richmond he met the lovely Mary Devlin, who afterwards became his wife. In 1857, he appeared as Richard III at Burton's Metropolitan for the first time before a New York audience, " with a brilliancy and force," says Ireland, " that surpassed the warmest expectations." During that same engagement, he appeared as Sir Giles Overreach, Richelieu, Shylock, Lear, Romeo, Hamlet, Claude Melnotte, Sir Edward Mortimer and Petruchio.

In 1861 he went to London, appearing at the Haymarket as Shylock. The visit was ill timed. The Civil War was brewing and, English sympathy being largely with the South, " Yankees " were not very popular. Booth was received coldly in " The Merchant," but later, when he gave " Richelieu," he aroused more enthusiasm. In Manchester, he was supported by Henry Irving, the English actor playing Laertes to his Hamlet, Cassio to his Othello, etc.

On his return to America, he appeared at the Winter Garden (formerly the Metropolitan) September 29, 1862, acting Hamlet, Othello, Richelieu, Romeo, Iago and other rôles of his repertoire. The following year his wife died, a crushing sorrow from which he never fully recovered. The same year, he and his brother-in-law, John Sleeper Clarke, became joint proprietors of the Walnut Street Theatre, Philadelphia, and the year following they joined William Stuart in leasing the New York Winter Garden, where, November 25, 1864, took place the memorable performance of " Julius Cæsar," with the three brothers, Junius Brutus, Jr., Edwin and John Wilkes, as Cassius, Brutus and Mark Antony respectively. That same month Edwin Booth appeared as Hamlet, which he enacted for one hundred consecutive nights, the longest run any Shakespearian play had ever known in America.

It was while he was thus at the zenith of his fame

217

THE THEATRE IN AMERICA

and powers that, like a bolt from the blue, came the blow which for a time threatened to engulf him and the entire Booth family in irretrievable disgrace and ruin. On April 14, 1865, while President Lincoln was watching a performance of the comedy " Our American Cousin " at Ford's Theatre, Washington, John Wilkes Booth, who was a Southern sympathizer, forced his way into the Presidential box and fired a pistol at the President. Seeing that his bullet had found its mark, Booth leaped from the box to the stage, breaking his leg in the jump. Then crying with theatrical gesture " Sic Semper Tyrannis! " (Thus tyrants shall all perish!), he made his escape through the stage door, where he had a horse in waiting.

Laura Keene, and her associates engaged in the performance, had heard the shot, but were too much dazed to realize what had happened. The audience, for a moment stupefied, rose the next instant in pandemonium. The President was hastily carried to a house near by, but all efforts to save him were unavailing and he died soon after. Meantime, hot pursuit had been organized after the assassin, who was finally overtaken and shot down by the pursuing patrol. Several persons were arrested for complicity in Booth's plot and executed.

Overwhelmed, by this catastrophe, Edwin Booth at once retired from the stage, but the following year, yielding to assurances that the public did not hold him responsible for a brother's guilt, he reappeared at the Winter Garden (January 3, 1866) as Hamlet, when he received a tremendous ovation, all the spectators rising as he came upon the stage and greeting him with cheers.

THE RISE OF EDWIN BOOTH

At the Winter Garden, during this season of 1866, Booth made some brilliant revivals of " Richelieu," " Othello " and " The Merchant of Venice." In March, 1867, the theatre was destroyed by fire and the following year the tragedian laid the foundation stone of Booth's Theatre, a splendid playhouse costing a million dollars, situated at the corner of Sixth Avenue and Twenty-third Street, New York. Meantime, Booth had become betrothed to Mary F. McVicker, an actress who played Juliet to his Romeo the night Booth's Theatre was opened to the public, February 3, 1869. The second production was " Othello," followed by Edwin Adams in " Enoch Arden." On January 9, 1871, " Richelieu " was revived with great splendor of costume and *mise-en-scène,* and on April 24 " A Winter's Tale " was put on at a cost of $40,000. No money was spared in realizing at this theatre all that was best in Booth's aspirations as a theatrical artist. Productions vied with each other in magnificence. The pace was too swift to be kept up. " Booth's management of Booth's Theatre was remarkable," says his sister and biographer, " for the continuity of its success, but the outlay was enormous." Finally, the strain on his mental and physical health became too severe and in 1873 Edwin Booth let the theatre to his brother, J. B. Booth. Bankruptcy followed and the tragedian was compelled to surrender all his personal property to his creditors.

After his relinquishment of Booth's Theatre, Edwin Booth never again participated in theatrical management. For the next twenty years he was a travelling star, the monotony of " starring " being relieved by occasional visits to London, where, on the invitation of Henry Irving, he appeared in 1881 at the Lyceum Theatre, playing Othello to Irving's Iago. In 1890, he joined the late Lawrence Barrett in a joint starring tour, but his health was already failing and he found himself unequal to the physical strain. His last appearance on the stage was at the Academy of Music, Brooklyn, April 4, 1891, as Hamlet.

A few years previously he had made a gift to the members of his profession of the residence he owned at 16 Gramercy Park, New York, together with all the books and art treasures it contained, to be used as a club and held in trust for future generations of players. The Players was incorporated in 1888 and is to-day the leading theatrical club in this country. For his own use, Booth had reserved a suite on the third floor of The Players, and here he died, June 8, 1893, in his sixtieth year.

Critical opinion differs as to Edwin Booth's rank as an actor. William Winter declares him the " foremost and best of American actors." The critic goes on to say:

Under the influence of Forrest, and later of Charlotte Cushman and E. L. Davenport, the American stage began to assume a distinctive character. Its growth, since then, in the elements of individuality and theatrical prosperity, has been rapid, continuous, and luxuriant. The transition from Forrest to Edwin Booth marked the most important phase of its development. Forrest, although he had a spark of genius, was intrinsically and essentially animal. Booth was intellectual and spiritual. Forrest obtained his popularity, and the bulk of his large fortune, by impersonating the Indian chieftain Metamora. Booth gained and held his eminence by acting Hamlet and Richelieu. The epoch that accepted

THE RISE OF EDWIN BOOTH

Booth as the amplest exponent of its taste and feeling in dramatic art was one of intellect and refinement. The tendency of theatrical life received then a favorable impulse which has never ceased to operate. Other forces have helped to accelerate progress, and to foster the higher elements of the drama; but it was the influence of Edwin Booth that cleared and smoothed the way. Wallack was cheered by it, in the management of that theatre which long held the first position. Jefferson, in consequence of it, more readily found a public that was appreciative of his gentle genius and delicate art. The brilliant career of Augustin Daly as a manager became more easily possible, and so did the thoughtful, ambitious, public spirited enterprise of Albert M. Palmer. That intellectual and noble actor, Lawrence Barrett, who made Booth his model, was, in a great degree, the direct consequence of it. Every appellant to the best order of public taste—Henry Irving, Ellen Terry, Genevieve Ward, Mary Anderson, Helena Modjeska, Ada Rehan, Richard Mansfield, Edward S. Willard, Charles Wyndham, Toole, Mrs. Langtry, the Kendals, each later votary of acting,—found a readier hearing and an easier conquest, because Edwin Booth's ministrations had developed acuteness of perception, diffused refinement, awakened emotion, imparted spiritual knowledge of a lofty ideal, and provided a high standard of dramatic art.[2]

Other critics, while conceding the lovable qualities of the man, are more reserved in their praise of his powers as an actor. In the opinion of Alfred Ayres:

Booth's place as an actor, great as he was as an entertainer, is not among the great; yet after the death of Forrest he was easily our best player of tragic parts. Mr. Booth had a good figure, a head of oriental beauty, a good, though not a big, voice, and his facility in articulating was phenomenal. No matter how rapidly he spoke, the words always came from him clean cut and sharply defined. With dramatic instinct he was generously endowed and he was a close student of dramatic situations. In repose he was singularly lacking—he was always gesticulating with his forearm or shaking his finger at somebody—and his reading was exceedingly

[2] Life and Art of Edwin Booth. By William Winter. Copyright by Jefferson Winter. Reprinted by permission.

faulty. Never, probably, has there been another actor with a great reputation that misplaced his emphasis as often as did Edwin Booth. Even in Hamlet, when he had played the part perhaps a thousand times, he was absolutely exasperating. But he could be in earnest, terribly in earnest, and earnestness makes amends for more sins twice over in a player than does any other one thing.[3]

John Ranken Towse says of him:

Less virile than the muscular Forrest, whom he succeeded, he excelled him in subtlety, brains, grace, and real dramatic fire, while, at his best, he was superior to E. L. Davenport—a far more versatile performer—John McCullough, Lawrence Barrett, and other less prominent rivals. . . . He was a great but not, I think, a very great actor, and a most accomplished artist, expert in all stage technique and artifice. . . . That Booth could give fine expression to the nobler attributes of humanity, if not in their highest imaginative development, he proved abundantly by his Brutus and parts of his Othello and Hamlet, but it is nevertheless a fact that he was most triumphant in characters containing a baser alloy. His alert manner, his flashing eyes, his crisp, somewhat metallic utterance, his capacity for fierce passion, his general suggestion of an agile mentality, constituted a most valuable equipment for parts in which the intellectual dominated over the moral or the sentimental. . . . He was a well graced actor, if ever there was one, and by his personal achievement he fairly won the distinguished place which he will always occupy in the annals of the American stage. But for the literary and artistic theatre itself, for the preservation or elevation of the art of which he was so able a professor, he did little or nothing. He was content during the greater part of his career, to accept and profit by the conditions which were undermining and ruining it. Able to fill theatres by his unassisted genius and prestige, he acquiesced in a system devised to fill the pockets of stars and managers, and habitually acted with scratch companies of incompetent and untrained players, histrionic scarecrows. In this way he helped to discredit the masterpiece in which he shone.[4]

[3] Edwin Booth. Article by Alfred Ayres in the *Theatre Magazine*, February, 1902.

[4] Sixty Years of the Theatre. Copyright, 1916, by John Ranken Towse. Funk & Wagnalls Company, Publishers. Reprinted by permission.

THE RISE OF EDWIN BOOTH

Booth's earnings as an actor were very large. His share of the profits of the Booth-Barrett combination in three years was $579,600, his weekly share being often more than $10,000. He was a bankrupt, yet, after giving away money right and left by the handful, and giving approximately $150,000 to the Players Club, he still left a fortune of about $600,-000. Such earnings had never been approached by any other player up to his time.

Contemporary with Edwin Booth and intimately associated with that actor during the latter years of his life, was an American tragedian greatly loved by the theatregoing public. This was Lawrence Barrett, characterized by William Winter as " one of the noblest figures of the modern stage."

Born at Paterson, N. J., in 1838, Lawrence Barrett made his first appearance as an actor at Detroit, Mich., in 1853. He was not seen in New York until January 20, 1857, when he played Sir Thomas Clifford in " The Hunchback " at Burton's Chambers Street Theatre. The following year he went to Boston where he remained two years, acting first at the Boston Museum and later at the Howard Athenæum. After another engagement in New York, when he was seen as Iago, he went South and became co-manager of the Varieties, New Orleans. In 1867 he visited California, where he appeared as Hamlet, and two years later, following appearances in England, he joined John McCullough in the management of the California Theatre, San Francisco.

Returning East, he was seen in 1871 at Booth's Theatre, New York, as Cassius in " Julius Cæsar," and a few years later he gave a fine performance of Yorick. In 1881, he appeared as King Arthur in William Young's tragedy, " Pendragon," and the following year was seen as Lanciotto in his own splendid revival of Boker's tragedy, " Francesca da Rimini." Later, he added Ganelon, the hero of William Young's blank verse tragedy, to his repertoire, which included, among other parts, Macbeth, Lear, Othello, Shylock, Wolsey, Richard III, Romeo, Benedick, Richelieu, Garrick, Claude Melnotte, Rienzi, Dan'l Druce, Harebell and Gringoire. " Most of the plays with which his name is identified," says William Winter, " are among the greatest plays in our language, and the spirit in which he treated them was that of exalted scholarship, austere reverence, and perfect refinement." The critic goes on:

He was profoundly true to all that is noble and beautiful, and because he was true the world of art recognized him as the image of fidelity and gave to him the high tribute of unwavering homage. His mental vitality, which was very great, impressed even unsympathetic beholders with a sense of fiery thought struggling in its fetters of mortality and almost shattering and consuming the frail temple of its human life. His stately head, silvered with graying hair; his dark eyes, deeply sunken and glowing with intense light; his thin visage, pallid with study and pain; his form of grace and his voice of sonorous eloquence and solemn music (in compass, variety and sweetness one of the few great voices of his dramatic generation), his tremendous earnestness, his superb bearing, and his invariable authority and distinction—all those attributes united to announce a ruler and leader in the realm of the intellect.[5]

It was, however, as Lanciotto in " Francesca da Rimini " that Barrett gained one of the great successes of his career. The play had originally been

[5] The Wallet of Time. Copyright, 1913, by William Winter. Moffat, Yard & Co., Publishers. Reprinted by permission of Jefferson Winter, Esq.

produced in 1855 and was revived by Mr. Barrett in 1882. Of his performance of the part Mr. Winter has this to say:

He formed the true ideal of Lanciotto—a great soul prisoned in a misshapen body, intense in every feeling, tinctured with bitterness, isolated by deformity, tender and magnanimous, but capable of frantic excess and terrible ferocity; a being marked out for wreck and ruin, and bearing within himself the elements of tragedy and desolation; and Barrett acted the part in one continuous, ever-ascending strain of tumultuous passion. By that means he made the piece a torrent of light,—luminous throughout its whole extent with his electric spirit.[6]

In 1887, Barrett combined forces with Edwin Booth and the two popular stars toured the country, the season beginning with a production of " Julius Cæsar " and the repertoire including " Othello," " Hamlet," " Macbeth," " Lear," " The Merchant of Venice," " Katharine and Petruchio," " The Fool's Revenge," " Don Cæsar de Bazan," " The King's Pleasure " and " David Garrick." The tour was eminently successful and was interrupted only by the death of Barrett, March 20, 1891.

Another actor of noble presence, contemporary with Booth and Barrett, was John McCullough, a tragedian of the heroic type whose personality and art endeared him to the American public.

Born in 1832, in Ireland, where his father was a small farmer, John McCullough came to the United States in 1847. At that time he was fifteen years old and had received so little education that he could not write. His family, which had followed him to

* The Wallet of Time. Copyright, 1913, by William Winter. Moffat, Yard & Co., Publishers. Reprinted by permission of Jefferson Winter, Esq.

America, settled in Philadelphia, and it was after witnessing a theatrical performance at the Arch Street
Theatre that young McCullough decided that no
career would suit him so well as that of an actor.
Fired with this ambition, he took lessons in elocution
and after some training with local amateur organizations, made his first professional appearance at the
Arch Street Theatre, August 15, 1857, as Thomas in
" The Belle's Stratagem." He continued acting at
this theatre until 1860, when he received an offer of
an engagement at the Howard Athenæum, Boston.
The following year he was again in Philadelphia, at
the Walnut Street Theatre, where he attracted the
favorable notice of Edwin Forrest, who offered him
leading parts in his support.

This proved the beginning of McCullough's
rapid advancement in public favor. He first appeared with Forrest in Boston in 1861, playing
Pythias to Forrest's Damon. His other parts at that
period included Laertes, Macduff, Iago, Edgar,
Richard, Icilius and Titus. When Forrest, in 1863,
produced " Coriolanus " at Niblo's Garden, New
York, McCullough appeared as Cominius. After
travelling with Forrest as his principal support for
some time, McCullough, in 1861, accompanied the
tragedian to California and in 1869 while in San
Francisco became manager of the California Theatre in partnership with Lawrence Barrett. He remained on the Pacific Coast eight years, producing
plays at the California Theatre on a scale of magnificence not yet seen in San Francisco. In 1874 he was
back in New York, where he made his first appearance as a star at Booth's Theatre as Spartacus in

THE RISE OF EDWIN BOOTH

" The Gladiator." After several more years' touring throughout the country, he appeared in 1877 at the Boston Museum, the engagement proving one of the most successful ever played. That same year he reappeared at Booth's Theatre, New York, as Virginius. To his repertoire he had also added such parts as Richelieu, Richard III, Othello, Metamora and Lear. In May, 1878, he appeared at the Boston Theatre, acting Claude Melnotte to the Pauline of Mary Anderson, and later that same year he was seen at the Fifth Avenue Theatre, New York, when he appeared as Ingomar to Mary Anderson's Parthenia. In 1881, he went to London, where he appeared at Drury Lane as Virginius and Othello with great success. Returning to America, he was again seen at the Fifth Avenue Theatre as Virginius and later as Lear. In 1883, his health began to fail and he showed the first signs of the mental trouble which a year later deprived him of his reason.

" The acting of McCullough, in all the parts that he played, was marked," says William Winter, " by profound sincerity." The writer continues:

His nature was splendidly self-poised, and that equilibrium enabled him, through years of patient labor, to hold a steadfast course and to surmount all the obstacles which opposed and ignore all the detraction which assails a man who is striving to achieve noble results in art. It also sustained him in the great Shakespearian characters which he essayed to personate, in each of which he was a remarkable, and in some of which a wonderful, figure.[7]

John Ranken Towse considers McCullough inferior to Barrett " in character, in intellect, in subtlety, in ambition and in range." He says:

[7] The Wallet of Time. Copyright, 1913, by William Winter. Moffat, Yard & Co., Publishers. Reprinted by permission of Jefferson Winter, Esq.

227

He was a good actor, within restricted limits, of heroic parts, for which nature had bestowed upon him the physical qualities in which Barrett was deficient. He was a man of noble presence, of powerful build, with bold Roman features and a voice that had in it the ring of the trumpet. A disciple of Forrest, he emulated the methods of his exemplar with considerable success, and in stormy bursts of passion he exhibited vast power. Moreover, he could assume a lofty dignity, in which Forrest was lacking, and had a notable mastery of virile pathos. He excelled in broad strokes, in the vivid contrasts between raging passion, portentous calm, and the inner convulsions caused by repressed emotions. But he was not an intellectual, imaginative or analytical performer. In great parts he was only second-rate. In Lear, for instance, he could stir his hearers to enthusiasm by the magnificent outbursts of passion which seemed to shake the theatre, and in the concluding scenes he depicted the pitiful state of the forlorn old king with simple and genuine pathos, but his impersonation as a whole, though theatrically effective, had neither grandeur nor subtlety. It was not Lear.[3]

The rapid growth and great wealth of the United States continued to attract to our shores at various periods not only the most distinguished of England's players, but also the most renowned of the Continental stars.

Daniel Bandmann, a German actor, came to this country in 1863, making his début at Niblo's as Shylock and became very popular here in Hamlet and other rôles. He went to England in 1868, but returned to America in 1870.

Tommaso Salvini, Italy's illustrious tragedian and one of the greatest actors ever seen in America, made his début here on September 16, 1873, when he thrilled a tremendous audience at the Academy of Music, New York, with his magnificent portrayal of Othello. Supported on that occasion by an Italian

---

[3] Sixty Years of the Theatre. Copyright, 1916, by John Ranken Towse. Funk & Wagnalls Company, Publishers. Reprinted by permission.

company—headed by Signora Piamonti as Desdemona—Salvini gave a performance so realistic and
terrifying that the spectators were held spellbound.
Later, when he engaged an English-speaking company to support him, no American actress could be
found willing to submit, as the Italian leading lady
had done, to the fury of his murderous attack as the
jealous Moor. The way in which he played the scene
is thus described by a spectator:

> Desdemona, not yet disrobed, alarmed by the menace in Othello's
> look and manner, gradually retreated as she replied to his interro-
> gations until she reached the left-hand corner of the stage by the
> footlights. As played by Piamonti—a lovely woman and magnifi-
> cent actress—she was the personification of pitiful, protesting love
> gradually resolving into speechless terror. Salvini, convulsed, with
> fixed and flaming eyes, half-crouched, slowly circled the stage
> toward her, muttering savagely and inarticulately as she cowered
> before him. Rising at last to his full height with extended arms,
> he pounced upon her, lifted her into the air, dashed with her across
> the stage and through the curtains (of the bed), which fell behind
> him. You heard a crash as he flung her on the bed, and growls as
> of a wild beast over his prey. It was awful—utterly, abominably
> un-Shakespearean, if you will, but supremely, paralyzingly real—
> only great genius, imaginative and executive, could have presented
> such a picture of man, bereft by maniacal jealousy of mercy and
> reason, reduced to primeval savagery.[9]

For several seasons, Salvini toured this country
triumphantly in the plays of his repertoire, "Sam-
son," "La Morte Civile," "Sullivan," "Ingomar,"
"Lear" and "Hamlet." In the Spring of 1876, he
appeared together with Edwin Booth in "Hamlet"
at the Academy of Music, Booth acting the Prince
and Salvini the Ghost. Alexander Salvini, a son of

---

[9] Sixty Years of the Theatre. Copyright, 1916, by John Ranken Towse.
Funk & Wagnalls Company, Publishers. Reprinted by permission.

Tommaso, came to America in 1881 and made his permanent home here, acquiring much popularity in romantic rôles.

Sarah Bernhardt was first seen in this country in 1880 at Booth's Theatre, New York, when she appeared as Adrienne in " Adrienne Lecouvreur."

This world-famous French actress was born in Paris in 1845 of French and Dutch Hebrew parentage and educated in a convent. Predestined, both by temperament and natural predilection, to a stage career, she entered the Conservatoire in 1861, and the following year carried off the second prize in tragedy. This gained her admission to the sacred precincts of the Théâtre Français, at which historic house she made her début, September 1, 1862, as Iphigénie in Racine's " Iphigénie en Aulide." She attracted little attention and, greatly discouraged, she retired temporarily, but continued to play burlesque and melodramatic parts at the Gymnase and Porte St. Martin Theatres. In 1867, she returned to the Odéon, where her performance as Donna Maria in " Ruy Blas " aroused much enthusiasm and led to a rearrangement at the Français. Here she remained until 1880, when she became a star and toured all over Europe. During her numerous tours of the United States she has been seen in the following plays: " La Dame aux Camélias," " Fédora," " Frou-Frou," " Phèdre," " Théodora," " Hamlet," " La Tosca," " Gismonda," " Cléopatre," " L'Aiglon," etc.

A peculiarly high-strung, temperamental woman, Bernhardt has been credited with many eccentricities, all of which have been adroitly used to advertise her. In her beautiful Paris home, she kept a young tiger as a domestic pet, much to the alarm of timid visitors, and a weird feature of her boudoir was a satin-lined coffin, concerning which a biographer says:

When Mme. Bernhardt is world weary she gets into this coffin, and covering herself with faded wreaths and flowers, folds her hands across her breast and her eyes closed bids a temporary farewell to life. A lighted candle on a votary table on her left and a death skull grinning on the floor add to the illusion.

Other distinguished continental stars seen here were Coquelin ainé, the famous French comedian who made his American début October 8, 1888, at Palmer's Theatre as Mascarille in " Les Précieuses Ridicules," Jane Hading, his leading woman and co-star, being seen the following evening as Claire in " The Ironmaster "; Mounet-Sully, the distinguished sociétaire of the Comédie Française, who made his début March 24, 1894, at Abbey's Theatre as Hernani; Mme. Réjane, another favorite French artiste, who was seen at Abbey's Theatre, February 27, 1895, in " Mme. Sans-Gêne "; and Eleanora Duse, the distinguished Italian actress, who was seen here for the first time at the Fifth Avenue Theatre, New York, January 23, 1893, as Camille.

Two foreign actresses of distinction who came to this country made America their permanent home. These were Mme. Janauschek and Helena Modjeska.

Mme. Janauschek, one of Europe's most celebrated tragic actresses, was first seen on the American stage at the Academy of Music, New York, October 9, 1867, as Medea. A week later, she appeared as Brunnhilde, one of her most famous rôles. On both of these occasions, she acted in the German language, not attempting to act in English until 1871, when, on October 10, she appeared at the Academy of Music in an English version of Mosenthal's " Deborah."

Janauschek was born at Prague in 1830. Her early life was one of privation and hardship, but, a woman of great intellectual force and indomitable will, she triumphed over all obstacles and from the time she first made her appearance on the stage at Frankfort in 1848 her success was assured. Kings and emperors showered gifts upon her until her collection of jewels was said to be the largest and most valuable ever owned by an actress. She continued acting before the American public for a number of years, meeting with great success in such rôles as Lady Macbeth, Mary Stuart, Deborah, Elizabeth, Catherine II, Hermione and the dual rôle of Lady Dedlock and Hortense in " Chesney Wold," a melodrama founded on Charles Dickens's " Bleak House." " Her face," says Mr. Towse, " was strong and expressive, her voice deep, full and vibrant, her port majestic and her vigor great." The critic continues:

Of the technique of her art she was a perfect mistress, and her versatility was remarkable in all characters compounded of strong intellectual or emotional elements. Neither by temperament nor disposition was she fitted for the softer, seductive heroines of modern social comedy. It was in great dramas that she shone, and when they disappeared from the stage her occupation, like Othello's, was gone. After holding a high seat among the queens of tragedy, she was, in her declining years, reduced to the necessity —as a mere means of livelihood—of appearing in the cheaper kinds of melodrama, which she often made extraordinarily effective by her still undimmed dramatic genius. No matter what the nature of her surroundings, she was a grand artist to the last, but the spectacle of her great abilities wasted on unworthy purpose was a melancholy one.[10]

Helena Modjeska, the distinguished Polish actress, was born in Cracow in 1840 and made her stage

[10] Sixty Years of the Theatre. Copyright, 1916, by John Ranken Towse. Funk & Wagnalls Company, Publishers. Reprinted by permission.

début in 1861. Later, she appeared at Warsaw where she had great success as Adrienne Lecouvreur. Her reputation now established, she continued acting in Warsaw, but her known sympathies with the sorrows of her native Poland having led to friction with Russian officialdom, in 1876 the actress and her husband, " Count " Bozenta, found it advisable to come to America, settling in Southern California, where they had a chicken farm. On August 20, 1877, having gained some acquaintance with the English language, Modjeska made her début at the California Theatre, San Francisco, as Adrienne Lecouvreur and won an immediate triumph, the critics hailing her as a great actress. That same year (December 22) she appeared at the Fifth Avenue Theatre, New York, also as Adrienne, the verdict of the metropolis confirming the opinion of other cities. In 1880, she went to England, appearing in an expurgated version of " La Dame aux Camélias," entitled " Heartsease." Returning to America, she was seen at Booth's Theatre. Another visit to Europe followed, after which she returned to this country and in 1887 acted in association with Edwin Booth. Her repertoire included over a hundred characters, among them being Juliet, Beatrice, Ophelia, Desdemona, Cordelia, Katharine, Rosalind, Camille, Frou Frou, Viola, Queen Katharine and Lady Macbeth. Although she never mastered the English language and always spoke with an accent, " no artist," says William Winter, " more delicate and subtle than Helena Modjeska has appeared among the women of the stage." He continues:

Her power was limited; but she exhibited a rare dramatic intelligence; the atmosphere of her mind and art was essentially poetic; her execution was marked by exquisite refinement and grace, and by perfect self-control and precision; she possessed innate distinction to an extraordinary degree; great personal charm; a winning, expressive voice; lovely simplicity of manner, and a rich, sensuous beauty; she manifested beautiful purity of spirit, and, within her special field, exceptional tragic force, amounting at times to authentic power.[11]

Modjeska was the first exponent of the Ibsen drama in this country. Her production in Louisville, Ky., of "A Doll's House" in 1883, under the title "Thora," aroused wide discussion of the great Norwegian, until then comparatively unknown in America outside of the library. Later, Ibsen's sombre plays became a favorite vehicle with our more intellectual players, other early interpreters being Beatrice Cameron (Mrs. Richard Mansfield), who was seen at the Garden Theatre, New York, January 31, 1891, as Nora; and Janet Achurch, who acted Nora at Hoyt's Theatre, New York, June 6, 1895. "The Pillars of Society" was produced for the first time in America by Franklin Sargent's students at the Lyceum Theatre, March 6, 1891. Three days later, the first professional performance of this play was given by Oscar Hammerstein at the Harlem Opera House, with J. D. Studley as Consul Bernick. Later Ibsen performers include Elizabeth Robins, Mrs. Fiske, Mary Shaw, Courteney Thorpe, Frederick Lewis, Ethel Barrymore, Wilton Lackaye, Alla Nazimova.

Henry Irving began his first American tour October 29, 1883, at the Star Theatre, New York, as Mathias in "The Bells." The following evening "Charles the First" was given, when Ellen Terry made her début on our stage as Queen Henrietta

[11] The Wallet of Time. Copyright, 1913, by William Winter. Moffat, Yard & Company, Publishers. Reprinted by permission of Jefferson Winter, Esq.

Maria. Other Irving productions seen in America included: "Louis XI," "The Lyons Mail," "The Merchant of Venice," "Richard III," "Hamlet," "Much Ado About Nothing," "The Belle's Stratagem," "Eugene Aram," "Twelfth Night," "Richelieu," "Nance Oldfield," "Becket," "Olivia," "Henry VIII" and "Faust." Tremendous success attended Irving's appearances in this country. In all, he made eight American tours, the total receipts amounting to nearly three and one-half million dollars.

Although not an actor of the first rank, Irving, whom England honored when he died in 1905 by burial in Westminster Abbey, was the most successful and conspicuous among the later English stars who visited this country. The actor's real name was Brodribb. Born in 1838, he was educated for a commercial career, but, finding himself unsuited for business life, and having had some success in amateur theatricals, he went to Sunderland in 1856 and made his début as a professional actor on September 18 of that year as Gaston, Duke of Orleans, in "Richelieu." Then he went to Edinburgh, where he stayed two and a half years, playing a great number of parts. He was first seen in London in 1859 at the Princess Theatre in an English version of Feuillet's "Roman d'un Jeune Homme Pauvre," but it was not until 1866 when he appeared as Doricourt at the St. James Theatre that he succeeded in attracting the attention of the metropolitan critics. The following year, he was at the Queen's Theatre, where he met Ellen Terry for the first time and where his playing of three parts, Bob Gassit in "Dearer Than Life," Bill Sykes in "Oliver Twist," and Robert Redburn in "The Lan-

THE THEATRE IN AMERICA

cashire Lass," won for him recognition as a past master in impersonating villains. In 1871, H. L. Bateman, the American manager, took a lease of the Lyceum and Irving was engaged with other London players to support the Bateman sisters.[12] The opening bill was not a success, but a month later, when " Pickwick " was put on, Irving made a hit as Alfred Jingle. Bateman, discouraged by the outlook, was now ready to give up, but, as a last resort, Irving persuaded him to stage " The Bells," an adaptation of " Le Juif Polonais," by Erckmann and Chatrian. Produced November 25, 1871, the play took London by storm, Irving's acting as Mathias electrifying the audience. Irving's reputation was now made. " Charles I," another success, followed, and then came " Eugene Aram," " Richelieu," " Hamlet," " Richard III," "The Lyons Mail," "Louis XI," etc., all of which added still further to the actor's fame. In 1878, the Batemans having retired, Irving became sole lessee of the Lyceum, which began its brilliant career under his managment, December 30, with " Hamlet," Ellen Terry, one of the most popular and charming Shakespearian actresses of our day, appearing for the first time under Irving's direction as Ophelia.

In the opinion of many critics, Irving was an intellectual rather than an emotional actor. " He could charm by his delicacy," says John Ranken Towse, " dazzle by his brilliancy and thrill by his intensity, but he could not overwhelm." The critic continues:

[12] Kate, Ellen, Isabel, and Virginia Bateman, known as the Bateman sisters, were the daughters of H. L. Bateman, actor and theatrical manager. Kate Bateman was born at Baltimore in 1842 and at the age of seven appeared at the Broadway Theatre, New York, acting Richmond to her sister Ellen's Richard III. In the Fall of 1851 the sisters appeared in London at the St. James Theatre in acts and scenes from Shakespeare. Isabel Bateman, born in Cincinnati in 1854, was also a child actress of considerable prominence.

THE RISE OF EDWIN BOOTH

He could be finely dignified and tender, as in Charles I; regal, subtle and pathetic, as in Lear; but not grand or awful; he could be beautifully paternal, as in "The Vicar of Wakefield," but he could not play the romantic lover. His Romeo was a dismal failure. It was in intellectual and eccentric characters, especially those in which there was a vein of sardonic humor or a taint of evil, that he was most successful, such as Mathias (in "The Bells"), Louis XI, Iago, Malvolio, Richelieu, Shylock or Benedick. . . . It would be difficult to exaggerate the value of his managerial services to the public and the theatre. He reawakened popular interest in the legitimate drama, showed managers once more how Shakespeare could be made to pay, demonstrated by financial success the efficiency of the artistic theatre as a commercial enterprise and the superiority of the stock over the star system, and gave a permanent uplift to the social status of the actor. He did for the poetic and romantic drama what Wallack's at its best did for literary artificial comedy.[13]

Among other distinguished German artists who came to America were Mme. Methua-Scheller, a charming actress in sentimental rôles who supported Edwin Booth as Ophelia; Marie Geistinger, a famous soubrette and one of the most popular German actresses that ever came to this country (1880); Ludwig Barnay (1883); Adolf von Sonnenthal (1885); Ernst von Possart (1889); Agnes Sorma (1897).

Genevieve Ward, the American Shakespearian actress, whose reputation was gained abroad, chiefly remembered for her performance of the adventuress in "Forget-me-Not," was first seen here in 1878. More recent English players of distinction include Wilson Barrett, the Kendals, Sir John Hare, Sir Charles Wyndham, Mrs. Langtry, Sir Herbert Tree, Sir Johnston Forbes-Robertson, Cyril Maude, Charles Hawtrey, Martin Harvey, E. S. Willard and others.

[13] Sixty Years of the Theatre. Copyright, 1916, by John Ranken Towse. Funk & Wagnalls Company, Publishers. Reprinted by permission.

CHAPTER XXVI

DALY'S, 1869–1899

THE early seventies inaugurated a particularly brilliant and interesting era in the history of the American stage. During the next twenty years—from 1870 to 1890—the art of the actor was seen at its best. After that the drama in this country began steadily to decline. Illiterate, sordid traders usurped the place of men of culture and training in the management of our theatres and gradual deterioration followed as a logical result of rank commercialism.

But in 1870, the coming cataclysm was yet too far distant to interfere with the enjoyment of playgoers. They could still find delight in the noble impersonations of E. L. Davenport, Edwin Booth, Lawrence Barrett and John McCullough, the delicious comedy of Joseph Jefferson, John Brougham, John Gilbert and William Warren. They welcomed to our shores such distinguished foreign stars as Ristori, Salvini, Bernhardt, Janauschek, Modjeska and Irving, and they basked in the radiant stage presence of those two beautiful and gifted Shakespearian actresses—Adelaide Neilson and Mary Anderson. Wallack's, still at the height of its prestige, successfully maintained its enviable position as our leading comedy theatre, although before long it was forced to lower its high artistic standard, having to contend against formidable and able competitors. The star of Augustin Daly was just rising and Albert M. Palmer soon began to make theatrical history at the Union Square Theatre.

Augustin Daly, one of America's most prominent and successful theatre managers, was born in 1838 at Plymouth, North Carolina, where his father, a former British sea captain, had established himself in the lumber business. In 1841, Captain Daly died and his widow brought her two sons, Augustin and Joseph Francis (afterwards Judge Daly), to New York. From his boyhood, Augustin was strongly attracted to the theatre, and for years he haunted the performances of the " Murdoch Association " and other amateur organizations, not with any idea of himself becoming an actor, but to familiarize himself with management. He was only eighteen when, without money or backing of any kind, he rented a theatre, hired musicians, borrowed costumes and with schoolmates for actors, invited the public to attend a performance that, in addition to two farces, included no less ambitious an effort than the second act of " Macbeth." The affair was a great success and when everything was paid only twenty-five cents profit was left for the youthful impresario. The experience, however, was worth many times that to Augustin Daly.

Three years later he entered journalism, becoming attached to the New York *Sunday Courier* as dramatic critic. Then came his first opportunity to write a play. Mosenthal, the German tragedian, had just created a sensation in Vienna with his "Deborah," a play dealing with the persecution of the Jews. Daly secured a copy, quickly adapted the piece for the American stage under the title "Leah the Forsaken," and Kate Bateman (one of the famous Bateman children now grown to womanhood) produced it in Boston, December 8, 1862, with great success. A few weeks later, the play was presented at Niblo's, New York, before a most enthusiastic audience. The success of this maiden effort encouraged Daly to persevere in playwriting, and the following year Mrs. John Wood, manager of the Olympic Theatre, New York, produced his adaptation of Sardou's "Le Papillon" under the title "Taming a Butterfly." Later, he adapted several French melodramas for Avonia Jones, daughter of the eccentric "Count" Joannes, and for some time managed a starring tour of that actress. His next play, a dramatization of Charles Reade's novel, "Griffith Gaunt," was produced at the New York Theatre, November 7, 1866, with J. K. Mortimer in the title rôle and Rose Eytinge as Rose Peyton. The following year, Daly leased the theatre for a summer season and produced a new melodrama written by himself, entitled "Under the Gaslight," the sensation of which was a man fastened to a railroad track and rescued just as the train reached the spot. The piece was produced August 12, 1867, with such success that Daly now found his reputation as a dramatist firmly established.

But these and similar efforts in the same direction were only a preparation for more congenial activities. Daly's ambition was to have a theatre of his own.

Opportunity came when the Fifth Avenue Theatre in
Twenty-fourth Street, which James Fisk, Jr., had
built for John Brougham, came into the market
after Brougham's failure as a manager. Daly saw
his chance and after some parleying with Fisk, who
had never heard of Daly and doubted his ability to
finance so important an enterprise, secured a lease
for two years. After redecorating and re-upholster-
ing the little playhouse very handsomely, Daly entered upon his managerial career August 16, 1869,
with a performance of Robertson's comedy, " Play."
The company he had organized was a remarkable
one, including as it did such old favorites as E. L.
Davenport, William Davidge, George Holland, D.
H. Harkins, Mrs. Clara Jennings, Mrs. Marie Wilkins, Mrs. Chanfrau and Mrs. G. H. Gilbert. Others,
not so well known at that time, but whose names after-
wards became household words, were: Agnes Ethel,
George Clarke, James Lewis and Fanny Davenport.
Later additions to the organization were: Clara Mor-
ris, then an unknown Western actress; Charles
Fisher, formerly leading man at Wallack's; Frank
Hardenbergh, popular in melodramatic parts; Sara
Jewett, an attractive young actress in sentimental
rôles; Ada Dyas, a capable English actress; Louis
James, the tragedian; Kate Claxton, of "Two
Orphans" fame. John Drew made his début in 1874.
Ada Rehan did not join the company until 1879.

Mr. Daly's first leading lady was Agnes Ethel,
a pupil of Matilda Heron. A good-looking woman
with a slight girlish figure and an appealing expression, she made her début as Rosie Fanquehere in
" Play," but attracted no particular attention until

the following year, when her success as Gilberte in
" Frou Frou " was the talk of the town. Other parts
in which she was seen were Lena in " Dreams," Jessie
Bell in " Daddy Gray," Fernande in Daly's adapta-
tion of Sardou's play of that name, Olivia and Viola
in " Twelfth Night," Hero in " Much Ado About
Nothing," Rosara in " She Would and She Would
Not," Lady Priory in " Wives as They Were," Con-
stance in " The Love Chase," Julia in " The Hunch-
back," Maritana in " Don Cæsar de Bazan," and
Leonie in " Checkmate, or A Duel in Love." In
October 1872, she left Daly and appeared at the
Union Square Theatre as the heroine of Sardou's
" Agnes," which had been written specially for her.

Fanny Davenport made her début a few weeks
later (September 29, 1869) as Lady Gay in " London
Assurance."

The eldest child of E. L. Davenport, the eminent
tragedian, Fanny Lily Gipsy Davenport was born
in London in 1850. She was brought to America
when four years of age and educated in Boston. Her
first appearance before the footlights was at the Howard Athenæum, July 4, 1858, when her father and
mother and the whole company stood in a group on
the stage singing the *Star Spangled Banner,* little
Fanny holding the American flag. Her first appearance in a play was at the same theatre in one of W. J.
Florence's burlesques. Later, she played the child
in " Metamora " and a number of such juvenile parts.
In 1862, she was seen at Niblo's, New York, in " Faint
Heart Ne'er Won Fair Lady." She then went to
Philadelphia and after acting for some years under
the management of Mrs. John Drew at the Arch

Street Theatre, she joined Mr. Daly. She was at that time very inexperienced, and there was nothing in her acting to suggest her father's genius. But she was strikingly beautiful, tall and handsome, and the good looks of the woman served to conceal the shortcomings of the actress.

From 1869 to 1877 she appeared at Daly's in a vast number of plays, among the rôles acted during that period being: Blanche in Daly's " Man and Wife," Elfie Remington in "Saratoga," Mrs. Wragge in Daly's " No Name," Lu in " Divorce," Baroness de Mirac in " Article 47," Nelly Wyckoff in " Diamonds," Marquise de Ceseranne in " Alixe," Mme. Guichard in " Monsieur Alphonse," Eugenia in " The Big Bonanza," Mabel Renfrew in " Pique," Lady Townly in " The Provoked Husband," Mary Melrose in " Our Boys," Camille, Polly in " Caste," Letitia in " The Belle's Stratagem," Peg Woffington in " Masks and Faces," Nancy Sykes, Lady Teazle, Ophelia, Lady Macbeth, Rosalind, Mistress Ford in " Merry Wives," Maria in " Twelfth Night "—a remarkable list ranging from the stately iambics of Shakespeare and artificiality of the old comedies to the storm and fury of modern melodrama. Her greatest success was in the Sardou plays —big spectacular dramas full of passion and violence, for which her temperament and tall, commanding physique well fitted her. Beginning in 1883, with "Fédora," she followed up that first success with " Tosca," " Cleopatra " and " Gismonda," and, heading her own company, toured the United States for several years. She died in 1898.

James Lewis, so long a popular comedian of the

Daly company, was a native of Troy, New York, and began his stage career as a burlesque actor in 1866 at Mrs. John Wood's Olympic Theatre. As a comedian he was irresistible.

"No one," says William Winter, "ever saw him without laughter—and it was kindly laughter, with a warm heart behind it. The moment he came on the stage an eager gladness diffused itself throughout his audience. His quaintness and unconscious drollery captured all hearts. His whimsical individuality never varied; yet every character of the many that he portrayed stood clearly forth among its companions, a distinct, unique embodiment."[1]

Mrs. G. H. Gilbert, the "grand old woman of the stage," a great favorite with the public for fifty years and a conspicuous member of the company until Mr. Daly's death in 1899, was born at Rochdale, near Manchester, England, in 1822. She began her long theatrical career as a dancer and in 1846 married G. H. Gilbert, also a dancer. Three years later they came to America. Mrs. Gilbert made her début at Chicago in 1851 as a dancer, her first appearance as an actress being at the Cleveland Theatre in 1857. Ten years later she made a big hit in New York at the Broadway Theatre as the Marquise in "Caste." From that time on, she was identified with aristocratic dowager rôles. Among her other parts were: Baronne de Cambri in "Frou Frou," Mrs. Vanderpool in "Saratoga," Carolina Cawallader in "The Big Bonanza," Aunt Dorothy in "Pique," Mrs. Bargiss in "Seven-Twenty-Eight," Mrs. Lamb in "Dollars and Sense," Eudoxia Quattles in "Love on Crutches," Zantippe Babbitt in "A

---

[1] From the Wallet of Time. Copyright, 1913, by William Winter. Moffat, Yard & Co., Publishers.

Night Off," Countess Pompion in "Old Heads and
Young Hearts," Dame Quickly in "The Merry
Wives," Mrs. Rackett in "The Belle's Stratagem,"
Lady Duberly in "The Heir at Law," etc., etc.

An interesting début occurred at the Fifth Avenue
Theatre on October 4 when Mrs. Scott Siddons, a
descendant of the great Siddons, was seen as Viola
in "Twelfth Night." A woman of exquisite beauty
and one of the most charming Rosalinds that ever
trod the stage, Mrs. Scott Siddons was born in
India in 1844 and first appeared on the stage at Nottingham, England, in 1866, as Lady Macbeth. The
following year she made her début at the Haymarket,
London, as Rosalind in "As You Like It," and soon
after came to America and made her first appearance
at the Boston Museum. She continued a favorite
with the American public for many years.

Another important acquisition to the company
the following year was that of Clara Morris, a young
Western actress, who made her début September,
1870, as Anne Sylvester in Daly's dramatization of
Wilkie Collins's novel, "Man and Wife." Agnes
Ethel had refused the part on the ground that it was
too immoral—this from the actress who had not hesi-
tated to play Frou Frou and Fernande—and Daly
was in a quandary until he happened to remember the
young woman who had called upon him with letters
of introduction from John A. Ellsler, of the Academy
of Music, Cleveland, where she had been acting.
There was something in the appearance of the newcomer that made Daly think he could entrust her with
the part. He telegraphed Ellsler: "Can she play
it?" Quickly came the answer: "Try her." The

result is theatrical history. The young actress took New York by storm and then and there entered triumphantly upon her long career as one of the most individual and successful players this country has produced.

As an actress, Clara Morris belonged in a class by herself. She was extravagant in gesture, crude in speech and manner, yet none understood human nature better or could portray with such tremendous power its conflicting passions. As John Ranken Towse says:

> She was, first and last, a natural born actress. If judged by her artistic equipment only, she could not establish a claim to any very high place in the ranks of her contemporaries. She was far behind many of them in artistic cunning, but she distanced all of them in flashes of convincing realism and in poignancy of natural emotion. She was often barely respectable as an elocutionist, she was habitually crude, and occasionally unrefined, in pose, gesture, and utterance; she had distressful mannerisms, she could not or did not attempt to modify or disguise her individual personality, her range was limited—she could not soar into the upper regions of tragedy—but, nevertheless, she showed, especially in emotional crises, a strong grasp of diversified characters within her own boundaries and illuminated them, at intervals, with such a blaze of vivid truthfulness that, for the moment, she seemed to be perfectly identified with them.[2]

It was about this time that Daly gave Bronson Howard, then a rising young American dramatist, his first opportunity. Born in Detroit in 1842, Howard had taken to journalism as a career and held important editorial positions on the staffs of several New York newspapers. A close student of the theatre, he had meantime dabbled in play construction

[2] Sixty Years of the Theatre. Copyright, 1916, by John Ranken Towse. Funk & Wagnalls Company, Publishers. Reprinted by permission.

and asked Daly to read a comedy he had written entitled " Saratoga." The play was produced December 21, 1870, and was a great success. It had a run of over a hundred nights, and proved the stepping stone to Bronson Howard's long and distinguished career as America's leading dramatist. Other successful plays by this author are " The Young Mrs. Winthrop," " Wives," " Old Love Letters," " One of Our Girls," " The Banker's Daughter," " The Henrietta," " Shenandoah," " Aristocracy," etc., etc.

The production of " Saratoga " was a notable event in the history of our theatre because the success of the play forced a change in the attitude of managers towards the native-made play. The American drama at that period was at very low ebb. The Indian plays, made popular by Forrest, had long since lost their hold on public favor, while the Yankee character comedies that gave to our stage such successful types as John E. Owens' Solon Shingle, W. J. Florence's Bardwell Slote, Frank Mayo's Davy Crockett, John T. Raymond's Mulberry Sellers, Chanfrau's Mose and Jefferson's Asa Trenchard, were forgotten almost as soon as the actors who created them had disappeared. The American drama —that is, plays written by Americans upon American subjects, giving faithful pictures of American life and manners—virtually did not exist. Our boards were crowded with French and English plays in which the characters expressed foreign ideas and behaved like foreigners. Howard's success gave fresh impetus to the cause of the struggling native playwright and paved the way for Clyde Fitch, Charles Hoyt, Augustus Thomas, William Gillette, James A.

247

Herne and other American playwrights whose successes gradually compelled recognition for the native drama. Bronson Howard was the pioneer. As Montrose J. Moses says:

In the early seventies he stood single-handed, with the Anglicism and classicism of Daly, Palmer, and Wallack as his chiefest opposition, and he forced the public gaze upon current thought and manners. . . . Popular opinion was led to value an importation, and to discount any serious treatment of American character or of American life. . . . Lester Wallack in no way encouraged native talent, even though his excellence as a stage manager helped to give the theatre an abundant amount of English comedy and tragedy. . . . The same may well be claimed of Augustin Daly, who nevertheless aimed to be American in " Under the Gaslight." But his was likewise a foreign ambition, for he mounted adaptations of French and German farces whenever he wished to depart from the Shakespearian or classical comedy repertoire of his New York theatres; he catered distinctively to culture. . . . Of the three prominent managers, Mr. Palmer may be said to have done the most to have encouraged native dramatic ability. He and Mr. Daly were both involved in the development of Bronson Howard.[1]

In 1872, Daly produced Adolph Belot's drama, " Article 47," in which Clara Morris made another sensation as Cora. " In the mad scene," Judge Joseph F. Daly tells us, " her acting was electrifying, and when the curtain fell she was the mistress of the American stage."

On January 1, 1873, the theatre was burned down and Daly took a short lease of the Worrell Sisters' New York Theatre (formerly the Church of the Messiah), opening it as the Fifth Avenue Theatre January 21, with an adaptation from the French entitled " Alixe," in which Clara Morris again scored. That same year

[1] The American Dramatist. By Montrose J. Moses. Copyright, 1911, Little, Brown & Co.

a new Fifth Avenue Theatre was built on Twenty-eighth Street and opened by Daly December 3 with a play by James Albery called " Fortune," Fanny Morant and Frank Hardenbergh delivering an original address written for the occasion by Dr. Oliver Wendell Holmes.

During the first season at the new house Daly presented a number of interesting bills. The novelties included several pieces from the French—Adolph Belot's " Parricide," Daly's own adaptation of " Folline " and Dumas' " Monsieur Alphonse," W. S. Gilbert's " Charity," and a dramatization of " Oliver Twist," with Bijou Heron as Oliver, Fanny Davenport as Nancy Sykes, Fisher as Fagin and William Davidge as Bumble. Louis James made a hit on this occasion as the most ruffianly Bill Sykes yet seen in New York.

The second season was devoted largely to old comedy revivals. On September 12, 1874, " The School for Scandal," " altered by Mr. Daly," was given with Charles Fisher as Sir Peter; William Davidge as Sir Oliver; George Clarke as Charles; B. T. Ringold as Sir Benjamin; Sol Smith Russell as Trip; Louis James as Joseph; James Lewis as Moses and Fanny Davenport as Lady Teazle. This was followed by a revival of Sheridan's " The Critic," with James Lewis as Puff, Louis James as Sir Christopher, William Davidge as Don Whiskerandos and Fanny Davenport as Tilburina. Bronson Howard's play, " Moorcroft," had its first production October 17, and this was followed by a revival of Hannah Cowley's " The Belle's Stratagem," with Fanny Davenport as Letitia Hardy, Louis James as Dori-

THE THEATRE IN AMERICA

court, Sara Jewett as Lady Touchwood, William Davidge as Old Hardy and James Lewis as Flutter. Charles Reade's "Masks and Faces" was given the same month with Fanny Davenport as Peg Woffington, and Fisher as Triplet.

It was during this season that John Drew made his first appearance in New York. He had been acting at his mother's theatre in Philadelphia when Mr. Daly engaged him for the part of Bob Ruggles in "The Big Bonanza." Later, John Drew joined Edwin Booth, playing Rosencranz to the latter's Hamlet. After that he travelled with Fanny Davenport, but in 1879 he again joined Mr. Daly and remained with him, acting leading romantic and comedy rôles with great success, until 1892. Very successful in dress-suit comedy, he also scored in such parts as Charles Surface in "The School for Scandal," Petruchio in "The Taming of the Shrew," Orlando in "As You Like It," the King of Navarre in "Love's Labour Lost." In 1892, John Drew left Daly to become a star under the management of Charles Frohman.

The season of 1875-6 opened brilliantly with a revival of "Saratoga." This was followed September 18th by the first production in America of "Our Boys," in which Fanny Davenport appeared as Mary Melrose, Jeffreys Lewis as Violet Melrose, Charles Fisher as Sir Geoffrey and Maurice Barrymore as Talbot Champneys. On December 14, "Pique" was given for the first time. In this play, which had a run of over two hundred nights, Fanny Davenport began her career as a star.

On May 79, 1877, the beautiful Adelaide Neilson,

whom William Winter declares the best representative of Shakespeare's Juliet and Viola in our time, began an engagement at Daly's as Viola in "Twelfth Night," and two weeks later she was seen as Juliet, the part for which she was most famous.

This popular Shakespearian actress, who had already been seen at Booth's Theatre in 1872, had a romantic career. Born at Leeds, England, in 1846, she began life as a factory girl, but, fond of reading, she was soon fascinated by the beauties of Shakespeare. She managed to obtain a little education, and, after taking a situation as nursery maid, eventually found employment in a theatre, her professional début taking place at Margate in 1868 as Juliet. The critics noticed her favorably and she continued to make progress until 1870, when she made a tremendous hit at Drury Lane as Amy Robsart. The same year she made another triumph as Juliet. In America, her other rôles included Rosalind, Viola, Imogen, Beatrice, Isabella, Pauline and Lady Teazle.

In 1877, Daly surrendered the management of the theatre to Stephen Fiske and began an extended tour through the South. During his absence, Mary Anderson was seen for the first time in New York. This famous actress—one of the loveliest and most popular players America has yet produced—made her metropolitan début at the Fifth Avenue Theatre, November 12, 1877, as Pauline in "The Lady of Lyons," supported by Eben Plympton as Claude Melnotte. A few nights later, she was seen as Juliet, Evadne and Parthenia.

Mary Anderson was born at Sacramento, California, on July 28, 1859. Her father was an English-

251

man, her mother a Philadelphian of German descent. Neither parent had any connection with the stage. The young girl left a convent school when she was fourteen, and, thrilled by seeing Edwin Booth in several of his rôles, she determined to become a Shakespearian actress. After studying elocution for a short time with George Vandenhoff, she made her stage début when only sixteen years of age, on November 27, 1875, at Louisville, Ky., as Juliet. Although a crude performance, as was only natural in one so young and inexperienced, a local critic described her first attempt as a " performance of extraordinary force, feeling and promise," its paramount beauty being its vocalism. " Mary Anderson's voice," says William Winter, " was always her predominant charm. Certain tones in it—so thrilling, so full of wild passion and inexpressible melancholy—went straight to the heart and brought tears into the eyes."

In March, 1876, the young actress was seen at St. Louis as Pauline Deschapelles, at New Orleans as Meg Merrilles and in September at San Francisco as Parthenia in " Ingomar." In January, 1877, she acted Lady Macbeth in Washington and later was seen as the Countess in Sheridan Knowles' " Love " and as the Duchess in "Faint Heart Ne'er Won Fair Lady." In 1881, at Troy, she appeared for the first time as Galatea in W. S. Gilbert's " Pygmalion and Galatea." In Boston, where she first appeared October 15, 1877, her success was immediate. The Boston Theatre was crowded to the doors nightly by the most cultured audiences ever seen in that city and the poet Longfellow and other literary celebrities were extravagant in their praise of the new star. Other rôles assumed by her were Bianca in " Fazio," Julia in " The Hunchback," Bertha in " Roland's Daughter," Clarice in " Tragedy and Comedy," Rosalind, Desdemona, Perdita and Hermione.

In each of these impersonations, and particularly as Galatea and as Perdita in " The Winter's Tale," her success was complete. Audiences everywhere went wild over her. Yet she could not be called a great actress. Her histrionic gift lacked versatility. At all times she satisfied the heart and gratified the eye, but she did not always succeed in simulating the deeper or more intellectual emotions. " In great parts, demanding imagination, passionate eloquence, or subtle discrimination," says Mr. Towse, " she was second rate." The critic continues:

From the beginning to the end of her public career, she was one of Fortune's darlings. Nature endowed her with rare beneficence. When, as a mere girl, she first entered upon the stage, she presented a figure of classic and virginal purity that was almost ideal. Her tall, lithe form was at once stately and graceful, the poise of her head was stag-like, and her face was radiant with health, innocence, and dignified beauty. It was by the spell of her personal charms that she instantly made her way into the heart of the American public, and she retired to a happy and prosperous privacy when still at the height of her popularity, while that spell was yet potent. A finer type of young American womanhood could not easily be imagined. Like Lady Teazle, " bred wholly in the country," she was accepted at once as the representative American actress of her time, was fondly called " our Mary," and quickly became the object of a widespread affection and admiration that might, without much exaggeration, be called national. As a novice she was placed by her worshippers on a pinnacle from which she was never deposed. Her memory is still surrounded by a glamour which no one could wish to dispel. Her beauty, her spotless character, her graciousness, her intelligence, her refined manner, and her unquestionable dramatic instinct and ability contributed greatly to the honor and glory of the American stage while she adorned it; but for all that, she was never a great actress or a great artist. She does not belong to the same category with Charlotte Cushman, Janauschek, Modjeska, Clara Morris, or Edwin Booth.[4]

In 1883, Mary Anderson paid a professional visit to England, where her triumphs were repeated. On her return to this country, she continued acting until 1889, her last appearance occurring at Washington early in the spring of that year as Hermione. In 1890, she suddenly retired from the stage to become the wife of Mr. Antonio de Navarro and took up her residence in England.

On Augustin Daly's return to New York in 1879, he secured a lease of Wood's old Museum, near Thirtieth Street and Broadway. This establishment, after extensive alterations, was opened September 18, 1879, as Daly's Theatre. Among the newcomers in the company were Ada Rehan, Emily Rigl, Charles Leclercq, Virginia Dreher, Fanny Morant and Otis Skinner, then at the beginning of his career.

Ada Rehan, the new leading lady, who made her début September 30 as Lu Ten Eyck in " Divorce," was born in Ireland in 1860, and educated in Brooklyn. Her first appearance on any stage was made at Newark, N. J., as Clara in " Across the Continent." In 1875, she joined Mrs. John Drew's stock company at the Arch Street Theatre, Philadelphia. Daly's attention having been drawn to her, he engaged her for a small part in his adaptation of "L'Assommoir,"

254

produced at Mrs. John Wood's Olympic. She remained a member of the Daly company until the
manager's death in 1899, and during that long period
established herself firmly in the favor of the playgoing public, acting over 200 parts, the principal
among them being Cherry Monogram in "The Way
We Live," the Countess in "Odette," Kate Verity in
"The Squire," Jeanne in "Serge Panine," Phronie
in "Dollars and Sense," Flos in "Seven-Twenty-
Eight," Annie Austin in "Love on Crutches," Nancy
Brasher in "Nancy and Co.," Lady Teazle in "The
School for Scandal," Katharine in "The Taming of
the Shrew," Rosalind in "As You Like It," Nell
Gwynn in "Sweet Nell of Old Drury," Peggy Thrift
in "The Country Girl," Sylvia in "The Recruiting
Officer," Hypolita in "She Would and She Would
Not," etc., etc. "From the first," says John Ranken
Towse, "Miss Rehan was in her element in every
variety of piquant, tender, mischievous, high-spirited, alluring, whimsical and provocative girlhood.
Her humor was infectious, her charm potent, her
pertness delicious, her petulance pretty and her
flashes of ire or scorn brilliant. She improved rapidly in artistry, and to the intuition of a clever novice
she quickly added the skill of the trained comedian."

In the middle nineties, Daly's star as a manager
was already in decline, but from 1880 to 1895, his
theatre enjoyed great vogue, the productions ranging
from elaborate revivals of Shakespeare and the old
English comedies to adaptations of spirited German
farce. Apart from the classics, there was little produced that had any real merit or permanent value,
but, thanks to the admirable Daly company, every-

thing was done well, in the true comedy spirit, and playgoers of discernment went to Daly's because they could not get quite the same dramatic fare elsewhere. Among the lighter pieces that found favor with his public were: "Divorce," "Wives" (adapted by Bronson Howard from Molière's "L'Ecole des Maris"), "An Arabian Night," "The Royal Middy," "The Way We Live," and "Needles and Pins," in which Ada Rehan, John Drew, Mrs. G. H. Gilbert and James Lewis all made great hits. Later bills were: "Dollars and Sense," "Love on Crutches," Pinero's "The Squire," and "The Magistrate," "A Night Off," "Nancy and Co.," "Love in Harness," "The Lottery of Love," "Railroad of Love," "The Great Unknown," "The Last Word," "Little Miss Million," "The Countess Gucki."

The Shakespearian revivals were on a most sumptuous scale. On October 14, 1886, Daly presented "The Merry Wives of Windsor" with great magnificence of *mise en scène*. Charles Fisher appeared as Sir John Falstaff, Otis Skinner as Page, John Drew as Ford, Ada Rehan as Mistress Ford, Virginia Dreher as Mistress Page, Edith Kingdon as Anne Page, and Mrs. G. H. Gilbert as Mistress Quickley. The following year, January 18, 1887, "The Taming of the Shrew" was acted in its entirety for the first time in America. John Drew was a spirited Petruchio and Ada Rehan achieved the great triumph of her career as Katharine. "As You Like It," revived in 1889, afforded Miss Rehan an opportunity for a beautiful performance of Rosalind. John Drew also made a hit as Orlando, and James Lewis scored as Touchstone.

Two seasons later (January 20, 1891) Mr. Daly made a brilliant revival of "The School for Scandal" with John Drew as Charles Surface, Harry Edwards—a favorite of the old Wallack Company—as Sir Oliver, Sidney Herbert as Sir Benjamin, George Clarke as Joseph and Ada Rehan as Lady Teazle. "Love's Labour Lost" was given March 28, 1891; "Two Gentlemen of Verona" in 1895, and "Much Ado About Nothing" in 1896. "Twelfth Night," revived February 21, 1893, ranked with the finest achievements of the American stage. Ada Rehan was the Viola, Adelaide Prince the Olivia, and Creston Clark the Orsino.

Back of the curtain, Daly was a stern disciplinarian and ruled his company with an iron hand. Like Wallack and other managers, he drew up a list of rules for the regulation of his players' conduct, and imposed heavy fines in the event of their infraction. He forbade any of his people to leave the city without permission even if not connected with the evening's bill, and even in the Greenroom they were not free to speak to visitors. Some members of his company resented his autocratic treatment. One to take offense was Ada Dyas, a capable English actress who left Daly and became very popular at Wallack's. Agnes Ethel had already left, and she was soon followed by Clara Morris, both actresses joining A. M. Palmer at the Union Square Theatre. Fanny Morant and Kate Claxton were others who seceded.

But with all his eccentricities, Augustin Daly will be remembered as one of the most distinguished theatre managers this country has ever had. Our stage was the richer for his activities and there was no one to take his place when he died. Not only did he create a remarkable stock company, but what is more important, he inspired public confidence and catered to a cultured and refined clientèle. No other American manager has been so successful in establishing and maintaining such a select following as he enjoyed. When a playgoer went to Daly's, he felt reasonably sure that he was going to see the best that American dramatic genius afforded. Since Daly's death, there is no theatre to which he can turn with such confidence. William Winter pays him this tribute:

He gathered the ablest men and women in the dramatic profession; he presented the best plays that were available; he made the Theatre important, and he kept it worthy of the sympathy and support of the most refined taste and the best intellect of his time. His fertility of resource seemed inexhaustible. He was quick to decide, and the energy with which he moved, in the execution of his plans, was the more splendid because it was neither deranged by tumult nor marred by ostentation. As long as he had a finely intelligent public with which to deal, and until actors of the old school began to die away, giving place to the cohorts of the drawing-room, he touched nothing that did not succeed. He earned a high renown, and he left an imperishable example. His character was marked by some eccentricities—for he liked to hide his feelings and to seem indifferent and hard—but it was a thin disguise. He had encountered much selfishness and much ingratitude, and his experience had made him stern in judgment and somewhat cold and austere in manner, but those who knew him well knew that his probity was like a rock, and they remember him as a man of inflexible principle, affectionate heart, and a temperament marked by simplicity, generosity, and tenderness.[6]

In 1884, Daly took his company to London, opening at Toole's Theatre with "Seven-Twenty-Eight."

[6]The Wallet of Time. Copyright, 1913, by William Winter. Moffat, Yard & Company, Publishers. Reprinted by permission of Jefferson Winter, Esq.

This was the first time that American actors had ever appeared in England as an organization, and was the beginning of several visits to Europe, the Daly company acting both in Berlin and Paris. The Continental engagements were not successful, but in England the reception of the American players was so cordial that in 1893 Daly was encouraged to open a theatre in London. The manager died in Paris in 1899.

CHAPTER XXVII

THE UNION SQUARE THEATRE

THE VOKES FAMILY. A. M. PALMER BECOMES MANAGER. SUCCESS-
FUL PRODUCTION OF "AGNES." STOCK COMPANY ORGANIZED.
"LED ASTRAY" AND "MY PARTNER." TREMENDOUS SUCCESS
OF "THE TWO ORPHANS." RICHARD MANSFIELD'S TRIUMPH
IN "A PARISIAN ROMANCE." STEELE MACKAYE. WILLIAM
GILLETTE. "JIM THE PENMAN." CLYDE FITCH. AUGUSTUS
THOMAS. "TRILBY." THE NEW YORK CASINO.

ONE of the most famous of New York's playhouses—the Union Square Theatre—began its interesting career in 1871 as a variety house. Sheridan
Shook, who controlled the lease of the Union Place
Hotel, on the south side of Union Square, built a
small theatre in the middle of the block, between
Broadway and Fourth Avenue. At first, the place
was under the management of Robert W. Butler, who
offered a varied vaudeville bill, including the Mar-
tinetti-Ravel troupe in pantomime, Marie Bonfanti,
the dancer, the Mathews family of gymnasts and
acrobats, Jefferson de Angelis, Harrigan and Hart,
etc. On April 15, 1872, the Vokes Family made
their American début at this house, opening in " The
Belles of the Kitchen." This famous organization
of English comedians, consisting of Fred, Fawdon,
Victoria, Jessie and Rosina Vokes, scored an immediate success in America and remained popular here
for many years.

But in spite of the Vokes' success and the many
attractive vaudeville features, the house failed to
attract patronage. Mr. Shook, therefore, decided on

a radical change of policy. Discontinuing it as a variety house, he reopened the theatre as a first-class "home of the drama" and engaged A. M. Palmer as manager.

Albert Marshall Palmer was the last of that famous trio of theatrical managers—Wallack, Daly and Palmer—the story of whose respective careers is practically that of the most glorious period of the American stage. The last survivor of a bygone theatrical régime, he belonged to that school of managers whom we find in control of the leading theatres of Europe—men of culture, refinement and scholarship, to the days when the stock company was at the height of its prosperity, when a refined management gave the drama both dignity and form, when there was a standard of public taste, when acting was cultivated as an art and had not yet degenerated into hero-worship, when the occupation of producing plays had not been turned into mere money-making.

The son of a Presbyterian clergyman, he was born at North Stonington, Conn., and in 1860 he graduated at the New York University Law School. Soon abandoning all idea of adopting the law as a profession, he interested himself in politics until 1869, when he became librarian of the New York Mercantile Library. He occupied that position in 1872, when Mr. Shook selected him as a likely manager for the Union Square Theatre.

Although wholly without experience in theatrical management, Palmer was well equipped to carry out Mr. Shook's ambitious programme. A scholarly, intellectual man, he had long been a student of the

261

drama, and only the best appealed to him. Yet it was no light task that he, a mere novice, was suddenly called upon to undertake. How could he attract patronage when he had not a play to produce, how could he hope to rival the prestige of Wallack's, the most famous theatre in America, just around the corner?

Luck helped him. A friend happened to know Agnes Ethel—Daly's leading woman—for whom Victorien Sardou was then writing a new play called "Andrea." Miss Ethel, piqued at Fanny Davenport's growing importance in the Daly company, was quite ready to discuss a contract with Mr. Palmer, and arrangements were completed for the production of "Andrea" at the Union Square. It was a shrewd move. Miss Ethel enjoyed a considerable following, and the première of a new play by Sardou was an event not to be ignored. The play, rechristened "Agnes," was produced September 17, 1872, and proved a big success, having a run of a hundred nights. In the cast were Agnes Ethel, Plessy Mordaunt, D. H. Harkins, F. F. Mackay, E. Lamb, George Parkes, Welsh Edwards, Mark Smith and Emily Mestayer.

This was the beginning of a series of triumphs, seldom interrupted by failure, during the eleven years that Mr. Palmer remained manager of the Union Square. "Agnes" was followed by revivals of the English comedies such as "London Assurance," "The School for Scandal," and "Money," and these in turn were succeeded by "Frou Frou," "Fernande," "Caste," "Jane Eyre" and "The Geneva Cross." In this last piece, Charles R.

THE UNION SQUARE THEATRE

Thorne, Jr., a forceful actor and popular leading man, made his first appearance with the Union Square Company, which now included: Stuart Robson, John Parselle, Eliza Weathersby, Clara Morris, Rose Eytinge, Kate Claxton, Maude Granger, Marie Wilkins, Emily Mestayer, McKee Rankin, F. F. Mackay, D. H. Harkins, Agnes Ethel, Mark Smith, Clara Jennings. J. H. Stoddart, Frederick Robinson, James O'Neill, Ida Jeffreys, Sara Jewett, Kitty Blanchard, Agnes Booth and Maud Harrison joined the organization later.

Early in December, 1873, Mr. Palmer presented an English version by Dion Boucicault of Octave Feuillet's drama, " Tentation," under the title " Led Astray." The piece was a great success and ran until May 14, 1874, when it was withdrawn to make place for " Camille," which was presented with this cast: Camille, Clara Morris; Armand, Charles R. Thorne, Jr.; Comte de Varville, McKee Rankin; Duval père, John Parselle; M. Gaston, Stuart Robson; Mlle. Olympe, Maude Granger; Mlle. Nichette, Kate Claxton; Mlle. Nanine, Kate Holland; Mme. Prudence, Emily Mestayer.

" Camille " was followed by Bartley Campbell's " Peril," which also scored a success, subsequently completely eclipsed by the same author's " My Partner."

But the greatest triumph of Palmer's managerial career came at the end of that year when he produced " The Two Orphans," It was only by the merest chance that he happened to stage this play, one of the biggest money-makers in dramatic history. None of those who had read the MS. could see any-

THE THEATRE IN AMERICA

thing in it; even the expert Dion Boucicault thought Palmer was making a blunder.

Adolph d'Ennery, the well-known purveyor of French melodrama, had written a piece called " Les Deux Orphelines," and the author, in consequence of a former misunderstanding, promised Hart Jackson, Mr. Palmer's agent, to let him have the play in compensation. A. E. Lancaster tells this interesting story of what followed:

> Jackson, on receiving the play, glanced through it, and told Mr. Palmer that it would never do for the Union Square, as it was a Bowery melodrama. Mr. Palmer, who had not examined it, told Jackson to get it translated and sell it to J. B. Booth for $1500, if no more could be got. Jackson set off to find Booth, and meanwhile Mr. Palmer thought it would do no harm to take a look at the play. By chance he picked up, at the translator's, the fifth tableau, which deals with Henrietta and the Nun and Marianne in the prison at La Salpetrière. He was so entranced by this scene that his eyes filled with tears, while, at the same instant, his heart gave an almost deadly jump at the thought that this treasure had passed from him for the paltry sum of $1500. Enter Hart Jackson. " Have you sold the play? " " No—Booth went to sleep over it." If Palmer never danced before he danced then, for he was hugging a treasure such as seldom comes to any manager more than once in a lifetime.[1]

The play was produced December 21, with Charles R. Thorne, Jr., as Maurice de Vaudrey; McKee Rankin as the brutal Frochard; F. F. Mackay as Pierre; Marie Wilkins as the ferocious La Frochard; Rose Eytinge as Marianne, and Kate Claxton, who made an immense hit as the blind orphan. The play was a tremendous success and had a record run of one hundred and eighty consecutive performances. Later, Kate Claxton bought the rights from

---

[1] A. E. Lancaster in an article in the *Theatre Magazine*, February, 1903.

Palmer and played the piece almost continuously for twenty years.

Among other notable successes produced during the next few seasons were " Rose Michel," introducing J. H. Stoddart in the character of Pierre, the old miser; " Miss Multon," a French drama adapted by A. R. Cazauran, Palmer's house dramatist and literary adviser, in which Clara Morris scored another triumph; " The Danicheffs," with James O'Neill, Charles R. Thorne, Marie Wilkins, Sara Jewett and other favorites; " A Celebrated Case," one of the most successful melodramas ever presented in this country, with Charles Coghlan as Jean Renaud and Agnes Booth as Madeleine; " My Partner," by Bartley Campbell, with Louis Aldrich as Joe Saunders; Sardou's " Daniel Rochat," in which Charles R. Thorne made a great impression as the husband in spiritual conflict with his wife; " The Rantzaus," from the French of Erckmann-Chatrian, in which John Parselle and J. H. Stoddart vividly portrayed the hatred of two brothers; and Bronson Howard's play, " The Banker's Daughter," which had a run of one hundred and thirty-seven performances.

On January 12, 1883, Mr. Palmer produced " A Parisian Romance," a drama adapted by A. R. Cazauran from the French of Octave Feuillet. This play gave Richard Mansfield—then practically unknown, but soon to become one of our most successful stars—his first opportunity.

The leading part in the play, that of the senile, lecherous old Baron Chevrial, had been given to J. H. Stoddart, who had been very successful in old men parts. But Stoddart had misgivings regarding the part, as he tells us in his Recollections:

I rehearsed the part for about a week, and then, being convinced that it did not suit me, I went to Mr. Palmer and told him I felt very doubtful as to whether I could do him or myself justice in it. He would not hear of my giving it up, saying that he knew me better than I did myself; that I was always doubtful; but that he was willing to take the risk. He also read a letter which he had received from some one in Paris giving advice regarding the production, in which, among other things, it was said that Baron Chevrial was the principal part, that everything depended on him, and that "if you can get Stoddart to look well in full dress, he is the man you must have to play it." I left Mr. Palmer, resolved to try again and do my best. Mr. Mansfield (whose position in the company at that time was only a minor one) was cast in the play for a small part, and, I discovered, was watching me like a cat during rehearsals. A lot of fashion-plates were sent to my dressing-room, with instructions to select my costume. As I had hitherto been for some time associated with vagabonds, villains, etc., I think these fashion-plates had a tendency to unnerve me more than anything else. So I again went to Mr. Palmer and told him I could not possibly play the Baron. "You must," said Mr. Palmer. "I rather think Mr. Mansfield must have suspected something of the sort, for he has been to me asking, in the event of your not playing it, that I give it to him. I have never seen Mr. Mansfield act; he has not had much experience here, and might ruin the production." At Mr. Palmer's earnest solicitation, I promised to try it again. I had by this time worked myself into such a state of nervousness that my wife interfered. "All the theatres in the world," said she, "are not worth what you are suffering. Go and tell Mr. Palmer you positively cannot play the part." Fearing the outcome, I did not risk another interview with my manager, but sought out Mr. Cazauran, and returned the part to him, with a message to Mr. Palmer that I positively declined to play it. The result was that Mr. Mansfield was put in my place.[1]

[1] Recollections of a Player. By J. H. Stoddart. Copyright, 1902, the Century Company.

THE UNION SQUARE THEATRE

Richard Mansfield was born in 1857 in the Island of Heligoland, Germany. His mother, Madame Rudersdorff, was a well-known singer. Mansfield began his stage career in England, playing small parts in the Gilbert and Sullivan comic operas. In 1882, he came to America and appeared at the Standard Theatre, New York, as Dromez, the miller, in Bucalossi's " Les Manteaux Noirs." Later that same year, he was seen in the cast of " Iolanthe " in Philadelphia. Then came the engagement for small comedy parts at the Union Square Theatre, followed by the golden opportunity which Stoddart's hesitancy brought about. Paul Wilstach, in his " Life of Mansfield," describes the pains to which Mansfield went to insure his success in the part:

When the part of Chevrial was given to him, Mansfield was fascinated with his opportunity, but he kept his counsel. He applied every resource of his ability to the composition of his performance of the decrepit old rake. He sought specialists on the infirmities of roués, he studied specimens in clubs, on the avenue, and in hospitals; and in the privacy of his own room he practiced make-ups for the part every spare moment. The rehearsals themselves were sufficiently uneventful. He gave evidence of a careful, workmanlike performance, but promise of nothing more. While he was working out the part, Mansfield scarcely ate or slept. He had a habit of dining with a group of young Bohemians at a table d'hôte in Sixth Avenue. The means of none of them made regularity at these forty-cent banquets possible, so his absence was meaningless. One evening, however, he dropped into his accustomed chair, but tasted nothing. " What's the matter, Mansfield? " asked one of the others. " Tomorrow night I shall be famous," he said. " Come see the play." [1]

The first night came and Mansfield's triumph was complete. After the terrific scene when the decrepit

<hr>

[1] Richard Mansfield—the Man and the Actor. By Paul Wilstach. Copyright, 1908, Charles Scribner's Sons.

old voluptuary falls dead, champagne glass in hand, the house went wild. The actor was recalled a dozen times, and the next morning, as he had said, he found himself famous. Other rôles in which he had great success were Dr. Jekyl and Mr. Hyde, Prince Karl, Beau Brummel and Cyrano de Bergerac.

Mansfield was a man of many parts. He spoke several languages, he was a graceful dancer, he sang well, he was an accomplished musician. As an actor, he was forceful, but undisciplined. He was artificial and stiff in manner, and had marked mannerisms and eccentricities which the unthinking mistook for genius. He had many admirers, and so prominent a critic as William Winter devoted two large volumes of biography to his memory. But his true place as an actor is probably that accorded him by John Ranken Towse, who says:

> During his mid-career he mastered most of the mechanical difficulties of his art, and greatly developed his powers of voicing the baser forms of passion. Thus in melodrama he was often exceedingly impressive. The loftier heights of tragic emotion he could not scale. That he had imagination was sufficiently proven by the range and variety of the characters he assumed, but he could only vitalize such ideals as could be expressed in the terms of his individual self. He was not really a versatile player except in the realm of eccentric comedy, where the mimetic faculty, which was strong in him, had full scope. Had he worked steadily along this line, he might have created masterpieces which would have won a permanent place in theatrical history. As it is, I cannot recall a single character, of any importance, that is now associated with his name. His personality only will endure in the memory of his contemporaries.[4]

The following year (1883) A. M. Palmer retired

[4] Sixty Years of the Theatre. Copyright, 1916, by John Ranken Towse. Funk & Wagnalls Company, Publishers. Reprinted by permission.

from the management of the Union Square Theatre and spent some time travelling in Europe. On his return in 1884, he became manager of the Madison Square Theatre, formerly the Fifth Avenue, and now owned by the Mallory Brothers, one of whom was a clergyman and editor of *The Churchman*.

After the fire in 1873, which drove out the Daly company, the little playhouse had been rebuilt and reopened in 1877 as the Fifth Avenue Hall. Various attractions appeared here until 1879, when the place was closed and reopened as the Madison Square Theatre with Steele Mackaye, the actor-playwright, as director.

Steele Mackaye, the author of " Hazel Kirke," " Paul Kauvar," and other successful plays, was an interesting figure in the development of the American drama. Born in Buffalo in 1842, he studied dramatic expression in Paris under Delsarte, and on his return to America became an exponent in this country of the Delsarte, or natural, method of acting. Two early plays, " Monaldi " and " Marriage," the latter an adaptation from the French of Octave Feuillet, attracted little attention, but " Rose Michel," an adaptation made for the Union Square Theatre, proved a hit and established his reputation as a playwright.

Backed by the Mallorys, Steele Mackaye now devoted all his attention to the management of the Madison Square Theatre. He introduced several novel features, one of which was the double stage, allowing for one scene to be set while another was being played before the audience, and began by producing his own plays. The first piece, " Won at Last," originally produced at Wallack's two years

previously, enjoyed a short run, after which, on
February 4, 1880, he presented " Hazel Kirke," a
play which proved a tremendous success and had a
run of five hundred nights. In the cast were Effie
Ellsler as Hazel Kirke, C. W. Couldock as Dunstan
Kirke, Eben Plympton as Lord Travers and Mrs.
Thomas Whiffen as Mercy. Other members of the
company at that time included Rose Coghlan, Ada
Gilman, Thomas Whiffen, Genevieve Stebbins, Ce-
cile Rush, Josephine Craig, Frank Weston, B. T.
Ringgold and Richard Brennan.

At this time, Steele Mackaye had gathered around
him several men destined before long to become figures of importance in the American theatrical world.
Henry C. De Mille, a former school teacher who
later became a successful dramatist, was employed as
play reader. Daniel Frohman was engaged as business manager. Gustave Frohman, who was in charge
of the travelling companies, had Charles Frohman
as his assistant.

Towards the end of the run of " Hazel Kirke,"
Steele Mackaye had a disagreement with the Mallorys, which resulted in his leaving the Madison
Square Theatre and opening the new Lyceum Theatre on Fourth Avenue and Twenty-third Street.

Meantime, the Madison Square Theatre continued to make successful productions. On June 1,
1881, William Gillette appeared for the first time
in his dual capacity of actor-dramatist, acting the
rôle of Professor Hopkins in his own play, " The
Professor."

One of the most successful and industrious of our
native playwrights, William Gillette was born at

270

Hartford, Conn., in 1857. He first went on the stage in 1875 at the Globe Theatre, Boston, as Guzman in " Faint Heart Ne'er Won Fair Lady." In 1880, he turned his attention to playwriting and for the next twenty years produced a great number of original plays and adaptations, ranging from farce to melodrama, the best known of which are " The Private Secretary" (an adaptation of a farce by Von Moser, entitled " Der Bibliothekar "), " Esmeralda " (with Mrs. F. H. Burnett), " All the Comforts of Home " (from the German), " Held by the Enemy," " Too Much Johnson," " Secret Service," " Sherlock Holmes " (with Conan Doyle), etc., etc.

" The Professor " ran one hundred and fifty nights and was followed by several other notable successes: " Esmeralda," with Annie Russell in the title rôle; Bronson Howard's comedy, "Young Mrs. Winthrop "; " May Blossom," by David Belasco, in which Georgia Cayvan, later the popular leading lady at the Lyceum, appeared as the fisherman's daughter, and William Young's comedy, " The Rajah," which ran one hundred and fifty nights.

William Young, a distinguished American poetical dramatist, began his career, like Boker, as a law student, but, attracted to playwriting, he went on the stage to acquire dramatic technique. His poetical play, " Pendragon," a tragedy from the legends of King Arthur, was produced in 1881 by Lawrence Barrett with great elaboration of *mise en scène,* and two years later his prose comedy, " The Rajah," met with almost equal success. In 1889, he produced another romantic tragedy, " Ganelon," in which Lawrence Barrett appeared in the title rôle. His best-known work is his dramatization of General Lew Wallace's popular story, " Ben Hur."

A. M. Palmer assumed direction of the theatre on September 1, 1884, and on September 29 startled the select clientèle of this staid little playhouse, of which one of the owners was a clergyman, by producing " The Private Secretary," an hilarious farce which has a low comedy clergyman as its hero. But no one took offense. A vast change had by this time taken place in the attitude of the public towards things theatrical. The old-time religious and moral scruples had been almost entirely swept away. The play proved a great success and enjoyed a run of two hundred nights.

Other interesting bills during the next two seasons included Henry Arthur Jones' " Saints and Sinners," W. S. Gilbert's " Engaged," Bronson Howard's " Old Love Letters," and William Gillette's war play, " Held by the Enemy," the forerunner of a number of successful dramas based on our Civil War.

The season of 1886–87 opened auspiciously November 1 with Sir Charles Young's melodrama, " Jim the Penman," the most noteworthy of all the Madison Square Theatre productions, in which Agnes Booth made a great hit as the devoted wife suddenly confronted with the fact that her husband is a forger. The play had a prosperous career, the brilliant cast including Frederic Robinson, W. J. Le Moyne, E. M. Holland, Louis F. Massen, Walden Ramsay, C. P. Flockton, Harry Holliday, William Davidge, Maud Harrison, Mrs. E. J. Phillips, H. M. Pitt, Herbert Millward, Agnes Booth, May Robson.

Another interesting première occurred the following spring when Annie Russell, a popular actress of great personal charm, was seen (April 28) as the heroine in a dramatization by George Parsons Lathrop and Harry Edwards of Tennyson's poem, " Elaine."

Other successful productions at this house included " Captain Swift," a drama by C. Haddon Chambers, in which Maurice Barrymore appeared as the picturesque hero, and " Aunt Jack," an English farce by Ralph Lumley, with a good part for Agnes Booth. These, in turn, were followed by " Beau Brummel " and " Alabama "—plays which brought to the front two rising American playwrights of great promise—Clyde Fitch and Augustus Thomas.

Clyde Fitch, one of the most prolific and successful of American dramatists, was born at Elmira, New York, in 1865. He began his career by writing for the magazines, but finding literature a slow and difficult road to wealth, he turned his attention to the stage. About this time (1889) he made the acquaintance of Richard Mansfield, who suggested to him the writing of a play based on the life of the famous fop, Beau Brummel. The play proved an enormous success and a controversy at once arose as to the credit for its authorship, the claim being made that it was mainly Mansfield's work, Fitch having been employed by the actor as an amanuensis. But Fitch continued to produce successful plays. In 1890, came " Frederick Lemaitre," written for Felix Morris, and this in turn was followed by " A Modern Match," " Pamela's Prodigy," " His Grace de Grammont "; " The Cowboy and the Lady," " The Moth and the Flame," " Nathan Hale," " Barbara Frietchie,"

" The Climbers," " The Girl and the Judge," " Captain Jinks of the Horse Marines," " Lovers' Lane," " The Girl with the Green Eyes," " Her Great Match," etc., etc.

Clyde Fitch made an immense fortune with his plays. " He will pass into theatrical history," says a biographer, " as one of our first native dramatists to possess distinctive qualities of wit, refinement and close observation of the life about him. In his abundance of detail and his handling of it, he has been surpassed by few writers. He had the professional touch, and a wonderful facility of composition. His art enabled him to transmute anything of value to stage use. His trivialities were perfect. He often lacked serious purpose in his plots, and made a mere convenience of them for the sake of detail, wit, characterization, episode and business, so that his very expertness, which made his plays so pleasing for the moment, is against the permanency of much of his work."

Augustus Thomas, who, at the present writing (1919), is regarded as America's most representative dramatist, was born in St. Louis, Mo., in 1859. He began his career by studying law, but later took up journalism, and after serving on the staffs of several newspapers in St. Louis, Kansas City and New York, finally turned his attention to the stage. His first play, " Editha's Burglar," adapted from Frances Hodgson Burnett's novel, was produced at the Madison Square Theatre in 1889. The success of this piece led to his joining A. M. Palmer's literary staff, and while thus engaged he handed Mr. Palmer the MS. of " Alabama," a play full of the atmosphere of Southern life and which, Colonel Henry Watterson said, did more in one night to put an end to sectional strife than he had been able to do in years. Presented April 1, 1891, " Alabama " scored a great success and Thomas now found himself a popular dramatist much in demand. Later plays from his pen include: " Colonel Carter of Cartersville " (1892), " In Mizzouri " (1893), " Arizona " (1900), " On the Quiet " (1901), " Colorado " (1901), " The Earl of Pawtucket " (1903), " The Witching Hour " (1907), " As a Man Thinks " (1911), etc., etc.

The production of " Alabama " proved the high water mark of A. M. Palmer's success as a manager. After that, he lost ground rapidly and never regained it. In 1891, he surrendered the Madison Square Theatre to Messrs. Hoyt and Thomas (for the exploitation of the Hoyt farces) and moved further up Broadway to Wallack's old theatre, at the corner of Thirtieth Street, of which he had secured control in 1888, the name " Palmer's " having been substituted for the historic " Wallack's."

It was an unfortunate move for Palmer. He was unsuccessful from the start, although he contrived to keep the theatre going for a few years. In 1895, Mr. Palmer partly retrieved his failing fortunes by the production of " Trilby," a dramatization of Du Maurier's novel—then the literary sensation of the hour—by Paul M. Potter. The play was first performed at the Garden Theatre April 15 with Virginia Harned as the barefooted heroine, Burr McIntosh as Taffy, John Glendenning as the Laird, Alfred Hickman as Little Billie and Leo Ditrichstein as Zou Zou. A particular hit was scored by Wilton Lackaye as the Mephistophelian Svengali.

Meantime, some interesting attractions appeared at Palmer's, including Mr. and Mrs. Kendal in repertoire, Digby Bell in " Jupiter," Henry E. Dixey in the Gilbert and Sullivan operas, Charles Wyndham in " David Garrick," John Drew and Maude Adams in " The Masked Ball," Viola Allen and William Faversham in Bronson Howard's " Aristocracy," Edward E. Rice's burlesque " 1492," Julia Arthur in " Lady Windemere's Fan," E. S. Willard in English melodrama, etc., etc. But the huge barnlike auditorium proved unsuitable for stock performance, and in 1896 Palmer finally gave up the struggle and retired from management.

Another success identified with the Union Square Theatre was Bronson Howard's comedy, " The Henrietta," which was seen at that house for the first time on any stage, September 26, 1887, with W. H. Crane in the character of Nicholas Vanalstyne and Stuart Robson as Bertie the Wall Street lamb.

One of the most popular comedians on the American stage, William H. Crane was born at Leicester, Mass., in 1845, and made his stage début at Utica, N. Y., in 1863. Later, he went out West and in 1877 formed that association with Stuart Robson which continued until 1889. During the two comedians' successful partnership, Crane was seen as the Dromio of Ephesus in the " Comedy of Errors " (1878), Sir Toby Belch in " Twelfth Night " (1881), Falstaff in " Merry Wives " (1885). In 1890, he scored a great hit as Senator Hannibal Rivers in " The Senator " and later was successful in such plays as " Brother John," " The Governor of Kentucky," " David Harum," etc.

A New York theatre highly popular in the early

THE UNION SQUARE THEATRE

eighties was the Casino, at the corner of Broadway
and Thirty-ninth Street, which was first opened to
the public in 1882 with Rudolph Aronson as director.
With its Moorish style of architecture and Oriental
furnishings, which gave it more the appearance of
an Eastern seraglio than a modern theatre, and with
its open-air roof garden, then a novelty in this country, the Casino was immediately successful and became known as the home of light opera. In addition
to " Erminie," which had the longest run of any
operetta ever produced in this country, there were
seen here in quick succession: " The Queen's Lace
Handkerchief," " Prince Methusalem," " The Merry
War," " Die Fledermaus," " Indigo," " Gypsy
Baron," " The Beggar Student," " Poor Jonathan,"
"Apajune," "Vice Admiral," "The Grand Duchess,"
" The Princess of Trebizonde," " The Drum Major,"
" The Brigands," " Madame Angot," " The Little
Duke," " Falka," " Nadjy," " Amorita," " The Tyro-
lean," and " The Yeomen of the Guard." To the
present generation the Casino recalls interesting
memories as the stage on which Lillian Russell,
Marie Tempest, David Warfield, DeWolf Hopper,
Francis Wilson, Marion Manola and Marie Jansen
made their reputations.

Lillian Russell, noted far and wide for her radiant
beauty, was born in Iowa in 1861 and educated at the
Convent of the Sacred Heart in Chicago, where her
singing voice was trained for choir work. In 1879,
she received an offer from E. E. Rice to appear in
the chorus of " Pinafore." The following year she
sang ballads on the stage of Tony Pastor's Theatre.
Her first appearance at the Casino was in " The Sor-
cerer," April 17, 1883.

THE THEATRE IN AMERICA

Francis Wilson, one of the most successful of American low comedians, was born in Philadelphia in 1854, and made his stage début at the Chestnut Street Theatre in that city in 1878 in " London Assurance." That same year he toured with Annie Pixley in " M'lss." He was first seen in New York at Haverley's Theatre January 14, 1880, in " Our Gobelins." He was in the cast of " The Queen's Lace Handkerchief " the night the Casino was first opened and subsequently made a great hit at that house as Cadeaux in " Erminie." Later, he starred in such pieces as " The Oolah," " The Merry Monarch," etc., etc.

In 1887 James Bailey, Frank W. Sanger, T. Henry French and Elliott Zborowski built a new playhouse at the corner of 40th Street and Broadway, which they called the Broadway Theatre. It opened March 3, 1888, when Sardou's " La Tosca " was produced for the first time in America, with Frank Mordaunt as Scarpia, Fanny Davenport as La Tosca, and Melbourne MacDowell as Mario. The following December " Little Lord Fauntleroy," dramatized from Frances Hodgson Burnett's story, was seen for the first time with Elsie Leslie as the youthful hero. The piece had a tremendous run in New York and was immensely successful all all over the country.

The Broadway Theatre remained a popular house until a few years ago, when it was given over to moving pictures. During its best days, the most prominent stars appeared on its stage, including Lillian Russell, Modjeska, Salvini, Rhea, De Wolf Hopper, Fanny Davenport and Lawrence Barrett. It was on the boards of this theatre that Edwin Booth said his last farewell to the New York stage, March 28, 1891, when he appeared as Hamlet.

CHAPTER XXVIII

RISE OF THE FROHMANS

STEELE MACKAYE AT THE LYCEUM. R. B. MANTELL, VIOLA ALLEN
AND JOHN MASON. MINNIE MADDERN FISKE. E. A. SOTHERN
AND JULIA MARLOWE. DAVID BELASCO ARRIVES IN NEW YORK.
LYCEUM STOCK COMPANY. CHARLES FROHMAN'S ENTERPRISES.
JOHN DREW A STAR. SUCCESS OF MAUDE ADAMS. EMPIRE THE-
ATRE, NEW YORK, OPENED. DEATH OF CHARLES FROHMAN.

STEELE MACKAYE, after his quarrel with the Mallorys, joined Gustave Frohman and Franklin Sargent in establishing the Lyceum School of Acting, for
the use of which a small theatre had been built on
Fourth Avenue, between Twenty-third and Twenty-
fourth Streets. In 1885, Messrs. Mackaye and Frohman leased the Lyceum Theatre and opened it April
6 in that year with Steele Mackaye's drama, " Dakolar," a piece partly suggested by Ohnet's novel, " The
Ironmaster." In the cast were three players who later
became great favorites—Robert B. Mantell, Viola
Allen and John Mason.

Practically the last of the Shakespearian actors,
Robert Bruce Mantell was born in Scotland in 1854.
After considerable success as an actor in the English
provinces, he came to America in 1878 and was first
seen at the Leyland Opera House, Albany, as Tybalt
in " Romeo and Juliet," with Mme. Modjeska. A
few years afterwards, he repeated his success in New
York, where he appeared in support of Fanny Davenport in " Fédora " and quite eclipsed the star by the

brilliancy and force of his acting. Later, he became a Shakespearian actor of considerable distinction.

Viola Allen, who played Madeleine in " Dakolar," was first seen on the stage at the Madison Square Theatre, July 4, 1882, when she succeeded Annie Russell in " Esmeralda." A charming and sympathetic actress, she was a great favorite in leading rôles for a number of years. She appeared in support of Tommaso Salvini in 1886 and was one of the cast of the war play " Shenandoah." In 1893, she joined the Empire stock company under Charles Frohman and later starred as Glory Quayle in " The Christian " and other plays.

John Mason (1858–1919), one of America's most popular leading men, made his stage début at the Walnut Street Theatre, Philadelphia, in 1878 and later went to the Boston Museum, where he played leading parts for many years. He was in the cast of " The Danischeffs " at the Union Square Theatre in 1884 and later acted in support of Edwin Booth. He was leading man with Mrs. Fiske, and in 1907 met with great success as Jack Brookfield in " The Witching Hour."

Early the following season (September 3, 1885) Minnie Maddern (the Mrs. Fiske of later years) was seen at the Lyceum as Alice Glendenning in Steele Mackaye's adaptation " In Spite of All." Of that performance a critic said : " Without the endowment of beauty, ungifted by the stage presence demanded by the populace, lacking breadth of figure and force of personality, she nevertheless manages by the rarest of all gifts to seize, by some inexplicable faculty of her own, upon the sensibility of her auditors and to do the most marvelously subtle, tender and pensive bits of acting which it has ever been our good fortune to witness." Four years later she won much applause as Mrs. Coney in " Featherbrain."

One of the most distinguished actresses of the American stage, Minnie Maddern Fiske was born in New Orleans in 1865. Both her parents were players and she herself was practically brought up on the stage, her début having occurred as the Duke of York in " Richard III," at the tender age of three. She was first seen in New York at Wallack's in 1870, when she appeared as Little Fritz in " Fritz, our German Cousin," with the German dialect comedian J. K. Emmet. At Booth's Theatre, in 1874, she was seen as Prince Arthur in " King John," with John McCullough. In 1882, at the age of sixteen, she abandoned child rôles and made her début as the frolicsome Chip, the ferryman's daughter, in " Fogg's Ferry." " She came forward," says a reviewer of that day, " like a new Lotta, young, slender, sprightly, quite pretty, arch of manner, rash in the matter of her stockings, as Lotta always was, and possessed of undeniable red hair." In 1884, she was seen for the first time in " Caprice," in which play, and " In Spite of All," she later toured the country.

In 1890, she married Harrison Grey Fiske and temporarily retired from the stage. On her reappearance in 1894, the public saw an actress of an entirely different quality, her method, as William Winter expressed it, " commingling impetuous volubility with intensity of repressed emotion." Now known as Mrs. Fiske, she became an exponent of the Ibsen drama, appearing with great success as Nora

THE THEATRE IN AMERICA

in "A Doll's House" (1894), Hedda Gabbler (1903), Rebecca West in "Rosmersholm" (1907), and Lona Hessel in "Pillars of Society" (1910). In 1897, she was seen as Tess in "Tess of the D'Urbervilles," and two years later appeared as Thackeray's heroine, "Becky Sharp," one of her most successful characterizations. Other rôles include "Frou-Frou" (1894), Giulia in "Little Italy" (1899), "The Unwelcome Mrs. Hatch" (1901), Mary in "Mary of Magdala" (1902), Leah Kleschna (1904), Cynthia Karslake in Langdon Mitchell's comedy "The New York Idea" (1906), Salvation Nell (1908), Hannele (1910), Mrs. Bumpstead Leigh (1911). The season of 1911 Mrs. Fiske revived "Becky Sharp," and the same year was seen in a new comedy by Langdon Mitchell, entitled "The New Marriage." In 1912, she was seen at the Empire Theatre, New York, in "Julia France," by Gertrude Atherton. Later, she appeared in "Lady Patricia," a play by Rudolph Bésier, and as Mary Page in Edward Sheldon's "The High Road." In 1914, she produced "Lady Betty Martingale," by John Luther Long, and in 1916 was seen in "Erstwhile Susan," by Marian de Forest.

Critical opinion differs as to Mrs. Fiske's rank as an actress. One critic writes with enthusiasm:

Emerging in the first maturity of her powers at the first flowering of the modern drama, Mrs. Fiske instinctively and surely identified herself with the best that was awaking in the theatre of Europe and America. With the production of "Tess" she came into her own. Her Tess, with its tragic, fateful power; her Becky, with its resourceful and gleaming comedy; her pathetic and ennobling Nell, are among the unforgetable things alongside Ada Rehan's Katharine and the Hamlet of Forbes-Robertson.[1]

[1] Alexander Woollcott, dramatic critic, *New York Times*.

RISE OF THE FROHMANS

Another critic takes quite the opposite view. He says:

In all her " creations " she presented her own identity without any substantial modification of speech, gesture, look, or manner. Situations, circumstances, differed, not the personality. It may be granted unreservedly that that personality was uncommon, piquant, provocative and interesting, and exceedingly effective in parts with which it happened to be in accordance. Her bright, inquisitive, slightly aggressive manner; her decisive movements and snappy utterances were admirably adapted to the light comedies—such as " Featherbrain "—in which she first won public favor. In that line her early work was full of promise. But her ambition, which was active and dauntless, inclined her to the more serious and emotional dramas, for which she had not the necessary histrionic or artistic qualifications. Her elocution was faulty and did not lend itself readily to emotional expression. She could be imperious, sarcastic, fiery, and angry, but the deeper notes of passion she could not sound, and her pathos was hard and hollow, without the true ring.[2]

At the end of the season of 1885, Daniel Frohman acquired a lease of the Lyceum and he sublet the house for two season to Helen Dauvray, who opened November 10 with a new play by Bronson Howard, entitled " One of Our Girls." In the cast was Edward H. Sothern, son of E. A. Sothern of Dundreary fame.

Born in 1859, E. H. Sothern began his stage career as a farcical comedian in such pieces as " The Highest Bidder " and " Lord Chumley," but his natural bent being more in the direction of the romantic drama, he entered that field exclusively and, after achieving success in Hauptmann's poetic play, " The Sunken Bell," and again later in Justin Huntly McCarthy's romantic drama, " If I Were King," finally developed into a popular Shakespearian star. An intelligent, if uninspired, Shakespearian actor, he presented the

---

[2] John Ranken Towse, dramatic critic, New York *Evening Post.*

plays with scholarly accuracy and great splendor of *mise en scène,* and in association with Julia Marlowe, an actress of great beauty and widespread popularity, succeeded for many years in making an affirmative answer to the frequently asked question: " Does Shakespeare pay? "

Julia Marlowe was born in England in 1870 and came to America when five years old. Her real name is Frost. She made her first appearance on any stage at Ironton, Ohio, in 1882 as a sailor in a juvenile " H. M. S. Pinafore " company. After remaining for some time in comic opera, she became interested in Shakespeare, appearing as Balthazar in " Romeo and Juliet " and Maria in " Twelfth Night." Later, she studied elocution with Ada Dow. Her début as a star occurred at New London, Conn., in 1887, when she appeared as Parthenia in " Ingomar." For some time the public and critics refused to take her seriously as a Shakespearian actress, but gradually her performances compelled attention. On December 12, 1887, she was seen at the Star Theatre, New York, as Juliet for the first time. Of this early performance John Ranken Towse says:

> It was a crude performance, naturally, but it was irradiated by unmistakable flashes of the true fire. She was a sylphlike creature, with wonderful dark eyes, a rich, liquid voice, and a face charming in repose and fascinatingly eloquent in animation. To the eye she was, in many respects, an ideal Juliet. Nine years later, when she had acquired much stage experience, she reappeared in the character. . . . It had gained much in artistic finish, smoothness, clearness, and consistency, but it had fewer of those electric flashes of natural intuition by which it had been illuminated formerly. More artistic in mechanical execution, it was less potent in virginal innocence and youthful fire. . . . In the potion scene she rose, in

her best moments, to tragic heights of emotional expression, but here again occurred unwelcome evidences of calculation in the prolongation of studied pauses and picturesque attitudes. She was not swept onward in the rush of horror-stricken imagination, as were Adelaide Neilson, Modjeska, and Stella Colas. Nevertheless, the performance, as a whole, was attractive, sympathetic, intelligent, and capable, and established her claim to a high place among the leading Juliets of her time.[2]

A few nights later she essayed the rôle of Viola in "Twelfth Night," which has remained one of her most popular impersonations, and from now on her repertoire was exclusively comprised of legitimate and classic rôles. Her best-known parts include Rosalind in "As You Like It," Ophelia, Beatrice in "Much Ado About Nothing," Julia in "The Hunchback," Kate Hardcastle in "She Stoops to Conquer," Barbara Frietchie, Mary Tudor in "When Knighthood was in Flower."

At the close of Helen Dauvray's season, the Lyceum passed under the direct control of Daniel Frohman, who opened May 3, 1887, with "The Highest Bidder," a new farce comedy by J. Madison Morton, in which E. H. Sothern made a hit in a lively comedy part. This was the beginning of the managerial career of the Frohmans who, from now on, were conspicuous in the affairs of the American stage.

Henry Frohman, a Hebrew, came to this country from Germany and began life here as a peddler, finally settling in Sandusky, Ohio, where he opened a small cigar factory. He had three sons—Daniel, Gustave and Charles, all of whom soon broke the confines of the small Ohio town to seek fortune in

[2] Sixty Years of the Theatre. Copyright, 1916, by John Ranken Towse. Funk & Wagnalls Company, Publishers. Reprinted by permission.

285

New York. None of them received much education, but they all had that shrewdness, energy and keen instinct for the theatre which is characteristic of their race. Gustave was the first to make connections with the theatre, having obtained a position as advance man for the Callender Minstrels. Through him, Daniel, who was then in the office of the New York *Tribune,* and Charles, who had been selling tickets in the box office of Hooley's Theatre, Brooklyn, also secured footing in the same line of business. In 1880, Daniel Frohman became business manager of the Madison Square Theatre and five years later acquired the lease of the Lyceum.

Fortunate enough to have a success on his hands from the start, Daniel Frohman now set about organizing a permanent stock company, the first members of which included Herbert Kelcey, an English actor who had appeared at Wallack's; Nelson Wheatcroft, a forceful " heavy " actor; W. J. Le Moyne, excellent in old men rôles; Charles Walcot, eccentric comedian and long a favorite at Wallack's; Georgia Cayvan, leading woman; Charles S. Dickson, Grace Henderson, Mrs. Thomas Whiffen, popular in old lady rôles, and Henry Miller and William Faversham, two English actors who later became stars. Additions to the company included Effie Shannon, a favorite in ingenue rôles; Henrietta Crosman, who later was a successful star; Elizabeth Tyree, Felix Morris, Katherine Florence, Edward J. Morgan, May Robson, Mary Mannering, Grace Elliston, Hilda Spong, Julie Opp and James K. Hackett. For stage manager, Mr. Frohman had secured David Belasco, whom he had brought from the Madison

Square and who, in association with Henry C. De Mille, also performed the duties of house dramatist.

This engagement marked the real beginning of the career of one of the most prominent and remarkable play producers of our time and to-day (1919) the leading theatre manager in America.

David Belasco was born in San Francisco in 1859, of English-Portuguese-Jewish stock. His father, a harlequin in the London theatres, attracted by the gold discoveries in California, came to America early in the fifties and settled in San Francisco. His son David was educated in a monastery, a fact which perhaps explains the manager's quasi-clerical attire which has been characteristic of his personal appearance all his life. But the quiet of the cloister did not suit the temperament of a lad filled with energy and a fierce desire to make his way in the world, and Belasco soon fled from the monks to join a circus. At a very early age he showed a keen instinct for the theatre and wrote his first play when only twelve years of age. After appearing for some time as a super at the California Theatre, he made his first appearance as an actor in 1871 in a small part in a play called " Help," at the Metropolitan Theatre, where he was also employed to copy actors' parts. Then followed a barnstorming tour of the various California and Nevada camps, the parts acted during the first two season including Robert Macaire, Hamlet, Uncle Tom, Marc Antony in " Julius Cæsar " and Raphael in " The Marble Heart." Returning to San Francisco, he was seen at Shiel's Opera House in a great number of plays. Later, he went to Virginia City, Nevada, then a rough mining town, and acted many parts at Piper's Opera House. Here he first met Dion Boucicault, who employed him to take dictation of a play. From Boucicault he learned much of what he knows of the art of playwriting. In 1874, he was back in San Francisco at the California, where he appeared in support of such important stars as Edwin Booth, John McCullough and Edwin Adams. Later, he went to Maguire's, where in addition to acting he was employed as house playwright. Some time was spent touring California with various stars, and then he secured a position at Baldwin's Academy of Music as assistant stage manager. In 1882, when Maguire lost control of the Baldwin Theatre, Belasco decided that his San Francisco career was ended and came to New York. He was then only twenty-nine years old, with a record of 170 parts acted and 100 plays written, adapted or altered.

His first play to attract any attention was " Hearts of Oak," written with James A. Herne and first produced at Hamlin's Theatre, Chicago, in 1879, Katherine Corcoran (Mrs. Herne) making her first appearance in that city in the rôle of Chrystal. His next play, " La Belle Russe," was first seen at the Baldwin Theatre, San Francisco, in 1881, with Jeffreys Lewis as Beatrice, the beautiful but vicious Englishwoman, and Maude Adams as little Beatrice. The play was seen a year later at Wallack's with Rose Coghlan in the title rôle.

The Mallorys engaged him as stage manager at the Madison Square Theatre at a salary of $35 a week. While performing these duties, he wrote " May Blossom." In 1886, Belasco, dissatisfied with his position at the Madison Square, left the Mallorys to join Daniel Frohman at the Lyceum.

During the fifteen years of its existence, the Lyceum was successful in catering to an intelligent and refined clientèle. The theatre never attained the brilliancy of Wallack's. It was not in any sense a rival of Daly's. The tone of the house and the quality of many of the plays presented was distinctly *bourgeois*. But if Daniel Frohman, in his effort to please popular taste, never attempted productions in the big manner of his famous predecessors, what he did do was done well. The plays given were well staged and excellently acted.

The first production by the stock company was a new play by David Belasco and Henry C. De Mille called " The Wife," which was presented November 1, 1887. In this piece Georgia Cayvan made a favorable impression as a repentant wife and Herbert Kelcey and Henry Miller also scored. The play was a great popular success, and while it was enjoying its long run, Belasco and De Mille turned out " Lord Chumley " for E. H. Sothern. The following season (November 13) " Sweet Lavender," by A. W. Pinero, was given for the first time and also had a long run. Then came " Our Flat," a successful farce, followed by " The Charity Ball," another society drama by Belasco and De Mille. Later bills at the Lyceum were " The Maister of Woodbarrow," by Jerome K. Jerome; " The Idler," by Haddon Chambers; " Nerves," by Comyss Carr; " The Dancing Girl," by Henry Arthur Jones; " Lady Bountiful," by A. W. Pinero; " Squire Kate," by Robert Buchanan; " Captain Lettarblair," by Marguerite

Merington; "Americans Abroad," by Sardou; "Sheridan," by Paul Potter; "An American Duchess," by Clyde Fitch; "The Amazons," by A. W. Pinero; "A Woman's Silence," by Sardou; "The Case of Rebellious Susan," by Henry Arthur Jones; "An Ideal Husband," by Oscar Wilde; "The Prisoner of Zenda," by Anthony Hope; "The Home Secretary," by R. C. Carton; "The Benefit of the Doubt," by A. W. Pinero; "An Enemy to the King," by R. N. Stephens; "Change Alley," by L. N. Parker and Murray Carson; "The Princess and the Butterfly," by A. W. Pinero; "The Tree of Knowledge," by R. C. Carton; "Trelawney of the Wells," by A. W. Pinero, and "Miss Hobbs," by Jerome K. Jerome.

In 1889, Daniel Frohman brought over from England Mr. and Mrs. Kendal, long-established favorites in refined domestic melodrama, who made their American début at the Fifth Avenue Theatre, October 7, in Sardou's "Scrap of Paper." The English stars proved immensely popular and toured the United States with the greatest success. In their supporting company were Violet Vanbrugh, J. E. Dodson, an excellent actor in eccentric old men parts who afterwards became a great favorite with our audiences, and Seymour Hicks, then a lad of eighteen and now a well-known actor-manager in London.

That same year also brought prominently before the public another of the Frohman brothers—Charles Frohman.

When Daniel Frohman became business manager of the Madison Square Theatre, his brothers Gustave and Charles were engaged to direct the tours of the "Hazel Kirke" road companies. This experience naturally led to Charles developing into a booking agent, and from this to being a producer on his own account was only a step. Then came the big opportunity which led to Charles Frohman becoming overnight one of the most prominent theatrical men in the country.

Bronson Howard had written a war play called "Shenandoah," a feature of which was Sheridan's ride. Its trial performance in Boston was a failure, and the managers, A. M. Palmer, T. Henry French and Henry E. Abbey, all three of whom held options, had little confidence in it. But there was a less important manager who had reason to believe in war plays. That was Charles Frohman. He remembered how successful he had been with Gillette's "Held by the Enemy." Prevailing upon "Al" Hayman, a San Francisco theatrical promoter, to take a half interest in the piece, he hurried to Boston and secured it. Produced at the Star Theatre, New York, on September 9, 1889, "Shenandoah" was a tremendous success. It ran for months and Frohman divided $200,000 with his financial backers.

Now firmly established as a producing manager, Charles Frohman took a lease of Proctor's Twenty-third Street Theatre and opened there September 8, 1890, with a new play by William Gillette called "All the Comforts of Home." In this play, Maude Adams, who played the rôle of Evangeline Bender, made her first appearance under Charles Frohman's management.

Maude Adams was born in 1872 at Salt Lake City, where her mother, Mrs. Annie Adams, was a mem-

291

ber of the local stock company. She went on the stage at a very early age, first with J. K. Emmett, and then as the child in " A Celebrated Case." Later, mother and daughter went to New York, where Maude was engaged to play the part of Moyna Sullivan in " The Paymaster " at the Star Theatre, September 17, 1888. The following year she joined E. H. Sothern's company, playing Louisa in " The Highest Bidder " and Jessie Dean in " Lord Chumley." Shortly afterwards, Charles Hoyt took her for the part of Dot, the young school teacher, in " The Midnight Bell," and on the termination of that engagement she received an offer from Charles Frohman.

Under Frohman's managerial wing, Maude Adams' rise to success was rapid, even phenomenal. She had no marked histrionic gift, there was not a rôle she attempted that a hundred other actresses could not have done as well or better, yet from the box office point of view she soon became the most popular actress and biggest money-maker on the American stage. Her first season as a star netted her forty thousand dollars and each succeeding season for many years the money poured in until she soon became the richest among living American players.

The secret of Maude Adams' success is not her art, but her personality—an elfish, diaphanous, elusive personality, the charm of which is irresistible and defies all criticism. The public flocked to see her, and the unsophisticated matinee maiden, who liked to regard her as an idealized girlhood, purchased her photographs in such numbers that the supply could not meet the demand. Meantime, Maude Adams was as shy and elusive as her manager. Quite unlike

the average player, she shrunk from public notice.
She was never seen in places where other actresses are
apt to congregate, and her life, never touched by the
breath of scandal, was that of a recluse. All this was
good advertising which, in this particular case,
brought substantial reward.

Charles Frohman's first stock company was organ-
ized at the Twenty-third Street Theatre in 1890. It
included Orrin Johnson, Frank Mordaunt, Emmett
Corrigan, J. C. Buckston, C. Leslie Allen, Sydney
Armstrong, Odette Tyler and William Morris.
Belasco and De Mille were commissioned to write a
new play for the company and this piece, "Men and
Women," was produced October 21. Other interesting bills that followed were "Thermidor," by Sardou; "The Lost Paradise," by Henry C. De Mille;
"The English Rose," by George R. Sims and Robert
Buchanan, and "Across the Potomac," a war play
by Augustus Pitou and Edward M. Alfriend.

In 1892, John Drew, so long leading man at
Daly's, became a star under the management of
Charles Frohman. Clyde Fitch had been engaged to
adapt for him a comedy by Alexander Bisson and
Albert Carré, and in this piece, called "The Masked
Ball," Mr. Drew, supported by Maude Adams, be-
gan his successful stellar career at Wallack's on Oc-
tober 3.

The following season, also, at Palmer's, Mr. Froh-
man produced Bronson Howard's play, "Aristoc-
racy," the company including Wilton Lackaye,
William Faversham, Viola Allen, Blanche Walsh,
Frederick Bond, Bruce McRae, Paul Arthur, W. H.
Thompson and J. W. Pigott.

In 1893, with the backing of " Al " Hayman and
Isaac B. Rich and William Harris, Boston managers, Charles Frohman opened the Empire Theatre,
a handsome new playhouse which had been built for
him at the corner of Broadway and Fortieth Street.
The opening bill, a melodrama of Indian warfare
called " The Girl I Left Behind Me," by David
Belasco and Franklyn Fyles, was a great success, the
play having two hundred and eight consecutive
performances.

Charles Frohman now organized what he called
the Empire Theatre stock company, including such
players as Robert Edeson, Ethel Barrymore, Elita
Proctor Otis, May Robson, Jameson Lee Finney, J.
Henry Benrimo, J. E. Dodson, Ida Conquest, Elsie
De Wolfe, Arthur Byron, Margaret Anglin, Henry
Miller, W. H. Crompton and others. It was a
stock company only in name, its individual members
being made stars at the first opportunity that offered.
The Frohman policy was entirely committed to the
pernicious star and combination systems which, from
now on, dominated the theatrical business in this
country.

The second Empire season began August 21, 1893
with " Liberty Hall," by R. C. Carton, and after this
on January 2, 1894, came " Sowing the Wind," a
play by Sidney Grundy, which had great success.
The following August " Charley's Aunt," one of the
most successful farces ever produced, was seen for the
first time, Etienne Girardot making a great hit in the
title rôle.

The season of 1895 was notable for several important Empire productions—" The Bauble Shop " and

"The Masqueraders," both by Henry Arthur Jones, and "The Importance of Being Earnest," by Oscar Wilde. Then came "Rosemary," a charming comedy of "old-fashioned sentiment," by Louis N. Parker and Murray Carson.

Maude Adams had such success in this last play that Frohman decided to make her a star, and he secured for her use a dramatization by J. M. Barrie of the latter's own story, "The Little Minister." Produced September 27, 1897, with Maude Adams as Lady Babbie and Robert Edeson as Gavin Dishart, the piece ran at the Empire for 300 consecutive performances, after which Miss Adams went on tour with the piece.

In 1899, Maude Adams essayed the rôle of Juliet and the following year she was seen for the first time in boy attire as the pathetic little Duc de Reichstadt in Rostand's Napoleonic play, "L'Aiglon." Two charming comedies, "Quality Street" and "The Pretty Sister of José," followed, and then came Barrie's spectacular "Peter Pan," which proved the greatest success of this popular actress' career. In 1911, Charles Frohman presented in America Rostand's sensational barnyard drama, "Chantecler," in which all the characters are birds and beasts, Maude Adams being cast for the rôle of the crowing rooster. For the first time, Frohman's unerring judgment had failed him. The play, as might easily have been foreseen, was only a success of curiosity, and Miss Adams, a frail, shrinking little woman, was woefully miscast in a rôle necessarily calling for an exhibition of the most lusty virility.

Frohman productions that were notably successful include W. H. Crane in " David Harum," a dramatization of the popular novel which netted half a million dollars for its promoters; William Gillette in " Secret Service," " Too Much Johnson " and " Sherlock Holmes "; Ethel Barrymore in " Captain Jinks " and " Alice Sit-by-the-Fire "; " Under Two Flags," " Are You a Mason," " A Message from Mars," " The Earl of Pawtucket," " The Tyranny of Tears," " Everyman," the morality play which first introduced Edith Wynne Matthison to our stage, " Madame X," " Raffles," " Passers By," " The Thief," " What Every Woman Knows," " Arsène Lupin," " The Twelve Pound Look," " Kismet " and " Grumpy." Among the stars under Charles Frohman's direction were John Drew, Maude Adams, William Gillette, Ethel Barrymore, Annie Russell, Julia Marlowe, Virginia Harned, Mrs. Patrick Campbell, Henry Irving, William Crane, William Faversham, Billie Burke, Julia Sanderson, Blanche Bates, Marie Doro, Nat Goodwin, Cyril Maude and Otis Skinner. Mr. Frohman controlled in New York the Empire, Lyceum, Knickerbocker, Garrick and Criterion Theatres, and also several theatres in other large cities in the United States. In London he controlled the Duke of York's, and at one time the Globe Theatre.

A man of amiable, forceful personality, Charles Frohman was well liked by all who knew him and made many friends both here and abroad. He was liberal in his relations with authors and actors, and his word was known to be as good as his bond. An extremely shy man, he kept out of the public view as much as possible. He always remained hidden on first nights and to most theatregoers and even to many of his own actors, he was only a name. Never having had the advantages of a good education, his attitude toward the theatre was that of the speculator rather than that of the artist. A firm believer in big names, he showed daring and boldness in his many enterprises and fairly earned his nickname, " Napoleon of the Drama." Notwithstanding his many successes, he died a poor man when on May 7, 1915, as a passenger on the ill-fated *Lusitania,* he fell a victim to German frightfulness.

CHAPTER XXIX

THE DRAMA IN OTHER CITIES

CHICAGO AS A PRODUCING CENTRE. THE BOSTON THEATRE, SEL-
WYN'S AND THE BOSTON MUSEUM. THE ARCH STREET AND
BROAD STREET THEATRES IN PHILADELPHIA. THE THEATRE IN
WASHINGTON. THE PRESIDENT AT THE PLAY. FAMOUS CALI-
FORNIA THEATRES. THE PASSION PLAY AT THE GRAND OPERA
HOUSE. THE BALDWIN THEATRE.

WITH the gradual disappearance of the famous stock companies and the general adoption of the combination system, New York became the acknowledged leader, the producing centre of America. Chicago, Boston, Philadelphia, San Francisco and other cities might continue to build luxurious new playhouses, but it was to New York that henceforth they must look for their plays. New York's supremacy in matters theatrical was unquestioned and from now on the history of the stage in the metropolis becomes virtually that of the rest of the country. The plays and players remain the same; only the theatres and the cities change. Mrs. Fiske, George Arliss, John Drew, David Warfield, Ethel Barrymore are as well known and feel quite as much at home in Philadelphia, St. Louis, Baltimore or Detroit as in New York. But no matter how popular the star, the play to-day must have the endorsement of Broadway to attract patronage out of town, and this has led to the vicious practice of forcing runs of poor plays in New York for the sake of the impression it will make " on the road."

One of the principal reasons for the decline of the theatre and the introduction of pernicious business methods was, as pointed out by a writer, the remarkable increase in the railroad mileage of the country and the adoption of the combination system:

> As soon as it became possible to transport productions complete from city to city, dramatic speculators began to arise, and the combination system sprang into life. It was quite evident that it would be much cheaper to move a company with scenery from one city to another than to maintain stock companies all over the land and to make new productions in every city of different plays. And so the fashion came into vogue of producing plays in New York, not with a view of making much money out of them there, but in anticipation of large returns "on the road." The system was profitable from the start. If a play simply paid the cost of its original production in the metropolis, managers were satisfied, because all the receipts in other cities, exclusive of the cost of travelling and the payment of salaries, were clear profit, and the season of such profits meant a small sized fortune. And so the system grew until there was scarcely a manager in the land who had not adopted it. The "combination system," it is called, and it is a very profitable one for the managers, but it struck a blow at the advance of dramatic art from which it will probably never recover.[1]

The only American city that challenges New York's unique theatrical position is Chicago, which of late years has acquired importance as a producing centre. A number of plays which were afterwards received with the greatest enthusiasm all over the country, for example, "The Man from Home," "Alias Jimmy Valentine," "Within the Law," etc., were originally produced in the Windy City. But even Chicago has no great confidence in its own verdict until the metropolis puts the seal of its approval upon a play. "The Man from Home" dragged along for several weeks to poor business and only became a pronounced success elsewhere. "Alias

---

[1] W. W. Austin in the *Theatre Magazine*, August, 1911.

Jimmy Valentine " opened on Christmas eve to about twenty-five persons in the house and played to two weeks of poor business, when Manager George Tyler suddenly carried it to New York, where it made an instant hit. Many plays have become great successes in other cities after a brief and very uncertain tryout in Chicago. " Disraeli," one of the most popular plays in George Arliss's repertoire, is among the number. The truth is that the theatregoing public in Chicago, as elsewhere, avoids a play until it is known to be really successful. There is only a very small coterie of real first nighters in Chicago who go to everything, irrespective of results. The remainder wait cautiously, are suspicious of every new play and are inclined to resent the fact that Chicago is used as a tryout town.

To the producing manager Chicago offers many advantages, commanding as it does the Middle West, the far West and leading the entire country west of Pittsburgh. The early theatrical history of the city has already been outlined in an earlier chapter. The oldest Chicago theatre now extant, the historic Mc-Vicker's, once the city's most rashionable playhouse and the Western home of America's most celebrated players, is to-day a popular-priced vaudeville house. The first McVicker's Theatre, built in 1857, and on the boards of which appeared Edwin Booth, the elder Sothern, J. H. Hackett, Lotta, Charles Kean, Mrs. Scott-Siddons and other famous stars, was destroyed in the great fire. Rebuilt in 1872, and remodelled in 1885, at a total cost of half a million dollars, the house was again destroyed by fire August 26, 1890, during the run of the war play " Shenandoah." Undeterred by his loss, once more Mr. McVicker rebuilt his theatre, opening March 31, 1891, with the Jefferson-Florence company in " The Rivals." McVicker's stock company, which ranked among the best in the country, included such distinguished players as James O'Neill, Louis James and Robert B. Mantell, and some of his productions, notably his revivals of " The School for Scandal," " A Midsummer Night's Dream " and " The Tempest," were among the most elaborate and correct the American stage has ever known. Mr. McVicker died in 1896, and two years later the old house passed under the control of Jacob Litt.

Another famous Chicago theatre—the Crosby Opera House, also swept out of existence by the great fire—was opened in 1865 by Grau's Italian Opera Company in " Il Trovatore," with Clara Louise Kellogg as prima donna. The theatre cost $600,000 and in its day was the finest theatrical structure in the West, even outrivalling with its art gallery and decorations the famous Pike's Opera House of Cincinnati.

The only theatre to survive the fire was the Globe, on Desplaines Street, where Charles Wyndham played his earlier engagements. The first theatre erected after the conflagration was the Academy of Music on Halstead Street, which was opened January 10, 1872, with " Ours." On the boards of this house appeared such popular stars as Lucille Western, Aimée, John McCullough, F. S. Chanfrau, Edwin Adams and Rosina Vokes. The house was destroyed by fire in 1878.

Hooley's, another historic Chicago playhouse, was first opened in 1872 with the Abbott-Kiralfy company. In 1898, the house passed under the control of Harry J. Powers, who remodelled it and reopened it the same year as Powers' Theatre, with Clyde Fitch's play, "The Moth and the Flame." Only first-class comedy and drama is presented at this house. It is also the home of many distinguished visiting stars.

The Auditorium, the largest theatre in Chicago, was opened December 9, 1889, with a musical programme headed by Adelina Patti. Later, Abbey and Grau presented grand opera there. The building has a seating capacity of over 4000 and the most elaborate hydraulic stage in the world. To-day it is devoted to spectacular melodrama and grand opera, and is the rendezvous of the *élite* during the opera season.

Among the more recent Chicago theatres, the Blackstone is, in normal times, the most fashionable house, playing only high-class comedy and drama. It is the Chicago home of various Frohman stars. At present, it is temporarily housing a mammoth moving-picture attraction. The Studebaker, perhaps the handsomest of Chicago's theatres, was built in 1898. Lately, it has been remodelled to resemble the interior of an Italian palazzio of the Renaissance. The Illinois is Chicago's most popular house, playing first-class musical comedy and musical revues. Wood's Theatre is the newest house, very handsome, the interior a symphony in autumn tints, playing A. H. Woods' attractions—comedy, drama and musical comedy. The Garrick is a commodious house, playing melodrama, comedy, drama and first-class musical shows. The Colonial, first-class musical comedy; the Princess, a small house, playing first-class farce and drama; the Cort, playing only farce and farcical melodrama; the Olympic, a popular-price melodrama house; the Playhouse, the smallest of the city's theatres, playing chiefly problem comedy and known as the temple of the " high-brow "—these are Chicago's latest theatres.

Among the older generation of Boston theatregoers, four playhouses are remembered with particular affection—the famous Boston Museum, the Howard Athenæum, the Boston Theatre and Selwyn's, afterwards the Globe.

The Boston Theatre, which stands on Washington Street, is to-day devoted to moving pictures. When it first opened, September 11, 1854, under the management of Thomas Barry, it was considered the most elegant as well as the largest theatre in the United States. " No other theatre in the world," says Eugene Tompkins, " has presented so many notabilities to the public, from tragedians and grand opera singers to negro minstrel and variety performers, from orators and clergymen to ballet dancers and athletes. Scarcely any world-famous artist in the last fifty years has missed making his or her appearance at the Boston Theatre." [2]

The house opened with " The Rivals," with this cast: John Gilbert as Sir Anthony Absolute, Mr. Pauncefort as Captain Absolute, Mr. E. L. Davenport as Fag, John Wood as Acres, Mrs. Barrow as Lydia Languish and Mrs. John Gilbert as Mrs. Malaprop.

The stock company was first seen in such plays as " The Loan of a Lover," " The Wonder," " The Love

---

[2] History of the Boston Theatre. By Eugene Tompkins.

Chase," "The Merchant of Venice," "John Bull,"
etc., etc., the stars of the first season including Julia
Dean, Edwin Forrest, James H. Hackett and E. L.
Davenport. On May 21, 1855, an Italian opera company began a short season, "William Tell" being
heard for the first time in Boston. The following
month the Ravels made their appearance, together
with Blondin, the tight-rope walker. Edwin Booth
opened at this house September 14, 1857, and two days
later played Iago for the first time in Boston. The
following week, he was seen for the first time as
Othello. In 1864, Messrs. Benjamin W. Thayer and
Orlando Tompkins became managers of the theatre,
the company at this time including E. L. Davenport,
J. W. Wallack, George H. Clarke, Benjamin G.
Rogers, J. M. Dawson, George Karnes, George Clair,
Shirley France, C. H. Wilson, Rose Eytinge, Rachel
Noah, Minnie Monk, Ada Monk, Annie L. Brown,
Mrs. Marshall and Harriet Orton. The following
year Frank Mayo joined the organization as leading
man and Fanny Davenport was seen occasionally in
minor rôles. The season of 1866–7 Edwin Booth and
John Sleeper Clarke were lessees of the house, with
J. B. Booth as acting manager. On November 3,
1868, Edwin Booth appeared as Macbeth to the Lady
Macbeth of Fanny Janauschek, she speaking her lines
in German to Mr. Booth's English.

In 1873, J. B. Booth, retiring from the management, was succeeded by L. R. Shewell, who organized
the following company: H. S. Murdoch, J. H. Fitz-
patrick, C. Leslie Allen, D. J. Maguinnis, J. W.
Hague, T. M. Hunter, W. H. Norton, George
W. Wilson, Rufus Scott, Harry Richmond, R. J.

Dillon, E. B. Holmes, J. O. Stevens, J. W. Gardiner, Harvey Collins, William Raynor, Charles Madden, Mrs. Thomas Barry, Olivia Rand, Blanche Hayden, Mrs. Charles Poole, Mrs. C. L. Allen, Hattie Stevens, Marie Uart, Carrie Prescott, Marion Follett, Annie Winslow, Emma Smiley, Iola Smiley, Carrie Jones, Misses Hoffman and Morgan. When Shewell relinquished control at the close of the season of 1877–78, Eugene Tompkins assumed the reins, which he continued to hold until his retirement in 1901. The first season under Mr. Tompkins' management opened August 23, 1880, with " Hearts of Oak," presenting James A. Herne and others. The company included: Mark Price, D. J. Maguinnis, C. Leslie Allen, M. J. Jordan, Frank S. Hartshorn, George R. Parks, Otis Skinner, S. E. Springer, J. T. Craven, H. E. Chase, J. W. Taylor, Arthur Moulton, H. A. Cripps, E. Y. Backus, Master Harry Woodruff, Margaret Lanner, Rachel Noah, Mrs. M. A. Pennoyer, Zoe Tuttle, Charlene Weidman and Mary Tucker.

In 1867, John H. Selwyn opened on Washington Street a theatre which became highly popular first as Selwyn's and afterwards as the Globe. The establishment of the new house, says Henry Austin Clapp, " had been regarded as a great event and the merits of its first three stock companies—of which Mrs. Chanfrau, Miss Carson, Miss Mary Cary, Mrs. Thomas Barry, Miss Harris, Miss Kitty Blanchard, Mrs. Wilkins, Miss Wells, Miss Fanny Morant, Mrs. E. L. Davenport and Messrs. Frederic Robinson, Stuart Robson, C. H. Vandenhoff, H. S. Murdoch, W. J. Le Moyne, G. H. Griffiths, Harry Pearson, H.

F. Daly and Harry Josephs were, at different times, members—were, it might almost be said, the chief theme of Boston's table-talk." [3]

The theatre opened with Sardou's comedy, " La Famille Benoiton," performed under the title " The Fast Family." Then were given " Dora," dramatized by Charles Reade from Tennyson's idyl; " The Spirit of '76," by Mrs. Daniel Sargent Curtis, and Robertson's " Ours," followed later by " School," " Home," " Caste " and other Robertsonian plays and dramatic versions of Dickens' novels. " Dora " proved an immense success. Says Mr. Clapp: " All the theatregoing population of Boston—then about half the population of Boston—went wild over ' Dora,' a purling piece, surface-ruffled only by Farmer Allen's tyrannical self-will and honest obstinacy, which were presented with heavy-handed effectiveness by Mr. Robinson. It was Dora herself, the gentle, persuasive Dora, the rustic but not rude, the meek but not insipid—beautiful, sweet, soundhearted to the core, like some perfect fruit ripened in a sunny nook of an English garden—it was this Dora that prevailed with everybody, in the person of Mrs. F. S. Chanfrau, whose style was as frank and unaffected as her face was lovely, her voice melodious, her manner gracious." [4]

The Boston Museum, from the year 1863 under the capable direction of R. M. Field, was for nearly half a century one of the most famous theatres in America. It was here, in 1849, that Edwin Booth made his first appearance on any stage, and from

[3] and [4] Reminiscences of a Dramatic Critic. Copyright, 1902. By Henry Austin Clapp. Boston: Houghton, Mifflin & Co.

1850 to 1870 were seen on its boards such prominent artists as Junius Brutus Booth, Edwin Adams, William Warren, Charlotte Cushman, George Vandenhoff, James W. Wallack, Eliza Logan, C. W. Couldock, Matilda Heron, Walter Montgomery, Agnes Robertson, and Mrs. John Drew.

On November 25, 1878, Gilbert and Sullivan's operetta, " H. M. S. Pinafore," was presented at the Boston Museum for the first time in America with Marie Wainwright as Josephine. Marie Wainwright, an American actress of great personal charm, was born in Philadelphia in 1853, and trained abroad for the lyric stage. She made her stage début at Booth's Theatre, New York, May 17, 1877, in " Romeo and Juliet," at George Rignold's benefit when he played Romeo to six Juliets. Later she was seen as the Princess in " Henry V," and then came her appearance as Josephine in " Pinafore." Afterwards she became leading woman for Lawrence Barrett and later starred with Louis James.

In 1879 William Seymour, so long associated with this famous theatre, joined the Museum as stage manager. He remained there ten years, afterwards going to the Tremont, where he was acting manager for Abbey, Schoeffel and Grau. In 1898, Mr. Seymour joined Charles Frohman as general stage director.

" The Boston Museum stock company was in its day," says Kate Ryan, " a powerful influence on the minds, morals and manners of all classes." The writer continues:

The decade between 1873 and 1883 saw the Boston Museum at the zenith of its greatness. Never before or since has such a

coterie of players graced an American stage. Here were produced
the works of Shakespeare, Sheridan, Goldsmith, Bulwer-Lytton,
Taylor, Robertson, the Morton farces, and the Gilbert and Sullivan
operas. These plays demanded actors possessing dramatic fire,
imagination, and intelligence; actors who could play in tragedy
and farce in the same night; actors capable of representing historic
traits, elegant manners, with pure diction and well-carried costumes. All this was the result of a broad experience and a sound,
fundamental training. . . . After William Warren's retirement in 1883, there was a marked change in the character of the
Boston Museum. The patrons missed the players with whom they
had become familiar, and whom they regarded rather as old friends
of long standing than as actors playing for their amusement. They
were accustomed to their traits and peculiarities, which explains the
popularity of the old English comedies, so frequently repeated that
they were as familiar as household words. There was a falling off
in the production of the old comedies and standard plays.[5]

Among Boston's more modern theatres are the
Boston Opera House, the imposing home for grand
opera built by Eben D. Jordan, the Majestic Theatre,
Hollis Street Theatre, the Wilbur, the Shubert, the
Plymouth, the Park Square and the Colonial. Then
there is the old Tremont, which still plays first-class
attractions, and the Castle Square, where in 1909
John Craig organized a stock company that justly
ranked as one of the best in the country, and which
to-day is devoted to two-a-day stock. Interesting
stock productions are also a feature at Henry Jewett's small Copley Theatre.

Philadelphia—up to the time of the Revolution
the leading show town in America—to-day ranks
fourth in theatrical importance. Of its famous old
playhouses, only the Walnut Street Theatre, still a
popular resort and bearing proudly its inscription

[5] Old Boston Museum Days. By Kate Ryan. Copyright, 1915. Boston:
Little, Brown & Co.

"oldest in America," still remains. The site of the old Southwark Theatre, till recently, was used as a distillery, and the ground on which stood the first Chestnut Street Theatre is now occupied by an office building.

The theatres of a later period, the second Chestnut Street Theatre and the old Arch Street Theatre, made famous by Edwin Forrest and Mrs. John Drew, are still interesting landmarks. The history of the Chestnut Street Theatre extends considerably over half a century. In the sixties appeared on its stage such favorites as Lucille Western, the Broughams, Couldock, W. E. Sheridan, Charles Santley, W. J. Ferguson, F. W. Sanger, and E. L. Davenport. In 1869 Laura Keene assumed the management of the house. She organized a strong stock company and opened September 20 with "The Marble Heart," the actress-manager playing the rôle of Marco and W. E. Sheridan appearing as Raphael the sculptor. Later, the house was the home of a resident stock company directed by William G. Gemmel. In 1878 Francis Wilson began his successful career at this house as Cool in "London Assurance." Early in the nineties the old theatre became the home of musical comedy and the lighter form of drama.

The history of the Arch Street Theatre has already been outlined * in earlier chapters. One of the most famous of Philadelphia playhouses, it was the scene of Edwin Forrest's earlier triumphs and the stage on which he produced all his original plays, "The Gladiator," "Metamora," "Broker of Bo-

* See Chapters on Edwin Forrest and Mrs. John Drew.

gota," and " Jack Cade." The Drews, so prominently
identified with the best traditions of the Philadelphia
stage, first became connected with the house in 1851,
when it was under the management of Mr. Hemphill. Later, Hemphill gave a lease to William
Wheatley and John Drew, and the house was reopened as Wheatley and Drew's Arch Street Theatre.
At the end of the second season, Drew retired and
John Sleeper Clarke, brother-in-law of Edwin
Booth and for many years leading comedian at the
Arch Street house, took his place in the management.
In 1860, at the invitation of the stockholders, Mrs.
John Drew assumed control of the theatre and organized her remarkable stock company. Great prosperity attended the venture until 1869, when the
introduction of the new " combination " system and
the building of more modern houses compelled the
disbandment of the organization.

Several new theatres were now competing for the
favor of the Philadelphia public. There were two
new theatres on Chestnut Street, Haverley's, and the
new house on Broad Street. They and the old Walnut and the new Park played all the best stars and
combinations and the Arch Street Theatre began to
lose its hold on public favor, although Joseph Jefferson and other prominent stars still remained faithful
and helped to maintain the prestige of the old house.

Among Philadelphia's more modern playhouses,
the Broad Street Theatre, built by Kiralfys for the
Centennial Exhibition of 1876, is the oldest. As a
theatre conducted on the combination system, it never
achieved the distinction of the older houses, but the
best attractions played there and for many years it

was Philadelphia's leading theatre. With its rounded turrets and unique style of architecture, the old Broad Street Theatre was long one of the Quaker City's most popular playhouses. The theatre is small, old and none too well appointed, but its auditorium is hallowed ground to all good Philadelphians and some of the most popular artists were seen there exclusively. This year (1919) the history of the playhouse as a legitimate theatre comes to a close, the establishment being devoted henceforth to motion pictures.

The Forrest and the Garrick, at Broad and Sansom, and Chestnut Street below Broad respectively, are comparatively new houses. They are large and modern in their appointments. Under the Shubert management come the Sam S. Shubert Theatre, the last built and largest, erected on the site of Horticultural Hall, at Broad below Locust; the Adelphi; the Lyric, both at Broad and Cherry Streets, and the remodelled Chestnut Street Opera House.

The Metropolitan Opera House, built by Oscar Hammerstein, holds 4000 persons and is very similar to the same manager's Manhattan Opera House, except that it has a more imposing location at Broad and Poplar Streets. The Academy of Music, at Broad and Locust, no longer stages opera, except the performances of the Operatic Society, an amateur organization.

The Little Theatre, at 17th Street and Delancey Place, originally a dramatic school, is similar to the Greenwich Village Theatre in New York in size, decorations and the intimate character of the plays given, except that it is situated in a fashionable neighborhood and is socially well patronized.

THE THEATRE IN AMERICA

Among leading American cities, Washington does not rank high in theatrical importance, although of recent years David Belasco has set the fashion of making it a producing centre. Many of Belasco's biggest successes, notably " The Darling of the Gods," " The Concert " and " Tiger Rose," were seen for the first time in our national capital. Audiences in Washington are perhaps more brilliant and interesting than anywhere in the country by reason of its cosmopolitanism and a large resident population of travelled Americans, but attractions seldom made money there until the Great War, when Washington's normal population was almost doubled and the three first-class houses—the New National, Belasco and Poli's—hardly sufficed to accommodate all who sought distraction from political and military duties.

The historic Ford's Theatre—half a century ago Washington's leading playhouse and the scene of that never-to-be-forgotten tragedy, April 14, 1865, when Wilkes Booth's bullet, fired into one of the boxes, killed Abraham Lincoln and plunged the nation into mourning—is now used for government archives. The theatre was closed immediately after the shooting, the building being purchased by the government for the Record and Pension Office of the War Department. The old theatre had a brilliant career up to the time of the assassination. Originally a Baptist Church, the premises remained unoccupied until 1857, when John T. Ford, backed by a number of prominent citizens of Washington, transformed it into a theatre. An excellent stock company was formed and the leading players of the day appeared on its boards.

Grover's Theatre, another favorite Washington playhouse of Civil War days, occupied the site of the present New National Theatre. It was noted for the excellence of its stock company and the care given to all its productions. President Lincoln was a frequent visitor to Grover's Theatre and usually occupied the President's box with Mrs. Lincoln and Secretary Seward. " During the engagement of Vestvali the Magnificent in 1864," says a writer,[1] " the President and his family attended the theatre as frequently as five nights in the week. The house advertisements often announced that certain plays would be performed ' at the request of the President.' "

Nearly all our Presidents have been fond of the theatre, from George Washington to Woodrow Wilson. The greatest precautions are taken when the President goes to the play. " When the President's secretary calls up one of the Washington theatres," says a writer, " and says that the President would like to see the performance, the management at once sends the tickets for a stage box, and then withdraws from sale all the tickets in the box or boxes immediately adjoining the President's box. These additional boxes may be sold to persons known to the management, but they are not on sale to the general public. If no one of sufficient importance appears to purchase them, they may be given to one of the secret service men who always come to the theatre with the President. For, no matter where the President goes, he is followed by the secret service men. Personally, he dislikes very much to have them accompany him to the theatre, but the chief of the secret service bureau

[1] A. T. Mudd in the *Theatre Magazine*, January, 1905.

in Washington has very vivid recollections of the national calamity that happened in a Washington theatre years ago. It is, therefore, an utter impossibility for any stranger to come very close to the President's box; although, of course, any crank could buy seats in the orchestra, near enough to see the President at close range." [*]

With the opening of the California Theatre in 1869, a brilliant theatrical era began in San Francisco. Under the joint direction of John McCullough and Lawrence Barrett, plays were produced on a sumptuous scale, and the most prominent stars filled long and successful engagements there. It was at the California Theatre, in 1877, that Helena Modjeska made her first appearance on the American stage in " Adrienne Lecouvreur."

On the stage of the new Metropolitan, a favorite house of the early seventies, the Chapman sisters, clever burlesque performers, appeared in " Little Don Giovanni " in 1873. Shiels' Opera House (afterwards Gray's) was first opened June 30, 1873. The following month Bella Pateman met with great success at this theatre in a dramatization of Wilkie Collins' " New Magdalen."

Early in the seventies, Thomas Maguire, an ex-cab driver, and Edward J. Baldwin, a former hostler, became very prominent in San Francisco theatrical affairs. Maguire's Opera House (afterwards the Bush Street Theatre) was opened in 1873, and a year later Maguire opened another house (the old Alhambra), engaging David Belasco as stage manager. In 1876, Baldwin's Academy of Music was first

[*] Will A. Page in the *Theatre Magazine*, May, 1908.

THE DRAMA IN OTHER CITIES

opened, with James A. Herne as stage manager, the house being inaugurated March 6, with Barry Sullivan in " Richard III." W. H. Crane, Louis James and M. A. Kennedy were in the cast. In 1880, the well-known English melodrama, " The World," by Paul Merrill, Henry Pettitt and Augustus Harris, was seen at this house. Baldwin retired from the theatre in 1882 and " Al " Hayman secured control, presenting, in 1886, one of the strongest theatrical companies ever organized in America, this notable company of stars including Robert B. Mantell, Joseph Haworth, W. J. Ferguson, Charles Vanderhoff, Rowland Buckstone, Henry Miller, Owen Fawcett, W. H. Crompton, Maurice Barrymore, Mary Shaw, Sophie Eyre, Louise Dillon, Kate Denin, Ada Dyer and others. The company opened May 31, 1886, with " Moths," from Ouida's novel. Later, July 12, Modjeska appeared here in Maurice Barrymore's play, " Nadjesda."

Other theatres of the seventies were Wade's Opera House, where George Rignold, the English star, was seen May 29, 1876, in his spectacular production, " Henry V," and the Grand Opera House, where Salmi Morse produced his Passion Play, March 3, 1879. Morse had written the play and James O'Neill, of " Monte Christo " fame, was very desirous to play the part of the Christ. Elaborate scenery was prepared by the promoters, Maguire and Baldwin, and David Belasco was engaged as stage director. O'Neill's Jesus made a profound impression, but the play offended many persons and aroused such religious frenzy among the ignorant that Irish Catholics assaulted peaceable Jews on the streets. Even

315

the manager himself was threatened with death. Finally a court injunction was issued, forbidding further performances, and the play was withdrawn. Belasco has written this interesting account of his share in the production:

How we scoured San Francisco—school, church, and theatre—for people to put in our cast! Every actor who was out of employment was sure of finding something to do in our mob scenes. I cannot conceive, in the history of the Theatre, a more complete or a more perfect cast.

We engaged two hundred singers; we marshaled four hundred men, women and children and infants in our ensembles. And in the preparation every one seemed to be inspired. . . . O'Neill, as the preparations progressed, grew more and more obsessed. He gave up smoking; all the little pleasures of life he denied himself. Any man who used a coarse word during rehearsals was dismissed. He walked the streets of the city with the expression of a holy man on his face. Whenever he drew near a hush prevailed such as one does not often find outside a church. The boards of the stage became Holy Land.

I also became a veritable monomaniac on the subject; I was never without a Bible under my arm. I went to the Mercantile Library and there studied the color effects in the two memorable canvases hung there, depicting the dance of Salome and the Lord's Supper. My life seemed changed as never before, and once more my thoughts began to play with monastery life.

The play traced the whole sequence of historical events leading to the Crucifixion and the Resurrection, and I remember how many effects we had to evolve for ourselves. In the Massacre of the Innocents we had a hundred mothers on the stage with their babies in their arms. In the scene where Joseph and Mary came down the mountain side, we had a flock of real sheep following in their wake. The entire performance was given with a simplicity that amounted to grandeur. All was accomplished by fabrics and stage lighting, and when O'Neill came up from his dressing room and appeared on the stage with a halo about him, women sank on their knees and prayed, and when he was stripped and dragged before Pontius Pilate crowned with a crown of thorns, many fainted.*

*My Life Story, by David Belasco. *Hearst's Magazine*, 1914.

THE DRAMA IN OTHER CITIES

The earthquake and fire of 1906 wiped out every notable theatre in San Francisco [10]—the Alcazar, California, Central, Columbia, Fischer's Grand Opera House, Majestic, Orpheum and Tivoli. Six months later, while the city was still struggling to make some order out of chaos, the old Central Theatre stock company began a season of melodrama in a tent. The Colonial Theatre, which was being built at the time of the cataclysm, was the first important playhouse to open, October 7, 1907. The Central Theatre, dear to lovers of melodrama, and Frederick Belasco's popular Alcazar, were restored to their patrons the same year. The opening of the $200,000 Van Ness Theatre, March 11, 1907, with Henry W. Savage's English Opera Company in "Madama Butterfly," afforded San Francisco society its first opportunity to wear full dress since the fire. The career of this theatre was short, for when the new Columbia was built in 1910, the temporary structure was torn down. The Valencia Theatre, a quarter of a million dollar structure, in the crowded Mission district, began in 1908 with a stock company and later played all the Shubert attractions. John Cort's fine playhouse, representing an investment of nearly a million dollars, began its prosperous career August 27, 1911.

---

[10] For these particulars of recent developments in San Francisco the author is indebted to an article by Mr. Horatio F. Stoll published in the *Theatre Magazine*, August, 1912.

CHAPTER XXX

DECLINE OF THE THEATRE

BEGINNING with the last decade of the Nineteenth century, the theatre in America already showed a marked and steady decline. The glorious nights of Wallack's, when the stock system was seen at the height of its prosperity, were now only a memory. Those managers of fine achievement, Augustin Daly and A. M. Palmer, had seen their best days. Clyde Fitch, Augustus Thomas and other native playwrights of promise were rising, but even their genius could avail nothing in face of the changed conditions. New men with new methods had come into the theatrical field. The making of money became the one and only aim of every effort. Of the great actors, not one remained. The stage was engulfed in a wave of commercialism that gradually destroyed the art of acting, elevated mediocrities to the dignity of stars, turned playwrights into hacks, misled and vitiated public taste, and the drama, from an art, became a business. "What," asks William Winter, "are the causes that have produced this deplorable effect?"

The major causes are the prevalence of Materialism, infecting all branches of thought, and of Commercialism, infecting all branches of action. The public is not blameless, because public opinion and sentiment—meaning the general condition and attitude of the public mind—reacts upon those who address the public. The

318

theatrical audience of this period (1908) is largely composed of vulgarians, who know nothing about art or literature and who care for nothing but the solace of their common tastes and animal appetites: on that point observation of the faces and manners of the multitude would satisfy any thoughtful observer: and, because the audience is largely of this character, the Theatre has become precisely what it might have been expected to become when dependent on such patronage. It has passed from the hands that ought to control it,—the hands either of Actors who love and honor their art or of men endowed with the temperament of the Actor and acquainted with his art and its needs,—and, almost entirely, it has fallen into the clutches of sordid, money-grubbing tradesmen, who have degraded it into a bazaar. Throughout the length and breadth of the United States speculators have captured the industry that they call " the Amusement Business " and have made " a corner in Theatricals." [1]

The success of Charles Frohman and the considerable expansion given to the theatrical business by the exploitation of his many enterprises, led to an attempt, in 1896, to create a theatre monopoly. A group of six theatre men, " Al " Hayman and Charles Frohman, owners of the Empire Theatre, New York; Marc Klaw and Abraham Erlanger, theatrical booking agents who had made a good deal of money with the Rogers Brothers and " Ben Hur "; Samuel F. Nirdlinger (Nixon) and J. Frederick Zimmerman, the Philadelphia theatre managers, met and decided to centralize their booking interests. Claiming that the system then in vogue for making routes for theatrical companies was in a most chaotic condition, they organized all the houses they controlled into a chain of theatres, " time " for which could be booked only through Klaw & Erlanger.

This was the beginning of the operations of the

[1] Other Days. Copyright, 1908, by William Winter. Moffat, Yard & Co., Publishers. Reprinted by permission of Jefferson Winter, Esq

Theatrical Syndicate. From now on, all attractions
—even the most important stars—were compelled to
submit to the whims and terms of the new theatrical
dictators. If they refused, as Mme. Bernhardt, David
Belasco and Mrs. Fiske had the temerity to do, they
found themselves barred from first-class houses and
forced to play where they could. Bernhardt took
refuge in a circus tent, Mrs. Fiske had to perform
in draughty ill-lighted halls, even in skating rinks.
David Belasco, finding the doors of all the Washington theatres closed to him when in 1904 he wished
to present Mrs. Leslie Carter in " Adrea," was compelled to rent Convention Hall, a vast barnlike building with a leaky roof. There was a violent rainstorm
during the performance and many distinguished
spectators, including Admiral Dewey, Secretary
Morton and Admiral Schley, had to sit through the
fourth act holding umbrellas.

It was an intolerable situation. The triumph of
the Syndicate meant the end of honest competition,
the degradation of the art of acting, the lowering of
the standard of the drama, the subjugation of the
playwright and the actor to the capricious whims and
sordid necessities of a few men who set themselves
up as theatrical despots.

There was instant revolt among the better elements of the theatre. David Belasco, Mrs. Fiske,
Henry W. Savage, Richard Mansfield, Joseph Jefferson, Nat C. Goodwin, J. K. Hackett, Francis Wilson and James A. Herne at once proclaimed their
independence and the theatre war was on. The Syndicate started to book attractions as it pleased, and
the insurgents were compelled to secure such inde-

pendent stages as they could find. The Syndicate grew in power and some of those who had been loudest in opposition succumbed to the lure of liberal terms until at last only Mrs. Fiske remained defiant.

But nothing that rests only on might can endure. A new theatrical power was then rising that was soon to bring about the downfall of the Trust. Three brothers, Lee, Sam and Jacob Shubert, of the most humble origin, had been active in theatricals in their native town, Syracuse, N. Y. Sam, who began as a program boy, was afterwards ticket seller in the Syracuse Grand Opera House. Later, he ran a stock company at the Bastable Theatre and gained control of a chain of stock theatres in that State. Meantime, he had taken his two brothers into partnership and in 1900 they went to New York, subleased the Herald Square Theatre and proclaimed themselves leaders of the Independent Movement in opposition to the Syndicate. Gradually, their chain of theatres grew. They secured the Casino, the Princess, the Majestic, the Lyric in New York, and before long controlled a chain of first-class houses from the Atlantic to the Pacific Coast.

Real warfare now set in. Cities that could support but one first-class house were compelled to have two—a Syndicate Theatre and an Independent theatre. The situation soon grew worse than that which the Syndicate pretended it sought to remedy, and the Trust was the first to sue for peace.

But the victory, while it broke up a close monopoly, did not bring any real relief. The drift toward commercialism in the theatre persisted. Instead of one master, there were now two. Fierce competition

resulted in overproduction and a superfluity of theatres. In the absence of the former high standard, the
stage became filled with trashy plays. Shakespeare,
except for E. H. Sothern and Robert Mantell, was
entirely neglected. The stock system was dead. Long
runs sometimes resulted in an actor being called
upon to play the same rôle for two consecutive years.
Thus it became impossible for the player to acquire
experience or versatility and the art of acting necessarily deteriorated. .

In 1909, a group of earnest theatre-lovers made
an attempt to stem the tide by agitating for an Endowed Theatre. The endowment of the theatre by
the State, which has proved so potent an educational
force in foreign countries, was believed to be imprac-
ticable under our system of government, but it was
thought that some wealthy men might be willing to
build and endow a repertoire theatre; that is, a theatre which changes its bill with frequency, presenting
the classics of the world's drama and the worthy
works of American dramatists in the best manner
attainable. More than a decade before, Henry
Austin Clapp, the well-known critic, had urged the
establishment in one of our largest cities " of a theatre dedicated to the higher culture of the histrionic
art which should be supported or 'backed' by the
munificence of two or more men of great wealth."
The idea gained adherents and the National Art
Theatre Society, comprising a thousand or more
intelligent theatre-goers pledged to further the cause
of a National Theatre, was organized under the
presidency of J. I. C. Clarke, a well-known publicist
and playwright. This worthy movement died for

lack of sustenance, but Heinrich Conried, while manager of the Metropolitan Opera House, presented the idea to the wealthy directors—the Vanderbilts, Morgans, Astors, Whitneys, Schiffs, Goulds, Belmonts, etc.—as a practical undertaking.

The suggestion was favorably received and immediately acted upon. A large plot of land was purchased on Central Park West and a magnificent edifice of marble and gold, the largest and most sumptuously decorated playhouse ever seen in the United States, was erected at a cost of several millions of dollars.

Mr. Winthrop Ames was appointed director and a stock company organized, comprising the following players: Rowland Buckstone, Louis Calvert, Ben Johnson, Albert Bruning, Pedro de Cordoba, Ferdinand Gottschalk, Charles Cartwright, Henry Stanford, William McVay, Howard Kyle, Jacob Wendell, Jr., Reginald Barlow, Charles Balsar, Rose Coghlan, Mrs. Sol Smith, Beatrice Forbes-Robertson, Olive Wyndham, Jessie Busley, Beverly Sitgreaves, Thais Lawton, Leah Bateman-Hunter, Vida Sutton. George Foster Platt was engaged to act as stage manager in association with Louis Calvert, and E. Hamilton Bell was appointed art director. For the opening production E. H. Sothern and Julia Marlowe were specially engaged for the star parts for "a limited period"—a bad blunder, as Walter Prichard Eaton points out, for it was a departure from the stock company idea from the very start.

The New Theatre opened its doors November 6, 1909, with a sumptuous revival of "Antony and Cleopatra," the cast being as follows:

THE THEATRE IN AMERICA

Mark Antony, E. H. Sothern; Octavius Caesar, A. E. Anson; M. Aemilius Lepidus, Rowland Buckstone; Sextus Pompeius, Ben Johnson; Domitius Enobarbus, William McVay; Eros, Charles Balsar; Scarus, Howard Kyle; Agrippa, Jacob Wendell, Jr.; Proculeius, William Harris; Thyreus, Henry Stanford; Menas, Lee Baker; Euphronius, George Venning; Demetrius, C. F. Hanan-Clark; Alexas, Lawrence Eyre; Cleopatra, Julia Marlowe; Octavia, Beatrice Forbes-Robertson; Charmian, Jessie Busley; Iras, Leah Bateman-Hunter; Canidus, Reginald Barlow.

A tremendous audience, one of the most brilliant and representative ever assembled in an American theatre, witnessed the opening performance, but that the undertaking would prove a failure was apparent from the first night. The command of unlimited capital had in this case proved not an advantage but a handicap. The idea of the millionaire promoters was that success in the theatre, as in Big Business, was merely a matter of spending money. So instead of building a small, intimate theatre where plays could be given their proper perspective, they had provided a vast auditorium, splendidly decorated, but with faulty acoustics and a stage so far away that the actors were almost inaudible. An attempt was subsequently made to correct these defects, but to no purpose. The opening performance, which was a ghastly failure, was followed by bills that proved more successful, notably fine productions of John Galsworthy's "Strife," "The School for Scandal," Maeterlinck's "Sister Beatrice," and "The Winter's Tale." Perhaps the one production at the New Theatre which scored financially as well as artistically was Maeterlinck's delightful fantasy, "The Blue Bird," produced October 1, 1910.

But the organization had the fatal defect of possessing no leading actors. "The company," says Mr. John Corbin, literary director of the theatre, "would have been utterly unable to cast Rosalind, Portia, Lady Macbeth, Juliet, Romeo, Hamlet, Lear, Othello —in fact, any of the really great parts. When the plays with no transcendent part were exhausted the classical productions came to a sudden end. Surely, a theatre without adequate leading actors is not really on a par with any adequate repertory theatre. And even with its very small salary list, the company was prohibitively expensive." [1]

In short, the well-meant scheme was a colossal failure, the wealthy backers pocketed their loss philosophically, and the theatre rapidly degenerated into a theatrical white elephant, too huge and expensive an establishment to suit any purpose except that of big spectacular productions to which it is now devoted.

A far less costly and much more practical application of the subsidized theatre idea is the Municipal Theatre of which there are several in the United States. The best known of these semi-official playhouses is that at Northampton, Mass., which was started in 1892, the house being the gift of Edward H. R. Lyman, a merchant of the town. During Mr. Lyman's travels in Europe, especially in Germany, he was much impressed by what the state-endowed theatres were doing for the people. On his return to Northampton he spent $100,000 in the erection of a theatre which he offered to deed over to the city authorities. A bill was passed by the State Legislature authorizing the town to accept the gift, and the Northampton Academy of Music was an accom-

---

[1] Article in the New York *Times*, December 21, 1918.

plished fact. The theatre did not have its own company until 1912, having to depend before that on the touring companies. The theatre is not only owned by the city, but the city also guarantees the support of the company. Each week a new play is given and the best touring companies are invited to play there. During the first half of the season 1918–1919 the following plays were presented at the Municipal Theatre: Eleanor Gates's " The Darling of the World " (first performance anywhere), Veiller's " The Thirteenth Chair," James Montgomery's " Nothing But the Truth," Kate Douglas Wiggins' " Mother Carey's Chickens " and Houseman's " The Gypsy Trail." The programme for the remainder of the season includes Vachell's " Quinneys," Martha Morton's " Her Lord and Master," Ibsen's " A Doll's House," Parker's " Rosemary," Shaw's " The Philanderer," Bernstein's " The Thief," Porter Emerson Brown's " The Spendthrift," St. John Hankin's " The Casillis Engagement," Tom Taylor's " Masks and Faces," " Jim the Penman," Arnold Bennett's " The Great Adventure," Stanley Houghton's " Hindle Wakes," Henri Berger's " The Deluge " and the Hattons' " Years of Discretion."

An interesting and important development of the present day stage has been the growth of the so-called Little Theatre movement. About 1912, there sprang up all over the United States organizations of amateurs who aimed to present works of a higher intellectual order than are usually seen in the commercial theatre, mostly one-act plays with fresh, vital themes that the ordinary manager would refuse to consider because he was unable to see " money " in them. This, of course, was an idea borrowed from André Antoine, the Paris Gas Company clerk, who, in 1887, started his Free Theatre to prove that " high-brow" plays would draw, notwithstanding the conventional theatre manager's deeply rooted conviction to the contrary. Antoine did not quite prove his case, for he was careful to see that each of his bills contained a distinct " punch " in addition to being " high brow," but there was no question as to his success. He brought out authors who have since become world famous, and his dingy little theatre on the Boulevard Strasbourg became the Mecca of the most intelligent theatre-goers in Europe. He also had the satisfaction of seeing one of his early productions, " La Chance de Françoise," the charming little comedy by Georges de Porto-Riche, afterwards put into the exclusive repertoire of the Comédie Française.

In America, the Little Theatre of Chicago, conducted by Maurice Browne, was the pioneer of over fifty of these independent stages. Mr. Browne, an Englishman with fine ideals, began his interesting experiment early in 1912, his company consisting of five professional actors and a dozen amateurs, who rehearsed every day without pecuniary compensation. Funds were raised to provide a theatre and quarters were found on the fourth floor of the Fine Arts building where a theatre seating ninety-one people was constructed. The first production included " Womankind," by Wilfred Wilson Gibson and " On Baile's Strand," by William Butler Yeats. Then came Granville Barker's paraphrase of Arthur Schnitzler's " Anatol," and plays by Euripides, Strindberg, Ibsen, Shaw, Dunsany, Houghton, Hankin, Yeats. Another Chicago organization of the same character, the Hull House Dramatic Association, was founded by Mrs. Laura Dainty Pelham in 1900. Composed entirely of working men and women employed for the most part in professions not generally associated with art, the Hull House Players began their career with melodrama, passed to domestic comedy and finally established their claim to serious recognition by a successful production of Ben Jonson's " Sad Shepherd." In 1910, they produced Galsworthy's " Justice " long before that powerful play was seen on the professional stage. Similar successful experiments in other cities include the Little Theatre of Indianapolis, founded in 1915 by Samuel A. Eliot, Jr.; the Vagabond Playhouse in Baltimore; the Laboratory Theatre of the Carnegie Institute at Pittsburgh; the Copley Theatre in Boston; the Little Theatre of Philadelphia, and the Wisconsin Players.

New York has several such " literary " theatres, the most conspicuous being the Washington Square Players—a group of enthusiastic theatre-lovers who, beginning as amateurs, gradually developed into professionals, opened a theatre of their own, and for several seasons presented bills that competed successfully with the best that Broadway had to offer. They, in turn, were followed by Stuart Walker and his famous Portmanteau Theatre, Frank Conroy's Greenwich Village Players, the Neighborhood Theatre in Grand Street, Grace Griswold's Theatre Workshop, the Provincetown Players and the East West Players. Of these little theatres and their influence, Walter Prichard Eaton has this to say:

DECLINE OF THE THEATRE

Their audiences numerically are but a drop in the bucket. Yet they are a sign, a portent which cannot be ignored. They are a protest against the easy, safe professionalism which has divorced our drama from all serious contact with the problems of actual life, which has reopened the gap between the American stage and literature—a gap which Herne, Fitch, Moody, Eugene Walter, George Ade and others seemed a few years ago on the point of bridging; which has left the public without any control over its esthetic expression in the playhouse. . . . The drama of to-morrow in America must be reborn out of the amateur spirit and the increasing number of amateurs who are giving themselves gladly to the task today is the most hopeful sign in our theatre.[2]

Open-air theatres, some of them modelled upon the general plan of the ancient theatres of the Greeks and Romans, have of late years become very popular in America, one of the best known being the Coliseum of the University of California, at Berkeley, Calif., erected in 1903, at a cost of $100,000 and the gift of Mr. William R. Hearst. With its seating capacity of 8000 it is small compared with the famous theatres of antiquity—the theatre of Dionysus at Athens held 27,000 spectators—but it is constructed in the true Greek spirit, with nineteen tiers of cement seats rising in a semicircle on the steep hillside and with a stage backed by a monumental cement wall classic in design, and divided into panels by fluted columns. In 1906, Sarah Bernhardt gave a performance of Racine's " Phèdre " at the Berkeley Theatre, and in 1910 Maude Adams appeared there as Rosalind in " As You Like It." The same year the students of the University were seen in a fine open-air production of " Oedipus." Margaret Anglin, an actress of distinction identified with the best in our

---

[2] Article in the *Theatre Magazine*, November, 1917.

theatre, has often been seen there in the Greek tragedies, " Antigone," " Electra " and " Medea."

The gloom of night and the beauty of Nature's
surroundings impart to these open-air performances
a distinct air of novelty. " Never," says a writer,
" can one forget the beauty of the scene as the audience of the great open-air theatre gathers in the twi-
light of a perfect summer day. When darkness comes
the tiers of seats and the fringe of eucalyptus gradually disappear while overhead the stars begin to twinkle. Then strong lights are thrown on the stage,
music from a hidden orchestra can be heard and the
players enter. The audience is spellbound and the
absolute quiet permits one to hear the rhythmic dialogue as well as in any closed theatre, for the acoustic
properties are absolutely perfect." [4]

Open-air performances on a large scale were first
given in this country during the summer of 1886,
when a splendid out-of-door production of Shakespeare's " As You Like It " was given at Manchester-
by-the-Sea, Mass. The cast on that occasion was a
notable one, including as it did Rose Coghlan, Agnes
Booth, Lillian Conway, Frank Mayo, Stuart Robson and H. C. Barnabee and his Bostonians, who
appeared as the Foresters. Later, at the same place,
there was a night out-of-door production of " A Midsummer Night's Dream," when Nat C. Goodwin was
seen as Bottom. Other notable open-air performances were those of " As You Like It," at Castle
Stevens, Hoboken, N. J., in 1891, and performances
of " As You Like It," " Merry Wives," " A Midsummer Night's Dream " at the Grand Union Hotel, Sar-

---

[4] Horatio F. Stoll in the *Theatre Magazine* for July, 1911.

atoga. In more recent years Mr. and Mrs. Charles Coburn's company and also the Ben Greet Players have made a feature of open-air performances. Percy MacKaye's masque " Caliban," produced on a mammoth scale and interpreted by such well-known players as Edith Wynne Matthison, Howard Kyle and Lionel Braham at the Stadium of the College of the City of New York in 1916, is still fresh in public memory. Interesting open-air performances and magnificent pageants have also been given from time to time in the splendid Harvard Stadium at Cambridge, Mass.—notably that of Maude Adams in " Joan of Arc " in 1909—the Yale Bowl, at New Haven, Conn., the Stadium of the College of the City of New York, and the Stadium at Tacoma, Wash. These enormous open-air structures being intended primarily for athletic games, they do not properly belong to the domain of the drama.

About the year 1910, the theatre had to contend with a new and formidable rival—the moving picture, a cheap and novel form of entertainment which, first introduced into the United States in 1896, has gradually grown tremendously popular. At first, the pictures were very crude and shown only in small halls called Nickelodeons—five or ten cents being charged for admission—but as the demand for the pictures grew and the possibilities of the business were realized, millions of capital were attracted, fine theatres exclusively devoted to " movies " were built, the best-known stars of the legitimate stage were engaged, and the making of the big spectacular films began. So large has the motion-picture business become it is estimated that in winter time there are 15,000 daily exhibitions, afternoon and evening, and in summer time many more than that. In the year 1917, the receipts taken in by motion-picture houses exceeded $175,000,000. In 1918, the total receipts were estimated at not far below two hundred million dollars!

Such a competitor as this could not fail to have its effect on the theatre proper. Not only did the legitimate theatre lose many of its regular patrons, attracted to the " movies " by the cheapness of admission, but it also lost some of its best actors, lured to the service of the " silent drama " by the almost sensational salaries the motion-picture magnates could afford to hold out as an inducement. Many theatres abandoned the legitimate drama entirely and became motion-picture houses. To-day, there are about 4300 theatres in the United States playing legitimate attractions. Many of them, however, have a mixed policy. They play vaudeville and pictures as a regular thing, breaking in on that program when a legitimate attraction is offered. About 33 per cent. of the theatres that formerly played only legitimate attractions are now presenting either vaudeville or pictures exclusively.

Apart from the harm which the motion picture has done to the legitimate drama by robbing it of theatres, actors, audiences and even dramatists (for some of our most popular playwrights devote much of their time writing for the screen) the success that has attended the growth of motion pictures in this country can hardly be looked upon as an unmixed blessing. At the outset, when the pictures first became popular, many of them were refining and educational in character, presenting interesting scenes in history, travel, science and nature study. But this was too slow a growth to suit the greed of certain film manufacturers who sought to increase their profits by turning out pictures making a special appeal to the sensual and the vicious. To such pictures as " Cabiria," " The Battle Cry of Peace," " The Birth of a Nation," " Intolerance," " Civilization," " Hearts of the World," " My Four Years in Germany," all masterpieces of the art of the cinema, only the highest praise can be accorded; but they, and a few other pictures of like calibre, are the conspicuous exceptions. The average motion picture shown to-day, when not revelling in scenes of violence and crime, is full of sickly sentiment and impossible heroics, while the so-called " comedies " are invariably of the slap-stick variety of humor, interspersed with much coarseness and vulgarity. When one stops to think of the vast audiences this sort of mental food reaches—millions of persons of both sexes, old and young, to whom these pictures are presented in such a vivid, realistic way as to make a profound impression, children of tender age being made familiar with scenes of lust and vice, which destroy their innocence and render them sophisticated before their time—it would seem that some sort of Federal control or censorship—not a self-appointed Manufacturers' Censorship Board which, of course, can hardly be expected to see anything to criticise in its own products—would be justified as a safeguard to public morals.

CHAPTER XXXI

NEW YORK THE THEATRICAL METROPOLIS

MR. WINTHROP AMES AND THE LITTLE THEATRE. MISS GRACE GEORGE'S STOCK COMPANY. THE RISE OF DAVID BELASCO. MRS. LESLIE CARTER. BLANCHE BATES. DAVID WARFIELD AND THE "MUSIC MASTER." FRANCES STARR. LEONORE ULRIC. NEW THEATRES. FAMOUS STAGE HUMORISTS—HOYT, HARRIGAN, GEORGE ADE, GEORGE M. COHAN.

To-DAY (1919), New York City, with forty-six playhouses of the first class, may boast of possessing more theatres than any other city in the world. Paris ranks second with thirty-six theatres, while London has thirty-two, the same number as Berlin.

Since the disappearance of the stock company, there has been no theatre in New York with a fixed policy, that is to say no one house of marked distinction or enjoying a special *clientèle* of its own, as in the days of Wallack and Daly. All the present-day theatres are conducted as purely commercial enterprises on the so-called combination plan, their respective stages being at the disposal of whatever attraction chances to come along, so that on the same boards may be seen one week a poetic play by Maeterlinck and the next week an indecent French farce. Exception should be made in favor of the Little Theatre, a small auditorium with no balcony and very small seating capacity but decorated and upholstered as exquisitely as a royal boudoir, where, under the intelligent direction of Mr. Winthrop Ames, are presented from time to time plays of a higher intellectual order than are usually to be seen in Broadway the-

334

atres. Two notable productions at this *maison d'élite* were John Galsworthy's sociological play, " The Pigeon " (1912), and the delightful fantasy " Prunella," by Laurence Housman and Granville Barker (1913).

Recognition must also be accorded Miss Grace George for her praiseworthy attempt to establish at the Playhouse, during the season of 1915-16, a stock company which included such fine players as Louis Calvert, Conway Tearle, Ernest Lawford, Mary Nash and others. The experiment was not of long duration. After reviving Langdon Mitchell's brilliant comedy, " The New York Idea," and producing for the first time in America George Bernard Shaw's satirical comedy, " Major Barbara," Miss George found that modern theatrical conditions imposed well-nigh insurmountable difficulties in the way of maintaining a permanent stock organization, and she was compelled, temporarily at least, to abandon her ambitious purpose.

Among America's leading play producers at the present time David Belasco is foremost. He stands alone in his field and has no competitor. As William Winter says, he is " sole survivor and transmitter of an earlier and better theory of theatrical management than is anywhere visible now."[1] Not only is he the owner of one of New York's most beautiful playhouses, but no manager is so successful as he in discovering new stars or in selecting plays that hit the public taste. The secret of Belasco's success is that he is never in a hurry. Unlike some of his brother managers, who hastily throw their plays on the stage,

---

[1] Life of David Belasco. By William Winter.

he takes his time. Each play is carefully prepared and rehearsed—sometimes as long as a year being spent on one production—and as a result he seldom has to record a failure. A Belasco première has come to mean one of the rare treats of the theatrical season.

Belasco's early career from the time he began as a super in San Francisco to the time when he first went to New York and joined the Mallorys at the Madison Square Theatre, has already been narrated in an earlier chapter. His subsequent activities as a dramatist have also been noted. It was not until 1895, when he presented Mrs. Leslie Carter at the Herald Square Theatre in "The Heart of Maryland," that he was successful as an independent producer.

Mrs. Leslie Carter, a woman with plain features but decided temperament and flaming red hair, was a Chicago society woman whose married life had been unhappy. Divorced by her husband, she went to Belasco, suggesting that he train her for the stage, and in relating her marital troubles displayed so much emotion that the manager thought he saw in her dramatic possibilities. She had no money of her own, but financial backing was secured from a Chicago manufacturer and Belasco began to teach her with a view to launching her as a star, notwithstanding the fact that public opinion was so much against Mrs. Carter that he had difficulty in finding stages on which to rehearse.

Mrs. Carter made her début November 10, 1890, at the Broadway Theatre in a play by Paul M. Potter called "The Ugly Duckling." The piece was coldly received, but the following year the new star was more successful in " Miss Helyett," a musical piece from the French. Meantime, Belasco was busy writing his new war play suggested by the poem *Curfew Shall Not Ring To-night,* in which Maryland Calvert, the heroine, in a thrilling leap, clings to and muffles the tower bell so it shall not give warning of the escape of her officer lover. After many delays due, according to Belasco, to the jealousies of rival managers, " The Heart of Maryland " was produced and proved an enormous success. Mrs. Leslie Carter was now recognized everywhere as a successful star. After playing in the piece three consecutive years she went to London, where she appeared at the Adelphi and was presented to King Edward VII.

The tide had turned for Belasco. Instead of being a mere hack playwright, he was a new theatrical magnate to be reckoned with, and from now on a new Belasco production was a theatrical event of importance.

In 1897, he produced at the Manhattan, New York, " The First Born," a tragic sketch of character and life in the Chinese quarter in San Francisco, and this was followed in 1899 by the production at the Garrick of " Zaza," from the French of Pierre Berton, with Mrs. Leslie Carter in the title rôle. Then came " Du Barry," seen at the Criterion Theatre, New York, December 25, 1901, with Mrs. Leslie Carter as the famous mistress of Louis Quinze, a stupendously costly production, amazing in its wealth of *mise en scène* and costumes, and " Adrea," written in collaboration with John Luther Long, produced September 26, 1905.

Meantime, Belasco was extending his interests and reaching out for new stars. In 1900, at the Herald Square Theatre, Blanche Bates, a young actress of striking personality who had previously been with Daly, made her stellar début under his management in " Naughty Anthony." This was followed in 1900 by the production of " Madam Butterfly," written with John Luther Long, in which Blanche Bates appeared as the unfortunate Cho Cho San, and the next year by " Under Two Flags," a new version of Ouida's novel by Paul M. Potter, in which Miss Bates as Cigarette repeated her former successes. Two years later Belasco made New York theatregoers gasp at the sheer magnificence of his production of the Japanese play " The Darling of the Gods." In this play, written with John Luther Long, Blanche Bates appeared as Yo San and George Arliss as the crafty Minister of War. Still another Belasco triumph was his own play " The Girl of the Golden West " (1905), with Blanche Bates in the title rôle, and on which Puccini afterwards based his opera, as he had done with " Madama Butterfly " before it.

But perhaps Belasco's most fortunate " find " was his engagement of David Warfield, a former variety actor who had met with considerable success at Weber and Fields' and other New York theatres, impersonating pathetically humorous Jewish types. Born in 1860 in San Francisco, where he was a program boy at the Bush Street Theatre, David Warfield is not a versatile actor, his form of dramatic expression being all in one key. But he possesses one precious gift that all actors may well envy—he knows how to touch the human heart. In the first play in which he

338

appeared under Belasco's management, "The Auctioneer," written by Lee Arthur and Charles Klein and produced September 23, 1901, he was seen as Simon Levi, the East Side Hebrew climber—a human study worthy of a Dickens or a Balzac. The play was a great success and was followed by a still greater triumph when on September 12, 1904, Belasco presented Warfield in "The Music Master." The story of a German musician, Herr Anton von Barwig, who, deserted by his wife in Vienna, comes to America and finds his long-lost daughter in his pupil, the play proved one of the phenomenal successes of the stage, and is still presented everywhere to crowded houses. More recent Warfield plays, "The Grand Army Man" (1907), "The Return of Peter Grimm" (1911), "Van der Decken" (1915), were not so successful.

In 1902, Belasco secured from Oscar Hammerstein control of the old Republic Theatre on West 42nd Street and after extensive alterations and redecorating, reopened it as the Belasco Theatre. It was at this house, in 1906, that Frances Starr made her first appearance under Mr. Belasco's management in "The Rose of the Rancho," a picturesque play of the Mexican border, by Richard Walton Tully, full of that local color and elaboration of detail for which Belasco is famous. The following year Mr. Belasco built a theatre in West 44th Street, which he at first called the Stuyvesant, but which on the passing of the older house was rechristened the Belasco. Here he produced Eugene Walter's "The Easiest Way," with Frances Starr as the young actress who treads the primrose path, "The Lily," with Nance O'Neil (1909), "The Concert," with Leo Ditrichstein (1910), "The Case of Becky," with Frances Starr (1911), and "Marie Odile," also with Frances Starr (1915).

Other Belasco productions were "The Secret" (1914), "A Celebrated Case," in co-operation with Charles Frohman at the Empire Theatre, New York (1915), "The Boomerang," with Martha Hedman and Wallace Eddinger in the case (1915), and "Polly with a Past," with Ina Claire (1917). During the season of 1916, Lenore Ulric, already favorably known for her work in "The Bird of Paradise," under the management of Oliver Morosco, made her first appearance under Belasco in an Indian play, "The Heart of Wetona." The following year Miss Ulric scored another great success in Willard Mack's melodrama, "Tiger Rose."

Belasco's contribution to the American drama is that of a producer and stage director rather than that of an author. His plays—mostly melodramas—have little permanent value, but as a creator of stage effects, in elaboration of detail, in arrangement of action and stage pictures, he is recognized to be without a master in the modern theatre.

Among the younger American play producers, Oliver Morosco, Arthur Hopkins, A. H. Woods and Selwyn and Company are to-day the most active.

Oliver Morosco, owner of the famous Burbank and Morosco Theatres in Los Angeles, California, went a few years ago to New York, where he became allied with John Cort, another Western manager who had extended his theatrical interests. One of the most notable of the Morosco enterprises was the production in 1913 of "Peg O' My Heart," with Laurette Taylor as the Irish heroine. Later the same management presented this actress in the war play "Out There." He also presented Emily Stevens in "The Unchastened Woman" (1915). In 1918, this manager built a fine playhouse in New York which he called the Morosco Theatre.

Arthur Hopkins, a manager with ideas, made his first bid for recognition in 1913 with the production of Eleanor Gates' fantastic play, "The Poor Little Rich Girl," Viola Dana appearing as the youthful heroine. This successful attempt was followed by "The Gypsy Trail," "Good Gracious Annabelle," "Be Calm Camilla," "A Successful Calamity"—the last three by Clare Kummer—and Nazimova in Ibsen repertoire. Mr. Hopkins deserves special credit for two fine productions—Tolstoi's "Redemption" ("The Living Corpse"), with John Barrymore (1918), and Sem Benelli's drama "The Jest," with Lionel and John Barrymore (1919). In 1918, Mr. Hopkins opened his own theatre in New York, a handsome playhouse called the Plymouth.

Quite a different type of producer is A. H. Woods, who, formerly in the ten, twenty, thirty cent theatres, was identified with such melodramas as "Nellie, the Beautiful Cloak Model." In 1913, Mr. Woods branched out as a Broadway manager and had great success with Bayard Veiller's play "Within the Law," in which Jane Cowl was featured, and also with the "Potash and Perlmutter" plays, presenting Barney Bernard and Alexander Carr. This season (1918–19) he scored another success with "Friendly Enemies," a war comedy in which Louis Mann and

341

Sam Bernard are featured. He also directs the tour of Julian Eltinge, the female impersonator, and built a theatre in New York bearing that actor's name.

The largest and most imposing theatrical structures in New York are the Century (formerly the New) Theatre—that costly and gigantic failure on Central West Park, mentioned at greater length elsewhere and now devoted to burlesque and big spectacular productions—and the Metropolitan Opera House, the splendid home of the world's most expensive songbirds, at 39th Street and Broadway, outwardly a barn but within a place of vast depths, religious silences and rich red and gold coloring. Here all during the winter opera season may be seen the *intelligenzia* of New York and the leading representatives of America's aristocracy of beauty, wealth and fashion.

Other leading and popular New York theatres include the Empire, built for Charles Frohman and still the headquarters of Maude Adams, Ethel Barrymore and other Frohman stars; the New Amsterdam, Klaw and Erlanger's "house beautiful," a sumptuously appointed theatre, with broad foyers, comfortable seats and nouveau art decorations that were once the sensation of the town; the Hudson, a fine theatre, generous in its lines and chaste in design; the Knickerbocker, a house of heroic proportions where Irving was seen for the last time and Rostand's "Chantecler" was first performed in America; the Belasco, a beautiful theatre full of the Belasco atmosphere, with dimmed lights and chiming bells to mark the rise of the curtain; the Lyceum, Daniel Frohman's headquarters; the Manhattan Opera House, built by the energetic Oscar Hammerstein for his campaign against the Metropolitan, and now used for big spectacular productions such as " The Wanderer," " Chu Chin Chow," etc.

Of late years there has been a marked change in the policy of theatre construction. Instead of erecting big, costly buildings with imposing façades as was formerly the custom, the new method is to build a smaller house, or *théâtre intime,* allowing of an auditorium with limited capacity so that no seat will be very far from the stage. Among these theatres may be mentioned the Punch and Judy, a quaint and charming little place with boxes like pews giving it a church-like atmosphere; the Maxine Elliott, one of the first of the intimate theatres and a lasting monument to one of America's most beautiful and popular actresses; the Playhouse, which led the theatrical uptown movement, and in the same street as the Cort and 48th Street theatres, all houses of about the same character and very attractive in design. Then a few blocks further downtown are the Booth and the Shubert—perhaps the most beautiful of all New York's many attractive theatres—the Comedy, the Princess, the Thirty-ninth Street, the Morosco, the Broadhurst, the Henry Miller, the Selwyn and the Central—the last three the newest of all.

These theatres are all beautiful architecturally and the last word in modern theatre construction, which means safety and comfort. Each house has individual distinction, the decorative scheme being original in design and treatment. If one must at times cavil at the dramatic fare provided, there can be no possible criticism of the house itself. The modern

American theatre is, without question, the safest, the most luxurious and the most comfortable in the world.

Our modern stage has produced several dramatists with a marked gift for interpreting the humor in homely American types, notably Charles H. Hoyt, Edward Harrigan, George Ade and George M. Cohan—master craftsmen who may be said to bear the same relation to the theatre as Mark Twain does to our literature. Charles Hale Hoyt (1860–1900) was born in Concord, N. H., and began his career in the cattle business in Colorado. Later, he took up newspaper work and began writing plays. His first piece, "A Bunch of Keys," written in 1883, was favorably received, and a later piece, "A Rag Baby," produced the following year, was also a success. His best-known play, "A Trip to Chinatown," enjoyed a long run at the Madison Square Theatre in 1890. Other pieces, "A Texas Steer," "A Temperance Town," "A Milk White Flag," "A Parlor Match," clever satires on contemporary events, were enormously popular and placed Hoyt in the foremost rank of successful dramatists of his day.

Edward Harrigan, actor, playwright and manager (1845–1911) used as types the Irish-Americans. At first associated with that other favorite comedian, Tony Hart, in such pieces as "The Mulcaney Twins," "The Mulligan Guards Ball," etc., Harrigan was as popular in his day as were Weber and Fields a generation later. In 1885, Tony Hart having retired from the firm, Harrigan took a lease of the Park Theatre, where he produced "Old Lavender" and "Pete" with great success. In 1900, he built in West 35th Street the theatre recently occupied by

Jacques Copeau and his French players, and here, surrounded by a capital company, including such favorites as John Wild, the blackface comedian; Mrs. Annie Yeamans, inimitable in elderly Irish rôles, and Ada Lewis, the " tough girl," he drew crowds with such pieces as " Reilly of the 400," " The Last of the Hogans," etc. But the managerial venture was not a success and Harrigan's Theatre soon passed under the control of Richard Mansfield, who reopened it as the Garrick.

A far more subtle and up-to-date humor is that of George Ade, a former newspaper writer whose particular genius, at first manifested in his Fables in Slang, soon found its place in the theatre. Born in Indiana in 1866, George Ade graduated from Purdue University, and, taking up journalism, was connected with several Chicago dailies. His first contribution to the stage, " The Sultan of Sulu," was successful enough to encourage him to persevere in the same field, and in quick succession came " Peggy from Paris," " The County Chairman," " The Sho Gun," " The College Widow," " Father and the Boys," etc., all pieces satirizing certain American characteristics and whose crisp dialogue and fresh, vigorous humor struck a new virile note to which the public was not slow to respond.

The most conspicuously successful of all these fun makers, if measured merely from the pecuniary standpoint, is George M. Cohan, actor, playwright, composer and manager. George M. Cohan, sometimes styled the " Yankee Doodle comedian " because of his fondness for waving the American flag on every possible occasion, was born at Providence, R. I., in 1878, both of his parents being players. He first appeared on the stage at Haverstraw, N. Y., when he was nine years old, playing the violin in " Daniel Boone." Next he toured with his father, mother and sister, the family having formed themselves into an organization known as the Four Cohans and presenting a piece called " Four of a Kind." After that, he played the title rôle in " Peck's Bad Boy." Meantime, the young actor was trying his hand writing songs. His first successful song, *Venus, My Shining Love,* was followed by *Hugh McCue, You Mick You,* written for Maggie Cline, and *Hot Tamale Alley,* written for May Irwin, *You're the Warmest Baby in the Bunch* and *Guess I'll Have to Telegraph My Baby.* Other song hits at that time were *If I Were Mr. Morgan, So Long May,* sung by Fay Templeton in " Forty-five Minutes from Broadway," and *The Yankee Doodle Dandy.* His most successful song, *Over There,* composed at the beginning of the war, had an enormous sale. He received enough royalties from that one song alone to make him a rich man. Between his song composing, Cohan did much playwriting. He expanded the sketch, " Running for Office," to a four-act play and followed this by " The Governor's Son," " George Washington, Jr.," and " Little Johnny Jones." Later plays from his pen are " The Yankee Prince," " Get Rich Quick Wallingford," " The Little Millionaire," " Forty-five Minutes from Broadway," " Broadway Jones," and many other pieces similar in character. In 1910, he had formed the partnership with Sam Harris which resulted in the building of the George M. Cohan Theatre and the Cohan and Harris Theatre.

For the explanation of George M. Cohan's almost phenomenal success one must not turn to his plays, for they are entirely inconsequential, although he is acknowledged an expert craftsman in the art of play-making. To a large part of our public Cohan represents the restless American spirit, the cheeky, go-aheadedness of the hustling Yankee. All the time he is on the stage he is in motion. His derby hat, worn jauntily on one side of his head, his face screwed up into a perpetual grin, his legs never still for a moment, coming on with a skip that soon develops into a hilarious dance, singing his own songs with nasal drawl and forever waving the flag, George M. Cohan delights millions of theatre-goers of a certain class and to-day boasts of a following that for numbers might well be envied by a Kean or a Booth.

This brings our chronicle down to the present time. To resume: the American theatre to-day (1919) may be said to be in a transitory state. As we have seen, a variety of causes gradually brought about its decline. The old stock companies became extinct and with them disappeared the actors. Art found itself compelled to give way to Big Business. A new era had set in, an era grossly commercial and conscienceless, with not an idea above piling up the dollars. As some of the managers characteristically express themselves: they are not in business for their health. What has been the result of this cynical, sordid attitude? Utter demoralization of the actor, the dramatist, the public. Instead of the maintenance, by means of the stock company, of a high standard by which all new acting and all new productions might be measured, the policy is to exploit ready-made stars, stage one piece after another, no matter what its ethics or its quality, and make all the money possible. Play production has degenerated into play speculation.

347

New pieces, hastily written, are pitchforked on to the stage, on the Art be d—— principle, in the hope that they will " go " somehow. The classics of the stage are seldom, if ever, acted, so that they are practically unknown to the present generation of theatregoers; the boards are flooded with meretricious rubbish. As to the actors, they are no longer engaged according to their ability to act, but solely according to their ability to draw—which does not necessarily mean the same thing. Many actors no longer take the trouble to act. If the public is content to let the popular leading man impersonate himself night after night, the actor, highly flattered at this public interest in his personality and quick to see how it can be turned to commercial advantage, naturally sees no reason why he should submerge his precious identity in attempting to present a distinct characterization. The manager, eager to profit by this absurd personal aggrandizement of the player, promotes it in every way possible. Highly imaginative press agents are employed to feed the newspapers with trivial gossip of the Rialto, and every actor and actress who attracts the slightest attention is at once made a star. Some insignificant little chorus girl with rumpled red hair and a simpering giggle, who may have received a little extra applause some night, is immediately promoted to stardom and has her name displayed in electric lights over the theatre portals as if she were a Cushman or a Rachel. The public is easily humbugged. Ignorant of what constitutes real acting—as theatregoers of to-day must be, having no standard to go by—they are quite ready to accept the makebelieve, and thus our stage has gradually declined until to-day some of our most prominent actors and actresses may appear in vaudeville or hire out their services to the " movies," without fear of losing caste in their profession. As Mr. Towse puts it:

To-day there are not on the American stage half a dozen players, male or female, who could bear the test of comparison with any one of fifty who were flourishing thirty or forty years ago. Of great actors there is not one. The best we have, in almost every department of drama—musical comedy and wild farce, of course, are not included in that category—are survivors of a past generation. Stars there are in plenty, but only two or three of them could by any stretch of courtesy be called first-rate actors. Most of them are specialists in the art of self-production, and, therefore, utterly unprogressive. The name of the new performers is legion, but the number of them who exhibit signs of brilliant promise is woefully small. In all the arts of production —in painting, lighting, machinery, and spectacle, even in playwriting—the stage is making progress, but the race of competent actors is threatened with extinction.[2]

Have the depths been reached? When one looks around at the sort of dramatic entertainment popular with theatre audiences nowadays and examines the quality of much of what passes for acting, one is forced to the conclusion that sooner or later a healthy reaction must set in and that the Drama, reinvigorated, will again come into its own. We have the most beautiful, the most comfortable, the safest playhouses in the world. For these improvements credit must be given to the commercialized theatre. There can be no question as to the enormous expansion of, and material improvement in, the theatre in this country— better and safer construction of theatres, greater attention paid to the comfort of the playgoer, increased financial prosperity of the actor—brought about directly unlimited capital was available for theatrical

[2] Sixty Years of the Theatre. Copyright, 1916, by John Ranken Towse. Funk & Wagnalls Company. Reprinted by permission.

enterprises. But there must be Art in the theatre as well as Business, or the drama and the histrionic art will languish and die. A reaction is inevitable. The drama is too vital a thing, too important a part of our civilization to be permitted to perish altogether. Salvation, as Mr. Towse says, can come only through the re-establishment of the stock company. The star system is already beginning to show signs of waning popularity. The making of stars has been overdone. The public, too often deceived, refuses to be imposed upon any longer. Some day in the not distant future the stock system must be restored. Then we shall see a revival of the art of acting. We shall have not only fine theatres, but also fine plays and all-round companies of fine players to interpret them—not one competent player surrounded by a number of mediocrities. We have dramatists who only await the opportunity that a non-commercial stage would hold out to them—Percy MacKaye, Augustus Thomas, George Ade, Avery Hopwood, Rupert Hughes, Margaret Mayo, Eugene Walter, Samuel Shipman, George Broadhurst, Rachel Crothers, Martha Morton, Frederic and Fanny Hatton, Rida Johnson Young, Philip Moeller, Alice Gerstenberg, Edward Sheldon, Clare Kummer, Josephine Preston Peabody, Owen Davis, Winchell Smith, Channing Pollock, Langdon Mitchell, A. E. Thomas, Booth Tarkington, Richard Walton Tully.

And might we not hope for the return of the most glorious days of the stock company when we have such acting material to draw upon as Mrs. Fiske, John Drew, David Warfield, Louis Mann, Fritz Lieber, Henrietta Crosman, E. H. Sothern, Julia

Marlowe, Frank Bacon, Lenore Ulric, Margaret Anglin, Louis Calvert, Lionel, John and Ethel Barrymore, Grant Stewart, Otis Skinner, Marjorie Rambeau, Alla Nazimova, Ferdinand Gottschalk, Blanche Bates, Grace George, Henry Miller, Frances Starr, Elsie Ferguson, Richard Bennett, Arthur Byron, George Arliss, William Faversham, Leo Ditrichstein, George Nash, William H. Crane, Edith Wynne Matthison, Arnold Daly, Constance Collier, Norman Trevor, Lyn Harding, Russ Whytal, Walter Hampden, H. B. Warner, Mary Shaw, Effie Shannon, Marie Tempest, Howard Kyle, Robert Edeson, Stuart Walker, Mr. and Mrs. Coburn, O. P. Heggie, William Hodge, Holbrook Blinn, Wilton Lackaye, Emmett Corrigan, Bertha Kalich, Guy Bates Post, William Collier, Maclyn Arbuckle, Helen Ware and many others who are not forgotten, but whom it is impossible to mention for lack of space.

There is nothing wrong with our theatres, with our players, with our audiences. The difficulty lies chiefly with those in control behind the curtain. The average American theatrical producer, primarily a man of affairs, has had neither the time nor the education to enable him to cultivate the drama as an art. Of the classic drama, its history, its traditions, he knows practically nothing. Any art, to prosper, must be fostered and practiced by an artist, a person of education and culture—not by a " business " man. Business is business and art is art and " never the twain shall meet." The American theatre awaits a modern Moses to lead the way out of captivity.

INDEX

INDEX

INDEX

355

INDEX

356

INDEX

357

INDEX

INDEX

INDEX

INDEX

362

INDEX

363

INDEX

INDEX

365

INDEX

Montez, Lola (Eliza Gilbert), ii, 163
Montgomery, Walter, ii, 307
Montressor Operatic Co., ii, 102
Moody, John, i, 9, 43, 55
Moody, William Vaughn, ii, 68
Moorcroft, ii, 249
Moral dialogues, i, 110
Morant, Fanny, ii, 249, 254, 305
Mordaunt, Frank, ii, 278
Mordaunt, Plessy, ii, 262, 263
Morosco, Oliver, ii, 340
Morosco Theatre, New York, ii, 343
Mormons, Drama among the, i, 346
Morris, Clara, ii, 85, 241, 245, 248, 263, 265
Morris, Felix, ii, 286
Morris, Lewis, ii, 52
Morris, Mrs., the first, i, 107, 111, 116, 123
Morris, Mrs., the second, i, 137, 145, 146, 163, 164, 165, 187, 225, 260
Morris, Owen, i, 99, 111, 116, 123, 260
Morris, William, ii, 293
Morse, Salmi, ii, 315
Mortimer, J. K., ii, 180, 240
Morton, Martha, ii, 350
Moses, Montrose J., ii, 248
Moths, ii, 315
Motion pictures, ii, 331
Mounet-Sully, ii, 231
Mountaineers, The, i, 218, 230, 336; ii, 32
Mount Vernon Gardens, New York, i, 258
Mourning Bride, The, i, 200
Mowatt, Anna Cora, ii, 66, 160
Mrs. Brougham's Theatre, New York, ii, 169
Mrs. Bumpstead Leigh, ii, 282
Mrs. John Wood's Olympic, ii, 210
Much Ado About Nothing (first time in America), i, 175; ii, 234, 242, 257
Mulligan Guards, The, ii, 179
Mulligan Guards' Ball, The, ii, 179
Murdoch, James E., i, 352; ii, 104
Murdoch Dramatic Association, ii, 98, 239
Murray-Kean Company, i, 23, 45, 46, 52, 54, 55, 57 to 95
Murray, Walter, i, 58
Music Master, The, ii, 339
My Husband's Ghost, ii, 137
My Partner, ii, 265
My Son at Last, ii, 194

Mysterious Husband, The, i, 173
My Young Wife and Old Umbrella, ii, 149

Nadjesda, ii, 197, 315
Nance Oldfield, ii, 234
Naiad Queen, The, ii, 123
Nancy and Co., ii, 256
Nash, Mary, ii, 335
Nassau Street Theatre, First, i, 22, 41, 45, 57
   Second, i, 90
National Art Theatre Society, ii, 322
National Theatre, Boston, ii, 151
   New York, ii, 105, 181
Natural Daughter, The, i, 254
Natural Son, The, i, 228
Naughty Anthony, ii, 338
Nazimova, Alla, ii, 234
Needles and Pins, ii, 256
Negro Minstrelsy, ii, 107
Neighborhood Theatre, ii, 328
Neilson, Adelaide, ii, 250
Nerves, ii, 289
New American Company, i, 136
New Amsterdam Theatre, New York, ii, 342
New Bowery Theatre, New York, ii, 178
New Columbia Theatre, San Francisco, ii, 317
New England, first appearance of actors in, i, 109, 112
New Exhibition Room, Boston, i, 224
New Hay at the Old Market, ii, 17
New Marriage, The, ii, 282
New Metropolitan Theatre, San Francisco, ii, 314
New National Theatre, Washington, D. C., ii, 312
New Olympic, New York, i, 291; ii, 172
New Orleans, Louisiana, Theatrical beginnings in, i, 338, 339, 340
Newport Theatre, i, 231
Newport, Theatricals in, i, 109
New President, The, ii, 192
New Theatre, New York (see Century), ii, 323
New Theatre Comique, New York, ii, 181
New Way to Pay Old Debts, A, i, 276; ii, 134, 140, 217
New York Athenæum, ii, 201
New York Idea, The, ii, 282, 335
Niblo's Garden, New York, ii, 24, 96

366

INDEX

INDEX

368

INDEX

INDEX

370

INDEX

371

INDEX

372

INDEX

373

INDEX

www.ingramcontent.com/pod-product-compliance
Lightning Source LLC
Chambersburg PA
CBHW081322090426
42737CB00017B/3004